A HAPPY LIFE:

From Courtroom to Classroom

A HAPPY LIFE:

From Courtroom to Classroom

Sidney B. Silverman

iUniverse, Inc.
New York   Bloomington

iUniverse books may be ordered through booksellers or by contacting:

iUniverse
1663 Liberty Drive
Bloomington, IN 47403
www.iuniverse.com
1-800-Authors (1-800-288-4677)

Because of the dynamic nature of the Internet, any Web addresses or links contained in this book may have changed since publication and may no longer be valid. The views expressed in this work are solely those of the author and do not necessarily reflect the views of the publisher, and the publisher hereby disclaims any responsibility for them.

ISBN: 978-1-4401-5085-2 (sc)
ISBN: 978-1-4401-5087-6 (dj)
ISBN: 978-1-4401-5086-9 (ebook)

Printed in the United States of America

iUniverse rev. date: 06/22/2009

Many relatives, friends, colleagues, mentors enriched my life. My children gave me joy—most of the time. One person, however, stayed with me through thick and thin. I can never repay all she has done for me. It is to her that I dedicate this book.

INTRODUCTION

AT SEVENTY-FOUR YEARS OF age, I received a master's degree from Columbia University. I studied alongside bright young students fifty years my junior. I read, researched, and wrote papers on Spinoza, Kant, Nietzsche, William James, Heidegger, and a school of ancient Greek philosophers. These great thinkers provided insight into morality, ethics, the essence of being, knowledge, God—yes, God—and there were many more wonderful classes.

I went to school only during the fall semesters. The rest of the year, I played golf and chess, swam, napped, and read. What did I like best? No question: being a student won hands down.

I wanted to mount a soap box and urge every old codger within shouting distance: "Return to school. If I succeeded so can you. Look, listen, I am no intellectual. My grades in high school and college were average. I was far from a superstar in law school. All you need is the will to learn. Your experience will compensate for any lack of gray matter." And then I thought of a better way. Why not write a book about my experience?

There was, however, a problem. How can I write about retirement without discussing what I retired from?

I graduated from Columbia Law School in 1957 and from the Graduate School of Liberal Arts and Sciences in 2007. In between, I was a trial lawyer plowing the rough and tumble world of stockholder litigation. There was a connection between courtroom and classroom: competition. In my practice, I had to win or starve to death. I developed a will to live. My nature, honed by competition, carried over to graduate school. There, I was not only a student but a litigator student; I tried to win. Grades measure success. I worked hard for As and was dismayed with anything less. I did get my share of As, but also some lower grades.

When I saw a master's degree was within my grasp, I turned to chess, a game I had played for many years. I read books, practiced against a computer program, and took lessons from a grand master. When I thought I was ready, I entered a tournament. My opponents ranged in age from twelve to fourteen. I won some games, but lost more. After several years of intensive study and play, I realized I did not have what it takes to be a good chess player. I gave up competitive chess; now I play for fun. Chess was a part of my retirement. A chapter on chess follows those on graduate school.

The final chapter is on health. The golden years is a euphemism; leaden would be more accurate, so too the painful years. I have had three hip surgeries (my left hip was replaced twice), two corneal transplants, and my heart runs on a battery. I can walk and see fairly well. At seventy-six, that's good enough.

Writing about aspects of my life allowed me to relive them. I tried hard to report honestly. Yet, it is possible that some occurrences were filtered through that all too human screen that sees events in a way pleasing to the observer. Viewed in totality, I believe my career, retirement, chess, and health are fairly presented. After many careful readings, I have found nothing to retract. Of course, what I found to retract, I already retracted.

Here, then, is my story.

PART 1

PRACTICING LAW

1
GETTING STARTED

THANKS TO SOME HIGHLY publicized reports of badly behaving lawyers, the legal profession has become the target of comedians and whoever it is that sends out comic material over the Internet. The comedy derives from grossly exaggerated portrayals of shockingly improper conduct. Lawyers, we are told, are beneath contempt, only marginally human. My experience as a lawyer has brought me into contact with hundreds of wonderful people, lawyers, judges, clients, clerks, office workers. Of course, people must look out for themselves in this world, but the legal community as a whole is populated by those who sincerely want to increase the amount of justice in the world. For every bad apple with a license to practice law, there are thousands of kind, intelligent, upstanding, and ethical men and women. I salute them. I am proud to salute them, and I hope that what follows will to some extent counteract our day's fascination with the bad apples.

I was not called to the bar; it happened by default. I studied Russian language at Colgate University and, upon graduation in 1954, planned to enlist in the army. The cold war with the Soviet Union was heating up and a proficiency in Russian could be put to good use. The army maintained an intensive foreign language program in Monterey, California. My Russian language professor assured me I would be tapped for the school. After Monterey, I would serve in Hamburg, Germany, live off base, my rank classified, and dress in civilian clothes. My professor also told me that in Hamburg, the ratio of women to men was nine to one. My immediate, post-college future seemed set, but the army turned me down because of a hip injury. I was not going to be a foreign spy. I needed to do something, something suitable for a college graduate. My choices seemed few. With a minimum of consideration, I enrolled in Columbia Law School.

In due course, I began work at a New York firm. As the most junior lawyer, I was relegated to the library and assigned small points of law to research. I wanted to get ahead quickly, but I felt I was on a slow and stodgy path to nowhere. The lawyers receiving responsible assignments were specialists. Many had gained expertise working for the government. I discussed my future with a sympathetic partner. Securities law was in its infancy but showed promise of booming. He suggested I work for the Securities and Exchange Commission in Washington, and then return to the firm. The partner predicted it would take five years to become an expert.

I got a job with the SEC in the department charged with regulating investment companies. I worked hard, advanced, and learned a lot. I lived in a large apartment with three other government lawyers. One of my roommates was Mordecai Rosenfeld, also a transplanted New Yorker. He was a Yale Law School graduate. He was smart, charming, and funny, but he had a serious drawback: his appearance. He had a large mop of black hair covering his forehead, making him appear to be what he was not, a lowbrow. His features, especially his ears, were outsized. Because of his homely appearance, he was shy until he got to know you. Then, he opened up. He was popular, but only with men. Like me, he was Brooklyn born and bred. We were homeboys and bonded.

In 1960, Rosenfeld and I said good-bye to Washington, returned to New York, and formed a partnership. We rented a one-room office for $75 a month in a rundown building in downtown Manhattan, and furnished it with an abandoned partner's desk and chairs stored in the basement of the building and "purchased" from the janitor for a tip of $10. The desk had two openings on opposite sides. He sat on one side and I sat on the other.

I was twenty-seven. I paid no attention to my shabby surroundings; what excited me was my name on the door. I was a partner in the firm of Rosenfeld and Silverman. My career had begun.

Rosenfeld had worked in New York for Abe Pomerantz, a lawyer who specialized in stockholder actions. He may have even invented them. It was Rosenfeld's idea to bring stockholder suits, and mine, as the specialist in investment companies, to sue the managers of mutual funds.

Our first client was my partner's four-year-old nephew, Joel Benjamin Rosenfeld. His father had purchased stock for his son at his birth, in One William Street, a mutual fund managed by Lehman Brothers. Under the law, any stockholder, even a four year old, can sue. The action is nominally against the corporation but only because it has failed to sue those who have wronged it. The corporation's claim is pursued "derivatively" by the stockholder on behalf of the corporation and the recovery inures to the corporation. The judge orders the corporation receiving the benefit to pay the plaintiff's legal fees. Otherwise, the corporation would be unjustly enriched. Lehman, then the quintessential and all-powerful investment banking firm, was our target.

Mutual funds are pools of liquid assets, contributed and owned by investors and managed by professional investment advisers. By pooling their money, small investors, who could not on their own afford to hire an investment adviser, can engage skilled money managers. Mutual funds are controlled and managed by their investment adviser. Under the law, one who assumes control over another's assets is a trustee and is held to the highest ethical and moral standards. Under the ancient common law, the trustee could not charge for his services; he served because it was his duty to do so. The rule was consistent with Kantian concepts of morality. One did what was right because it was right and not from inclination, pleasure, or desire for reward. Modern law relaxes this ban and allows a fiduciary to be paid, provided that the fee is fair.

Lehman charged the One William Street fund 0.005 percent of its net assets, the standard fee charged by fund managers. Lehman also managed another investment company, Lehman Corp, a closed-end investment company. It was customary to charge closed-end funds a flat fee rather than a percentage of assets, and Lehman charged Lehman Corp an annual fee of $250,000. Both funds were about the same size and held stock in the same companies. We thought that the percentage fee charged One William Street flunked the fairness test. It came to about $1 million, four times the fee charged Lehman Corp.

While in Washington, we scribbled out the complaint. After opening our office in New York, we turned over our handwritten draft to a public stenographer who typed it. On our second day in practice, the two partners walked to the federal court and together handed the complaint to a clerk for filing. We were off and running.

I was impressed with myself. In just three years, I had leapt from the library and the lower echelons of the Securities and Exchange Commission to senior partner and co-head of a litigation firm handling a million dollar lawsuit.

Simpson, Thatcher, and Bartlett, a large and powerful law firm, represented Lehman. They were understandably perplexed when they received the complaint; Rosenfeld and Silverman was not listed in any directory of lawyers in the New York telephone book, or even on the directory in the lobby of the building given as its address. The firm thought the suit might be a hoax. An investigator was hired; he came to our office and quickly all doubts were resolved. Rosenfeld and Silverman did in fact exist; both of its partners were members of the New York bar.

On the morning of our third day in practice, Rosenfeld got to the office early and when I arrived was in an agitated state. He held in one hand our only reference book, Wiesenberger's *Manual of Investment Companies*. The book listed every investment company and its adviser, the rate and dollar amount of fees charged, the officers and directors, the ten-year growth in net assets, and the yearly and compounded rate of growth of the fund's investments.

Rosenfeld began a harangue, speaking quickly and loudly. His hands moved in time with his words: "I was up all night studying Wiesenberger. From the hundreds of funds, I picked the twelve with the worst performance records but who paid their advisers among the highest fees. Poor performance should not be rewarded; the adviser should, instead, be penalized. A straight percentage fee makes no sense. Take a mutual fund that has $1 billion of net assets and charges a flat fee of 0.005 percent which comes to $5 million. Whether a fund is $500 million or $1 billion, the advisers must evaluate all available publicly traded stocks, and then determine the percent of the fund's assets that should be invested in particular stocks. Say the manager decides that 2 percent should be invested in General Motors and its stock is selling for $50. If the fund is $1 billion, the manager buys 400,000 shares; if $500 million, then 200,000. Why should the manager get twice as much for what amounts to the same amount of work or thought? Maybe the fee should be slightly more because of the additional responsibility, but not twice as much. In fairness, the fee of 0.005 percent should be reduced as the assets grow. Let's bring more suits." The last line was said slowly and softly. Rosenfeld grinned from one oversized ear to the other and sat down.

We had a problem: we lacked clients who owned stock in the funds Rosenfeld had targeted. He suggested, "We canvass our relatives and friends. If they own shares and are willing to be plaintiffs, fine. Otherwise we purchase for our relatives a few shares in each of the funds." Under the law, a plaintiff must be a stockholder at the time of the wrong. In our cases, the wrong was a continuing one, as the excessive fee was charged each day. A new stockholder could attack present and future fees, but not past ones. The point was to correct the practice of excessive fees, which our newly honed shareholders had standing to do.

We checked with our family and friends. A few owned shares in the right funds, but for the most part we purchased shares, for my mother, Rosenfeld's mother, my sister, and his brother. The fledgling firm thereupon commenced a dozen new suits against America's oldest and mightiest investment banking firms.

Rosenfeld's selection of poorly performing funds was clever. It answered the argument invariably made when compensation is attacked as excessive: "How can you put a price tag on the Mozart of finance?" The funds had grown large through aggressive sales campaigns, rather than smart investment decisions. The managers were certainly not Mozarts. We joked that the managers relied on their *tuchas* (derrières to those who do not speak French), not their brains in purchasing stock, and that it took the same *tuchas* to manage such funds, regardless of size. We called the suits the "same *tuchas* cases."

We were able to draft the complaints and get them filed without the assistance of any other lawyers or even a secretary, but had no grasp of tactics. The powerful firms representing the mutual funds and their advisers blindsided us. The law gave them twenty days to respond to the complaints but the period was more often extended than observed. In each case, the defendants made requests to extend the twenty-day period. We knew the requests had to be granted but failed to appreciate the significance of the fact that the adjourned date for all thirteen actions was the very same. On the due date, the opposing firms served every conceivable motion supported by outsized legal memorandums, oxymoronically called briefs. We were overwhelmed by the flood of paper.

Rosenfeld arranged a meeting with Pomerantz, the dean of the stockholder bar and his former mentor. The first thing you noticed about Pomerantz was his size: he was fat. The second was his gift of gab. He occupied a large corner office at the end of a corridor. I was there not more than ten minutes when Pomerantz rose, walked to the back of his office, and opened a door to a small closet containing a sink on one side and a bar to hold coats on the other. He closed the door but the noise announced his activity; he was urinating into the sink. When he opened the door, he pointed to the sink and said, "I call it my pissing bowl. You are free to use it anytime."

Pomerantz loved the cases but criticized the way they were started; "A federal judge assigned the thirteen cases will immediately sense that the lawyers, not the clients, were the instigators. This is a crime, called barratry. You could be disbarred." Suddenly I fell from the co-head of a litigation firm handling thirteen big cases to a disgraced lawyer, my career ended.

Pomerantz took pity on us. He offered to amend the complaints by replacing our relatives with stockholders who owned shares long before the commencement of the actions. The amendments caused automatically the withdrawal of our thirteen complaints. The defendants then had to remake their motions against the amended complaints. By this process, our cases were replaced by new ones and our crimes buried. Pomerantz said his firm would take charge and we would assist. He proposed a division of fees, sixty–forty, in favor of his firm. We, of course, accepted the generous offer.

Years later, I learned that a Pomerantz contract was not as sacrosanct as, say, an international treaty. In order to gain control of identical stockholder actions started by several different lawyers, he promised the others shares in the fee. None knew it then, but Pomerantz gave away more than 100 percent of the fee. If he lost, it made no difference. The fee was contingent and 150 percent of zero is zero. If the case was won and a fee awarded, Pomerantz called all the lawyers to a meeting. Sitting around his large conference table, he glowered at each lawyer, and then said: "I worked hard to win the case and get us a big fee. Based on my commitments to you, I gave away more than 100 percent of the fee. It is wrong that I work, you make money, and I get nothing. The understanding must be revised. My firm gets 50 percent and you share the balance equally." The others protested. Typical were cries of, "Abe, I would not have given my case to you for a chance to earn 10 percent of the fee." Pomerantz prevailed. He did it over and over again and got away with it. Why? He was the best, and a small share of his fee was better than what the others could earn on their own.

After a lot of work extending over several years, the funds' advisers agreed to reduce their charges and Pomerantz was awarded a fee based on a percentage of the benefit realized by the funds. Since the funds were benefited, they should have paid the fees, but to make it more palatable to the judges who had to approve the fees, Pomerantz required the advisers to bear the expense. The fees, in the aggregate, exceeded $1 million.

Pomerantz tried to chisel us, but we hung tough. I said, "These were our cases, not yours. We worked hard on them. We have a contract and I'm not giving up even 0.005 percent." He laughed and, probably for the first time, honored a deal. The day Rosenfeld and I received our share was a singular day in our lives. We held the check in the air, clicked our heels, and gleefully shouted, "Poor no more."

Pomerantz taught us the trade. He also introduced us to lawyers who referred cases to him. Soon they turned over cases to us that were too small for the Pomerantz firm.

Rosenfeld and I had a viable law practice. You would think that two formerly poor young lawyers, now successful would stay together. I often thought we should have, but we did not. In 1964, I was the law offices of Sidney B. Silverman; he was the law offices of Mordecai Rosenfeld. Rosenfeld and Silverman was no more. Neither of us could get over what seems now a petty incident. The breakup of a law firm is a lot like a divorce. We had been close friends, members of each others' wedding party, and we socialized out of the office as well as spending five days a week together. After the split, we never talked to or saw each other again.

2
LEARNING MY TRADE

IN STOCKHOLDER ACTIONS, THE plaintiff knows only what the corporation has chosen to disclose. Much more is required to prepare a case for trial. And that much more takes the form of discovery requiring the corporation being sued to produce documents and make witnesses available for pretrial examination. New York law provides, however, that in stockholders cases discovery may not go forward without a court order. The reason: a history of abuse. Frivolous cases were settled, because the cost of complying with discovery was much larger than the possible settlement.

Without discovery, the stockholder is prevented from gathering evidence, and good cases, as well as bad ones, are unable to proceed. To obtain a court order, the stockholder lawyer must demonstrate that the action has merit. The order must first be approved by the clerk before it is submitted to the judge. The clerks routinely made me wait for hours until they reviewed my application. More often than not, they claimed a minor error prevented submission, and I had to start all over again the next day. After the clerk's approval, I waited for days for the judge to sign the order; sometimes he did, most times he did not.

All this changed after Hugo Rogers entered my life. He was appointed a referee by a state court judge to advise whether a settlement was fair and to issue a report. This was the usual procedure in stockholder actions. I was the proponent of the settlement and seized the opportunity to make an important friend. Rogers, a strikingly handsome and dignified man, was the former head of Tammany Hall and in the late 1940s had been borough president of Manhattan. When I met Rogers, he held no political office. A politician out of office should have no clout, but the former politico's appearance and demeanor exuded power. The clerks knew him. When we entered the clerks' offices, the chief greeted Rogers and asked, "What can I do for you today?" Rogers introduced me and said that Mr. Silverman will explain the application. The clerk listened attentively, found the application in order, and took it directly to the judge. Within a short time, the order was signed. Why did Rogers help me? He got a small share of my fee.

After a while, I went alone to the chief clerk. "Remember me?" I said, "I'm Sidney Silverman. I usually come with Hugo Rogers but he could not make it today." It took longer, but I got the order signed and saved some money.

Rogers also helped me maneuver in other areas. I joined a luncheon club called the Lawyers Club. It was located on the top floor of an old downtown building and its dining room had great views of New York Harbor and the Hudson River. Its outstanding feature was a floor to ceiling stained glass window. Rogers was my first guest. As we waited to be seated, he said the only tables worth sitting at were those alongside the stained glass window. To the question, "How do I get such a table?" he replied, "Give the maitre d' a couple of dollars." I left Rogers, moved ahead of others waiting to be seated, and spoke to the maitre d': "Hello, captain. My name is Sidney Silverman. I'm here with Hugo Rogers, former borough president. When it is my turn to be seated, I want a table by the window." I slipped him $5. When my time came, the maitre d' greeted me by name and escorted us to a table by the window. It cost me an extra $5 every time I lunched at the Lawyers Club, but I always had one of the best tables. Someone who saw me seated at one of those special tables and did not know any better might have thought I defended the mighty corporations I sued.

Rogers had other tricks. My wife and I were his guests at a formal dinner. The main dish was steak. To the waiter's question, "How do you like your steak?" we both replied, "Rare." Rogers took out a $10 bill, ripped it in half, and gave one half to the waiter. He said, "If their steaks are rare, you will get the other half." After bringing us our steaks, the waiter hovered. I cut into my steak and it was rare. Rogers handed the waiter the other half of the bill. My wife nudged me and said sotto voce, "I lost my appetite. Let's leave." To which I whispered back, "We can't. I need him."

While I had argued motions, written briefs, examined witnesses before trial, and settled cases, I had yet to try a case. I was anxious. What if I was inept? Most of my cases were in New York or Delaware. My first trial, I thought, should take place in a distant state. If I were a disaster, the news might not reach New York and I could change fields.

I had a case pending in Denver, Colorado, that came to me through a lawyer who referred his clients to Pomerantz. He had rejected the case as too small and suggested I might take it. The client, Nat Gluck, and the lawyer came to my office.

Gluck was a retired blouse manufacturer living in Brooklyn. He was short, wore open-collared shirts under a plaid jacket, and always seemed in need of a shave. Gluck was obsessed with the stock market. He owned shares in hundreds of corporations. In order for the stockholders to cast votes on the election of directors and other matters placed before them, corporations send proxy solicitation material (proxies) to shareholders. The proxy, among other things, sets forth the compensation of the board members and principal officers, and every material arrangement, or "deal," they have with the company. Such deals are called self-dealing transactions. Gluck read the proxies carefully and circled in red every suspicious deal. He was so outraged by self-dealing that he literally turned red when reading the passage, as he always insisted upon doing. Before we met, he took the proxies to his lawyer. After our first meeting, he called only me. "Who needs a middleman? In the blouse business, I did, and I resented it. Once I met you, I knew I could deal direct."

What did Gluck get out of suing? The cases he brought were discussed in proxies and press releases. On nice afternoons, Gluck sat on a bench in his neighborhood, surrounded by other old, retired cronies. Gluck discussed his lawsuits, showed the complaint and the company's press releases. Among his crowd, he was a big man, a corporate warrior. Bragging rights were all Gluck wanted and all he got.

The facts in the Denver case were straightforward. They involved a man named Harry Trueblood and a small oil and gas company, Consolidated Oil and Gas. Trueblood was the chief executive officer and chairman of the board. He owned a one-thousand-acre sheep farm in the Rocky Mountains that he had purchased for $50,000, $50 per acre. A classic case of self-dealing arose when Trueblood sold the farm two years after he purchased it to the oil and gas company for $500 per acre.

Although self-dealing transactions are disclosed, important details needed to put flesh and blood on the bare bones are shielded from stockholder scrutiny. Discovery levels the playing field. In Consolidated Oil, I took lots of discovery, knew as much as the defendants, and was ready for trial.

Trueblood and the directors conceded, as they had to, that the sale was a self-dealing transaction. They disputed the allegation that the transaction was unfair and in fact contended that the corporation received a great bargain when it bought the property.

I established my case by putting into evidence the self-dealing transaction and the relevant documents surrounding it. That was all I needed to do. The burden then shifted to the defendant directors. They had to prove the transaction was fair and that in approving it, they exercised sound business judgment.

Under questioning by the company's lawyer, all seven directors testified. At the end of each director's testimony, it was my task to cross-examine. My only trial experience was as Pomerantz's assistant. He was a skillful trial lawyer and an excellent teacher. He advised: let the judge know at the beginning exactly where you are going. A good lawyer's first question should resemble a headline in the *Daily News*. I knew from the depositions that the price of $500 per acre was Trueblood's asking price and the directors had not proposed a lower price. My opening questions ranged from: "There was no arm's-length bargaining or bargaining of any kind because you accepted the price asked by Mr. Trueblood and made no effort to obtain a lower price, is that correct?" to: "You rubber-stamped Mr. Trueblood's offer because you were more interested in helping him than in protecting the stockholders, is that correct?"

The witnesses were shocked by the bluntness of my questions. They were unaccustomed to criticism and angered that a young lawyer from New York was treating them in this rough way. The witnesses all denied my opening questions. One of them shook his finger at me and said, "You are wrong. The board worked hard to make sure the deal was fair."

I liked that answer. I wanted the case to turn on whether the deal was fair at the time it was made. In follow-up questions, I got into the nitty gritty of the arrangement. The company had planned to convert the sheep farm into a ski resort and residential community, a costly project Trueblood could not afford. In such circumstances, a purchaser can obtain a bargain price. As it turned out, the corporation gave Trueblood a ten fold profit on his original investment. That was the only appealing part of the case.

The big issue, and the one on which I lost the case, was whether the land was worth at least $500 per acre. The sheep farm was on Eagle Mountain, a suburb of Vail. At the time the case was started, Vail had just begun operations. By the time of trial, it was one of the most popular and successful of ski areas. *Sports Illustrated* ran a feature on Vail, complete with a picture of a $500,000 home owned by one of the Murchisons, the Texas billionaire oil, cattle, and real estate kings. There was no question that by the time of trial, the land was worth many times more than $500 per acre. I argued that the present value was not the correct criterion. What mattered was the value at the time of purchase. In my opinion, none of the directors who approved the purchase of the land could have known what the land would be worth in the future. But, all of them claimed to.

Trueblood testified that he was willing to return the corporation's money plus interest and repurchase the land from the corporation. It is impossible, and rightly so, to get damages on a deal that turns out to benefit the corporation. Anyone but a young, unsophisticated lawyer, concerned with finding out whether or not he is a capable trial lawyer, would have understood the principle involved and would have dropped the case.

Although I lost the case, I gained confidence. It was my first trial and I did a good job. I also learned a valuable lesson, one I never forgot. In a stockholder case, you must make sure that the transaction harms the company; an evil purpose is not enough. The Eagle County deal was arranged as an accommodation for Trueblood; he could not have sold the land to an unrelated party for $500 per acre. Further, he had no intention of benefiting the corporation and would not have parted with the land, if he had known that in a few years it would be worth fifty times as much as he had paid for it. While it was wrong to use corporate assets to assist their CEO, as it turned out, the corporation was benefited, not harmed.

Years later, the importance of the real estate development dwarfed the company's other activities and it changed its name from Consolidated Oil to the Eagle County Development Corporation. Some years later, Trueblood died and the attorney who opposed me became president of the company. I was happy for the lawyer. He had been kind to me and complimented me on my trial preparation. He said, "You have squeezed everything you could out of a very weak case. I would not like to defend a good case against you." It cost him nothing to be nice to a young, inexperienced lawyer, but it meant so much to me.

3
MAKING LUCY CRY, TWICE

I DEVELOPED A FOLLOWING AMONG certain litigious-minded stockholders. They had two things in common: they loved to star in corporate actions and they were all Gluck's bench mates. My big problem was not getting cases, but deciding among the many offered. Since my fee was contingent on success and each case involved a large investment of time, I tried hard to select winners. But I'm human and all too often circumstances, other than the merits, clouded my judgment. A cloud appeared when Philip Rosen said, "You must sue Lucille Ball. I own stock in Desilu Corporation. Lucy is a great comedienne but a bubblehead in business. Desi was a top-notch businessman, the president of the company, and received a salary of $500,000. He got a separate salary as an actor. When he died, Lucy became president at the same salary. Her salary as an actress is also $500,000, making her total compensation $1 million."

I knew compensation cases can be won only if the amount in question constitutes waste. Waste is defined as a sum no rational, knowledgeable person would approve. Lucy's combined compensation was large, but not by Hollywood standards. The odds of winning were low. I took the case anyway. Why? Famous actresses are rarely parties in corporate litigation. With Lucy as a defendant, the media would be all over the case and, who knows, I might see my name in boldface print.

Lucy was represented by Mickey Rudin, a famous Hollywood lawyer. At her deposition, I asked not a single question about her services as a performer. I asked business questions: How many shares of common stock were outstanding? What were the rights of the preferred stockholders? Who was the largest creditor? And many more such questions. Ball broke down in tears, and said, "Desi would know the answers." If Ball knew nothing about the basic financial affairs of the business, she was not filling Desi's shoes and should not receive his salary.

After the deposition, I asked Lucy for a glossy photograph. She smiled at me and flirted by blinking her beautiful blue eyes. "Of course," she said. "Come to my office. And to whom would you like me to inscribe the photo?" I had promised our maid I would return with a signed photograph. I said, "Sign it from Lucy to Lucy." She did and then asked, "Who is Lucy?" "She is our maid and a devoted fan of yours." Lucy screamed, "Mickey, his maid!" and started to cry again.

Before I left, Rudin took me aside and told me of instances where Ball appeared as a guest star on other programs for the nominal fee of $500. In return, the other performers appeared on Ball's show for $500. But for this reciprocal arrangement, Desilu would have paid the guest stars top fees of about $20,000 per appearance. He showed me compensation arrangements of other stars. Ball's total remuneration, including her salary as president, was plainly below market. The lawyer said he would never agree to pay me a fee. "You made Lucy cry, you bastard. I know you are close to Abe Pomerantz. I will be in touch with him."

Shortly after I returned from Los Angeles, Pomerantz called and invited me to lunch at his usual place, the Democratic Club of New York County. This grand mansion on Park Avenue and Thirty-seventh Street, built for Joseph Raphael De Lamar in 1906, served as the club house for Tammany Hall. (It is now the Polish Consulate.) The place reeked of depravity. There, I am sure, every sleazy deal in New York County was hatched. Lawyers negotiated with county leaders for the right to run for judge or assemblyman or state senate on the Democratic ticket, a certain road to election. The Surrogate of the county, the judge in charge of the property of dead persons (estates), made patronage appointments over lunch, drinks at the bar, or in the card room, in favor of party regulars who were awarded big fees for safeguarding the interests of widows and orphans whose only real need of protection was from the guardian the surrogate himself had appointed! Corrupt politicians were the reigning heroes of this palatial establishment. They paced the floors smiling and waving to acquaintances and even to strangers. I know. They smiled and waved at me.

The enormous central hall of the mansion had been reconfigured as a dining room seating over a hundred diners at widely separated tables, undoubtedly to prevent eavesdropping. Pomerantz was known at the club and we were promptly seated and handed menus. He looked at the day's offerings and exclaimed, "Sidney! They have salami and eggs on the menu. That dish has killed more Jews than Hitler." He then ordered the killer dish while I searched in vain for something even vaguely healthful. The kitchen had never heard of salads or fish. I settled for cheese blintzes and sour cream.

After we ordered, Pomerantz turned to the business at hand. "Rudin called. He does not want Lucy to be put through a trial even though he is sure she will win. If you dismiss the case, he will pay me $10,000, which I will turn over to you." I turned it down. "It's illegal to take an under the table payment to drop a stockholder's case. For a lousy $10,000, every lawyer on the West Coast will have something on me." I was too polite to Pomerantz to add, "and on the East Coast as well."

"I'm prepared to drop the case and eat my time and expenses," I said. Pomerantz approved and agreed to tell Rudin.

I lived up to my end of the bargain, but did Pomerantz relay my decision to Rudin? To this day, I believe he did not. He probably got the money and kept it. Pomerantz was not known to pass up a buck.

4
A WHALE SWALLOWS A GUPPY

MY WIFE AND CHILDREN spent the summer in Amagansett, a three-hour train ride away. I stayed alone in New York during the weeks and joined them on the weekends. With no pleasant distractions, I got to the office early and stayed late. There was also another reason: I had too much work. One hot June morning, I rose at 4:00 AM, hopped on a subway and at 5:00 AM, began work. By the end of the day, I was exhausted and had hardly made a dent in the pending load. I needed help. I called a professor at Columbia Law School who taught a course in securities law and asked if any of his second-year students were available for work during the summer. He sent two and I hired both.

Their job was research. It was time-consuming and, since the office lacked a library and the Internet was not yet invented, they worked at the County Bar Association library. I incorporated their work into briefs and I made it through the summer. They must have loved their work. When they graduated they came to me for jobs. I turned them down. By that time, I had taken on two lawyers and had neither work nor room for more. The students went on to become superstars. Years later, I bragged that they got their start with me.

After the summer of 1970, I vowed never again to work alone. I made a concerted effort to hire a lawyer. I contacted employment agencies and placed ads in the *New York Law Journal*. The lawyers with good academic credentials and experience declined my offer. They aspired to become partners and doubted whether a solo lawyer would ever admit them to partnership. I could have hired dozens of lawyers with mediocre credentials, but my cases were contentious and I wanted to be in the trenches with only the best.

One day I read an ad in the *Wall Street Journal*. It said: "Would you hire Madame Curie if she could work from only 10 to 3? We have married women who are talented accountants, lawyers, copywriters, bookkeepers, and secretaries who must be home after school to care for their children but are eager to work part-time." I called and the agency sent two lawyers, Jewel Bjork and Joan Harnes. Both were older than I, Bjork by several years and Harnes by more than five. They had excellent academic records, were married to successful men, and lived in Manhattan's best neighborhood, the Upper East Side. I could not help noticing that one, Bjork, was stylishly dressed and attractive. I hired them both at the salary stipulated by the agency, $10,000.

In 1970, law firms discriminated against women. When women were hired, it was for work in dead-end departments, not litigation. My new associates began work at 10:00 AM. They were on diets and took no lunch hour or other break. They ended their day at 3:00 PM. Their work was as good as their credentials and they were fast. They accomplished in five hours what a good lawyer might do in eight. Bjork and Harnes worked mainly on briefs, a time-consuming task. I was free to develop new business and prepare cases for trial. The arrangement worked. We won cases and business poured in. The women's salaries and their time spent in the office increased dramatically. They worked at night from their apartments and on weekends from their country homes. One night at midnight, Bjork, who was still in the office, confronted me angrily: "I thought I would be working fifteen hours a week, not a day. Goodnight, Mr. Silverman." When I asked what time she would be in the next day, she smiled sweetly and said 9:00 AM. Bjork was a socialite and very much part of the establishment. My work was anti-establishment. Yet, she loved it.

My big case in 1970 concerned a guppy swallowing a whale; the guppy was Leasco Corporation, the whale, Reliance Insurance Company. Leasco was founded by Saul Steinberg shortly after he graduated from the University of Pennsylvania. While at college, Steinberg wrote a paper describing a business plan that would enable an upstart company to compete with IBM in the leasing of its computers. In the 1960s, computers were both expensive and quickly outdated, prone to early obsolescence. Rather than buy computers that might soon be outmoded, many businesses preferred to lease them. IBM, a conservative company, assumed that when the lease expired the computers would be valueless and therefore sought to amortize the full price of the computers over the terms of the lease. Steinberg's college paper suggested that the computers did not have to be scrapped when a new generation arrived, but could be sold in underdeveloped countries, principally Latin America. Steinberg reasoned that by anticipating a residual value for the computers, they could be leased on terms more favorable than those offered by IBM.

When he graduated, Steinberg formed Leasco and put the plan in operation. With financing provided by banks, Leasco purchased computers from IBM and leased them for less than IBM was charging. Each year, Leasco reported rising earnings They were paper profits based on the assumption that the computers could be sold at the end of the lease. If they could not, the "profits" would turn into losses. Wall Street believed, paradoxically, the upstart, not IBM, the manufacturer of the computers. Stocks trade at a multiple of earnings and companies with growing earnings, known as growth companies, trade at a high multiple. Leasco was the street's darling. Its stock price soared as the market accepted Leasco's paper profits as though they were real, honest-to-goodness cash earnings, and assigned a high multiple to them.

Reliance was an old-line fire and casualty insurance company that conservatively and properly reported its earnings and assets. Reliance, like other insurance companies, required premiums to be paid in advance, sometimes for periods covering five years. The premiums eventually would be applied to pay claims, but in the interim constituted "float," money that the insurance company holds. Based on actuarial experience, Reliance anticipated that over time it would payout in claims an amount equal to its premium income. Pending payout, Reliance made money investing the float and kept the return. In effect, Reliance was in two businesses: insurance and investments. The operations of the former were at break-even but provided the float for the profitable investment business. Yet, Wall Street valued Reliance as though it were only a stodgy insurance company and overlooked its strong investment activities. Reliance traded at an undervalued market price.

Reliance also had an undisclosed asset arising from the requirement that insurance companies set aside funds—in insurance jargon, reserves—in order to satisfy the claims of policyholders. The reserves are typically invested in safe securities, readily convertible into cash. Insurance companies are rated by independent services, based in part on the ratio of their reserves to premium income, the higher the ratio, the better the ranking. Reliance stood at the top of its class. In fact, its reserves were so extensive and the ratio so high that Reliance had surplus surplus, reserves far in excess of state law requirements. A management more interested in making deals than in running a responsible insurance company, could legally separate the surplus surplus and use the money to acquire other companies. An aggressive management more concerned with earning money for stockholders than meeting the claims of policyholders, might also invest the remaining surplus in speculative securities, exposing policy holders to risk although potentially benefiting stockholders. Reliance was a prime target for acquisition. It had a solid balance sheet, a strong business, and surplus surplus.

To prevent premature trading on inside information, the acquirer usually assigns a code name to the target company. Steinberg lusted after Reliance and assigned it the code name "Raquel Welch," then Hollywood's leading sex bomb. There was, however, a serious obstacle to the takeover. Leasco was a fraction of the size of Reliance. In fact, Reliance's surplus surplus was much larger than the capitalized value of Leasco, its stock price multiplied by its outstanding common stock. Leasco could purchase Reliance only by printing stock and using the newly minted shares to pay for the insurance company. Since a share of Leasco traded for more than a share of Reliance, a share-for-share exchange would give Reliance stockholders, in the cockeyed market, a premium for their stock. Stockholders are not a loyal bunch. It is common knowledge that if you offer a premium, even though the premium consists of inflated stock, they will accept. Steinberg won. The Reliance stockholders accepted at face value the absurdly high market price of Leasco's stock and exchanged their undervalued Reliance stock.

We represented a Reliance stockholder and brought a class action on behalf of all Reliance stockholders. As often happens in securities litigation, the real issue is obscured. Here, the real issue was fairness. Leasco's stock was worth far less than its market price and Reliance's stock worth far more. Because the exchange offer was voluntary, the case could not proceed on fairness. If Reliance stockholders believed their shares were worth more than a share of Leasco, the remedy was simple. They could refuse to tender them, that is, to sell them to Leasco. If enough Reliance shareholders refused to tender, the deal would crater.

We needed a new theory and disclosure provided the key. We contended that Leasco's offer was false and misleading because it did not disclose what had motivated it to make the offer: Reliance's surplus surplus. We argued that if full disclosure was made, the Reliance stockholders would have realized that an alternative and more attractive plan was available to them. The surplus surplus could be distributed as a dividend. It was worth more in cash than the Leasco stock and, to boot, the Reliance stockholders would keep their stock.

The case was filed in the federal court for the Eastern District, located in downtown Brooklyn, and assigned to the wisest, kindest, and most patient judge in the federal system, Jack B. Weinstein. We needed all of Judge Weinstein's qualities to survive.

I believe that most federal judges would have dismissed our case on motion. There is no entry on a balance sheet called surplus surplus and no accounting guidelines to determine it. An expert can make a calculation, but it will be an estimate. Furthermore, surplus surplus may have been unique to Reliance. What was certain was that no insurance company had ever boasted of having surplus surplus. Judge Weinstein let it go to trial, although expressing doubts about the merits. The trial lasted two weeks. The critical issue was whether surplus surplus could be calculated with sufficient precision to be disclosed. Reliance argued it could not and if it disclosed too high or too low an amount, it might have to deal with a different kind of lawsuit.

Reliance's CEO, George Roberts, was an honest and dedicated insurance man. Since Reliance had stockholders and policyholders, he wore two hats: one to enhance profits for the stockholders and the other to protect the policyholders. There was no question Roberts favored the interests of the policyholder and opposed the Leasco takeover, because he believed Steinberg would use the excess reserves to make speculative investments and endanger the company's ability to pay claims. Steinberg, a deal man, would be prone to sell the policyholders down the river. Roberts fought hard, but when defeat was inevitable, he accepted a large increase in salary plus stock options to stay on and run the insurance operations. He did not sell out, it only looked that way.

At Roberts's deposition, he refused to acknowledge the term surplus surplus, but called it excess surplus. I asked him many times, in different forms, the same question: how can excess surplus be determined? He kept deflecting the question by saying he had never made the determination. I never gave up. Finally, his lawyer screamed, "You have asked that same question ten different ways! I will let the witness answer just once more and that's it." The anger was contagious. Red in the face and out of control, Roberts yelled, "If they had asked me to make that determination, I could have done so damn quickly." Like Steinberg, I found my own code word for the Leasco action: "the damn quickly case."

The lawyer defending Roberts was young. He had just been made partner and complained about the financial burden that exalted status conveyed. The day he became a partner, he signed a loan agreement with the firm's bank and turned over the funds to the firm to pay for his share of the firm's assets. The interest on the loan was deducted from his monthly draw. The net effect was that his take-home pay was less than his salary as an associate had been.

Late Friday afternoon, during the first week of trial, a lawyer for one of the defendants examined a director who was a Chicago lawyer and a former commissioner of the Securities and Exchange Commission. The direct examination ended at about 5:00 PM. The lawyer asked that my cross-examination proceed and court remain in session until it was concluded. The purpose: to allow the witness to return to Chicago for the weekend and not have to come back the following Tuesday, the next trial day. Judge Weinstein said that he was ready to stay late.

I objected. I said the day began at 9:00 AM, I was tired, and did not believe that I could fairly discharge my responsibilities. I did not disclose the real reason. I ordered a daily transcript of that day's testimony and wanted to review it over the recess to prepare my cross.

The judge reached a Solomonic ruling: the witness would not have to return and I would not have to cross-examine him that evening. Instead, when court resumed, the examination would proceed over the telephone. The witness was provided with a complete set of documents and instructed by the judge not to look at any documents unless directed by me.

I again objected. I said I found it an advantage to look at a witness's face and would be prejudiced by a telephonic cross-examination. A witness's demeanor, I said, was important to the trial judge. Judge Weinstein overruled my objection stating that the credibility of this particular witness was not in issue and if there were prejudice to me, I could raise it on appeal. Court was then adjourned to Tuesday morning.

After court, Rogers Derring, who represented a defendant other than the witness, invited me to dinner. We ate in an old Brooklyn Heights steak house. I relaxed, had two martinis and a steak. Derring told about his family's summer project. They owned an island off the coast of Maine. Every summer the family spent a month there. There was no electricity, only a house in progress that Derring, his wife, children and his children's friends were building. The family slept in tents, cooked over a fire, and took their sailboat to the nearest town to buy provisions. During the day, they worked on their house, swam, fished, and sailed. Derring said they went to bed at sundown and, in order to read, woke by early light. I asked when he expected to be finished and he said he hoped never.

Outside the restaurant, we met by chance a young lawyer working on the case for the firm representing the witness whose cross-examination was delayed. He was a friendly fellow and we told him about our dinner, including the two martinis. He told the partner in charge. When court reconvened on Tuesday, an angry lawyer told the judge that although Mr.

Silverman claimed to be too tired to complete cross-examination, he had plenty of energy left to down two martinis and a steak. Derring turned to his fellow colleague-in-arms, pointed his finger at him, and with outrage and anger said, "Mr. Silverman was my guest. I resent any adverse use being made of our dinner." The judge told everyone to calm down. He said, "Mr. Silverman claimed to be too tired to cross-examine, not too tired to drink martinis or eat a steak. Let us proceed with the telephonic cross-examination."

I killed the witness on cross. At one point, we heard him yell to his secretary, "Damn it, get me a glass of water right away." He did not realize that his voice carried over the speaker phone and we, sitting in the courtroom, sensed the pressure he was under. I looked at the judge and he smiled back at me.

At the end of cross, I said my examination had not been impeded by conducting it over the telephone and withdrew my objection. By so doing, I scored brownie points with the judge.

Bjork and Harnes assisted me at the trial. They sat at counsel table, on either side of me. Bjork, glancing at the threesome, said ironically, "A rose between two thorns."

After the trial, we reversed our roles; I assisted them in writing the brief. The brief was a masterpiece. The only better analysis was that underlying Judge Weinstein's decision. We won a very important case, perhaps my most important case. We celebrated our victory in an unusual way, by moving to fancy new quarters.

Harnes lived on Park Avenue and Bjork on Fifth Avenue. When they started work, my offices were downtown, a good distance away, in the Woolworth building and consisted of three rooms: a reception room where the secretary sat, my office, and a conference room shared by Bjork and Harnes. They lobbied for more space and argued that if we moved to midtown, they could spend more time at work. In the past, I took no pride in my office. The space and the furniture were unimportant. My work excited me. That and being the boss made the dreary surroundings shine. My attitude changed when we moved. We found beautiful space at a premier address, One Rockefeller Center, and moved in the spring of 1972. There were three private offices; my office, a large corner office, a reception area large enough for two secretaries, several chairs and a couch, and a combination library and conference room. I bought new furniture. The office looked spiffy, reflected an aura of success, and, yes, I was proud.

5

THE GUNSLINGER, THE SLOB, AND A BIRD

THE STOCKHOLDER PLAINTIFF HAD been good to me. He applauded when I won and was uncritical when I lost. Why uncritical? He was unaffected by the result as his stake was so small. In class actions, the plaintiff lawyer is the real winner or loser. I longed to represent a flesh and blood client who owned the case and would rejoice in victory and lament in defeat. The Dr. Rolfe case satisfied this longing.

Rolfe lived and worked in Cleveland. He was a physician, specializing in ophthalmology. He was in his late fifties with a nest egg of $300,000, which he turned over to an analyst at White Weld. The analyst did well and after five years, the doctor was worth $1.3 million.

One day at work, Rolfe's financial adviser collapsed and died. White Weld suggested the account be assigned to the analyst's assistant. The doctor, now a millionaire, could not accept the idea of an assistant handling his account and said no. The firm then recommended Akiyoshi Yamada, a young hotshot money manager of the type called "gunslingers." Rolfe met with Yamada, was impressed, and retained him with the following provisos: the stocks and their replacements would remain in the custody of White Weld and the brokerage firm would exercise oversight of Yamada's activities.

The gunslingers were crooks. They purchased for pennies large amounts of stock in worthless companies. They then manipulated the price of the company's stock by trading with each other at progressively higher prices. As the price rose, they sold their own holdings to the accounts they managed, hoping as the final step to unload the worthless securities on an unsuspecting public. They were often, however, unable to complete this final step. Their clients were left holding the bag. They complained to the SEC, whose investigation led to a criminal indictment. Yamada was an active player; in fact, one of the ringleaders of this group.

Yamada was convicted of stock fraud and sent to jail, but Rolfe, one of his victims, lost his entire stake of $1.3 million.

The complaint named Yamada as a defendant and Rolfe had an open-and-shut case against him. But he was probably broke or, if he had money, we would probably not be able to find it. The only viable defendant was White Weld.

The doctor had two claims against White Weld. The firm had failed to supervise Yamada's trading activities and was negligent in recommending him. Brokerage firms were held liable for failing to supervise, but only when the customer's account was managed by an employee. No court had as yet held a brokerage firm liable for losses caused by an independent investment manager recommended by the firm. The case against White Weld was weak. Courts are reluctant to hold one independent contractor (White Weld) liable for injury caused by another independent contractor (Yamada). The brokerage firm's lawyer was so confident of victory that he wasted no time making motions and asking for an immediate trial. Trial was scheduled for the summer of 1975.

Before the trial began, Harnes asked me for a favor. Her son, John, a junior at Harvard, was burned out and at loose ends. He had no job for the summer and did not want to return to college. She asked if I could find work for him. The litigation bags, big boxes with large handles (some firms used duffle bags), I lugged to court were large and heavy. John was tall, young, and strong and could handle the bags. I hired him for the summer. John's first day at work was a Sunday, the day before the trial was to start. Rolfe was also in the office. He was our first witness and had to be prepared. The defendants had taken his deposition and we had produced documents, including several letters written by Rolfe to Yamada. In the letters, Dr. Rolfe enthusiastically endorsed Yamada's plans to double or triple his account.

My game plan was to present Rolfe as an old man nearing retirement whose investment objective was the conservation of his capital. The defendants sought to present him as a greedy fellow, willing to accept a high amount of risk to quickly double or triple his worth. I was unhappy with the letters. Read literally, they suggested that the doctor approved of speculative investments. On close inspection, however, it was clear that the letters were written in desperation after Rolfe had incurred large losses. The doctor hoped that by doubling or tripling what was left in his depleted account, his losses could be recouped.

With John and the doctor present, I played two roles: me examining the doctor and the doctor answering the questions. Then I switched. I cross-examined the doctor and answered for him. At all times, my presentation of Rolfe's proposed testimony was consistent with the doctor's prior testimony and the way I wanted to present him. Then, I asked the doctor the very same questions. His answers were much different from those I had proposed in my role-playing just minutes earlier. His answers would have doomed the case. I was frustrated. Why couldn't he remember and repeat the prepared answers?

John asked to prepare Dr. Rolfe in another room. I worked on other matters for the trial but held little prospect for success. For us to win, the judge would have to stretch the law, a process he would not undertake if he believed Rolfe understood the risks and encouraged Yamada. John and the doctor returned to my office. I questioned him again. This time the doctor's responses were satisfactory. At trial, the doctor was our first witness. Although he forgot much of his trial preparation, his overall testimony was not a total disaster.

The second witness was our expert, Martin J. Whitman. He was one of those guys who looked old probably even at birth. If there was a prize for the worst dressed investment banker anywhere in the world, Whitman would win hands down. His table manners were shocking. Most of the time, he used his fingers instead of a fork. He loved salad dressing, poured it onto lettuce, picked up a fistful of leaves, and slurped. The dressing cascaded down his chin and onto his tie. He spoke in clipped sentences using only those words necessary to convey his meaning.

While his surface was rough, Whitman was all substance. He graduated summa cum laude from Syracuse and held a degree from the Institute for Advanced Studies at Princeton. He was an adjunct professor at Yale's School of Management. Whitman was brilliant, sincere, and honest. He had a large circle of friends and was truly loved and admired. In my small world, Whitman was the brightest star. At sixty, he was discovered by the leading financial institutions and became a major player in world markets. At eighty-three, he remains active in his own firm and is as modest and unassuming as when we first met. Any doubts about Whitman's achievements can be resolved by checking Wikipedia.

Whitman is extraordinarily rich but lives modestly. Dressed in jeans and a moldy old sweater, he once met with a contractor and discussed necessary but expensive work on his country home. The contractor asked Whitman if he could afford to pay. Whitman made a typical Whitman remark: "I'm poor, but I have lots of money." Michael Todd, the flamboyant theatrical producer, said, "I've been broke but never poor. Poor is a state of mind." Marty drives a Honda and has lived in the same apartment for over forty years. Lots of money has not changed Marty. He was born poor and never changed his state of mind.

Whitman analyzed the doctor's portfolio at the time it was turned over to Yamada. He divided the securities into three categories: high quality, low quality, and lowest of the low. A high quality stock had good earnings and a sound balance sheet. A low quality stock had no or little present earnings but a good business and prospects of becoming a high quality stock. The lowest of the low were stocks without earnings or prospects for earnings, little if any assets, and no discernable business. Before Yamada got his hands on Rolfe's portfolio, it consisted of high quality stocks with a sprinkling of low quality stocks. After Yamada took over, he sold all the stocks and purchased stocks that were the lowest of the low. Whitman's testimony made the case against Yamada very strong, but I still needed to tie in the brokerage firm.

Bigotry gave me the break I needed.

Henry Roth was Yamada's lawyer. He practiced on his own from an office in the wastelands of Queens. He was short and plump. Most lawyers wear suits to court. Roth wore the same maroon corduroy jacket throughout the trial. His shirts were frayed and his shoes scuffed. Although defendants' lawyers generally lunch together, the white shoe lawyers representing White Weld refused to break bread with Roth.

Yamada did not attend the first day of trial, so that day Roth lunched alone. The next day, I invited him to join us and paid for his lunch. I did this throughout the trial. At one lunch, we discussed the case and the likely outcome. We had made a strong case against Yamada and, in addition, the brokerage firm's witnesses were placing all the blame on him. Since Yamada did not intend to testify, a judgment against him was certain. I said that if the judge pinned the tail on Yamada, he would likely exonerate the brokerage firm. Such an outcome would not be good for Yamada or the doctor. While Yamada was broke, he was young and might someday make money. A judgment against him would burden him for years. Since my client was old, he wanted to collect now. He could only do so if the brokerage firm was found liable. I suggested to Roth that we dismiss the case against Yamada if he had evidence against and was willing to implicate the brokerage firm. The lawyer made no immediate comment, but at the end of the day he asked if he and Yamada could meet me that night at my office.

At the meeting, Yamada's lawyer insisted upon a written agreement. The general form states that the case will be dismissed against the witness if he testifies truthfully. In order to avoid a claim by the other side that the testimony was purchased, it is prudent to enter into the agreement before hearing the proffered testimony. I was unwilling to buy a pig in the poke and insisted on a preview. I asked Yamada's lawyer to tell me what he believed Yamada's testimony would be. Here's where my kindness to the man the other lawyers avoided, where my investment in his lunches paid off. Roth's take sounded good; so before hearing Yamada himself, I signed the agreement. It provided that if Yamada appeared at the trial and answered every question fully and honestly, we would dismiss the case against him. I recognized that I was taking a chance in dismissing the case against the only defendant whose culpability was certain, but I recognized that my client wanted money, not an empty judgment.

Yamada was tall and powerfully built. Like most con men, he was charming. He described the scheme. He and a few other money managers purchased dormant securities for pennies. They then resold the securities to each other's accounts at ever-increasing prices. He said he hoped the heavy trading by his group would attract interest in the stocks and entice the public to purchase. Unfortunately for Rolfe and the other accounts, the public did not bite and the clients were stuck. Then, Yamada helped establish liability against White Weld.

He said he was concerned the firm might blow the whistle on the poor quality stocks going into Rolfe's account; instead, the firm complained that Yamada's trades were not generating enough commissions. To keep the firm happy, he directed business to it from other accounts. He said that White Weld was the only reputable firm handling transactions in the bogus securities and the other brokerage firms were owned by members of the gunslingers group. Yamada was astonished that White Weld's surveillance officers did not detect the fraud since the trading pattern was so unusual. He said Rolfe was unsophisticated and did not have the foggiest notion of what was going on in his account. When the meeting ended at midnight, I knew I had made a good deal.

The next day, Yamada testified. He was even more charming in court than in my office and his testimony was very helpful. On cross-examination, White Weld's lawyer suggested he had fabricated a story to avoid personal liability. Yamada said he did not fear a judgment as he had no money and planned to return to Japan. The hostile cross-examination of Yamada served a purpose, but one different from its intent. When the lawyer got into the substance of Yamada's testimony, he reacted with more damning testimony against the brokerage firm. He said brokers at White Weld threatened to blow the whistle unless Yamada generated more commission business. White Weld was now tied to the scheme.

A friend of mine observed that in trials, there were times when we should thank God for our opponents. I thought that if they had not snubbed Yamada's lawyer, if they had not treated Yamada so rudely on the stand … I looked up towards the sky and closed my eyes.

After cross, the judge questioned Yamada. I detected a shift in the judge's attitude. Prior to Yamada's testimony, the judge referred to Dr. Rolfe as "the plaintiff." During the course of the day's questioning of Yamada, the judge made repeated reference to "the doctor." I read the change as a sign that in the judge's eyes, Rolfe was emerging as one of society's dedicated servants, a medical doctor. At the conclusion of Yamada's testimony, I was satisfied that he had lived up to his end of the bargain, so I supported the request that the case against him be dismissed.

When the trial was over, the judge asked for post-trial briefs. The plaintiff's brief came first, then the defendant's, and then our reply. As John was familiar with the facts, I asked him to prepare a first draft. I spent several hours with him going over the format of a brief. The judge was an intellectual and John a classics major. I asked him to weave in references to Greek mythology. He equated White Weld with Cyclops, the one-eyed dragon who, plied with wine, closed his one eye. "White Weld, plied with commission income, like Cyclops with wine, closed its eye and Rolfe's account was decimated." His brief was better than I had any right to expect from an untrained and inexperienced college student. Harnes revised her son's factual presentation and added legal analysis. The brief, a mother and son collaboration, was a fine job.

In his decision, the judge found the brokerage firm liable but limited its damages to Rolfe's brokerage fees paid to the firm. The judge split the pie, reasoning that White Weld should not profit, but should not be liable for Rolfe's losses.

We appealed the damage ruling to the Court of Appeals and White Weld cross-appealed the determination of liability. The appellate court reversed the damage ruling and affirmed White Weld's liability. The case was sent back for a new determination on damages. On remand, the judge gave the doctor a full recovery of $1.3 million, plus interest. The decision was a landmark case. It appeared on the front page of the *New York Law Journal* and was discussed in many academic law journals.

After Rolfe received his money, he called me and asked if I would recommend an investment adviser, "One that will make lots of money for me." The doctor had learned nothing. With tongue in cheek, I replied, "Are you serious? If I were to recommend an adviser and he turned out to be a bum, you could sue me, citing Rolfe vs. White Weld against me." I did, in fact, recommend an adviser for Rolfe, Whitman, our expert in the case. He managed Rolfe's money very well and the doctor had a happy and uneventful retirement.

Several months after the case was over, I had a settlement meeting in another case. After I made an offer, the lawyer prepared a handwritten memorandum and asked me to sign it. Since his client had not accepted it, only my client would be bound. The request was unusual. I asked for an explanation. After some hesitation, he said he heard that in the Rolfe case, I had repeatedly reneged on offers to settle. He did not want to take my offer back, get approval, and then learn I had changed my mind.

What he had heard about the course of settlement talks in the Rolfe case was a half truth. Before trial, I offered to settle Rolfe's claim for $150,000. The offer was rejected and the counter-offer of $75,000 was rejected by me. After trial, but before the decision, White Weld accepted my offer of $150,000, which it had previously rejected. I said circumstances had changed and the offer made before trial was no longer available. I offered $300,000 and it was rejected.

After the decision on appeal, White Weld offered to pay $300,000. I advised Rolfe to reject it as I thought we had a good chance of achieving a full recovery. There were no further talks.

After I explained the course of the settlement talks, the lawyer was nonplussed; he insisted I sign the memo. I replied, "I'll sign if you put in a provision that if a bird appears in the sky, I can walk away from the offer." He left. A few hours later, a settlement agreement in the amount of my offer, signed by his client, arrived by hand with a note: "I hope you saw no birds." So, two wise guys came to terms.

The corporate litigation bar is relatively small, but I never heard any more flak about the Rolfe settlement talks.

6
HER SON JOHN
AND THE UNFRIENDLY JUDGE

JOHN HARNES RETURNED TO Harvard in the fall. The following year, upon graduation, he worked for us during the day and attended Brooklyn Law School at night. It was a classic case of a reverse progression. John went to Buckley, one of New York's finest independent schools, and then St. Mark's, an elite boarding school, and then Harvard. His grades were bad at Harvard and only Brooklyn Law School would accept him.

After he graduated from law school, I thought John should work with a large firm where he might have a future; he had none with me. No firm wanted him. They said they preferred candidates who graduated from Brooklyn College and then from Harvard Law, and not the other way round. John stayed with me for a few years but then a problem developed which convinced me he had to move on. We tried a case before Milton Pollack, a judge in the New York federal court. Before becoming a judge, Pollack defended stockholder cases. He was undeniably smart, but arrogant and nasty. When he was a lawyer, I had several cases against him and we clashed. Our first battle involved Schenley Industries and its CEO, Lewis Rosenstiel.

A stockholder sued Rosenstiel accusing him of looting Schenley. The case was a strong one and a settlement was pending in the Chancery Court in Delaware. Although a stockholder can enter into a settlement on behalf of the corporation, it does not become final until a judge approves. Before the judge decides, notice of the pending settlement is mailed to all stockholders and they are given the right to object.

The settlement notice attracted a lot of stockholder anger. Rosenstiel was getting away with murder. Lawyer after lawyer specializing in stockholder cases was approached to oppose the settlement; all refused. Why? They feared the plaintiff's lawyer for Schenley would retaliate by objecting to one of their phony settlements. Not so the fearless and brand new law firm of Rosenfeld and Silverman. They filed an objection.

We tossed a coin as to who would argue. I won. Pollack represented the defendants. He had reddish blond hair which looked dyed, and leonine features. He was pompous and self-assured. Pollack attacked me early in my argument before the judge: "Who is Mr. Silverman? He has not made his mark in the liquor or chemical business. In fact, I have not heard of him as a lawyer. Why should we listen to him?" I replied: "It is true I am just starting and Mr. Pollack is renowned. Fortunately for the cause of the Schenley stockholders, justice is blind and their cause will be determined on the merits." Pollack grew nastier as the argument proceeded. Whenever I discussed the merits of the case and the lack of merits of the settlement, Pollack interrupted me. When I objected to his rude behavior, Pollack said he could not remain silent while I was misleading the court. At one point, I took matters into my own hands and angrily told a lion of the Bar, sotto voce, "Go fuck yourself."

I lost; the settlement was approved. I do not want to make excuses for losing but at that time Delaware courts were strongly pro-defendant. Delaware earned revenues from companies incorporating there and the courts, to encourage the process, tended to favor the directors. One law professor, after analyzing Delaware decisions, wrote that the state, in its desire to attract corporate business, "Had won the race to the bottom."

Some years later, President Nixon appointed Pollack to the federal bench in New York. When he became a judge, I wondered whether he would treat me fairly. I did not have long to wait. Shortly after he became a judge, one of my cases was assigned to him. The answer to my question came early in the case and it was loud and clear: No. I thought I was getting somewhere in my cross-examination of a witness when Pollack interrupted and said, "Mr. Silverman, no more of your wise guy, smart aleck questions. They are not helping the court. I will now ask a question." The judge then turned to the witness and asked, "Did you exercise business judgment in approving the contract?" That was the ultimate question in the case. If the witness's lawyer had asked it, I would have objected on the ground that it was leading and called for a conclusion. But a lawyer cannot object to a judge's question. The witness answered yes. Pollack turned to me and said, "You see, Mr. Silverman, when the right question is asked, the court is helped." Pollack decided who was going to win before hearing the evidence and never changed his mind. My side was going to lose.

Pollack had discretion to decide the factual claims against us and was confident his decision would be upheld on appeal. The rule on appeal protects a trial judge's findings of fact, unless they are "clearly erroneous." In practicable application, findings are affirmed if they are supported by any credible evidence. Such evidence existed, although it was outweighed by contrary evidence.

We had raised an issue at trial not raised in the complaint and the defendants had not objected to that. Courts will normally decide all issues that have been fairly and fully tried, regardless of whether they have been included in the complaint. Not Judge Pollack. The claim rested on a legal question and so, if it was decided against us, could be raised on appeal without deference to Pollack's decision. We would have a good ground for appeal. Pollack was not only the judge, but my adversary. He knew an appeal could be taken only on claims ruled upon. So, he announced he was not going to rule on the claim and that the parties should not waste time briefing it. There was a slim avenue open. I could petition the Court of Appeals for a writ of mandamus. If obtained, the writ would command Pollack to determine the claim. He would, of course, find for defendants, but I would then have a good ground for appeal.

John worked with me at the trial. It was his task to prepare the first draft of the petition and then give it to his mother for revision. I read the revised petition and did not like it; there were personal attacks on Pollack in it. He deserved them and more, but it was a bad litigation tactic. I spoke with both John and his mother. I said, "Take out all personal attacks on Pollack; they will irritate the Court of Appeals and distract from our argument." Harnes said she had already removed many and agreed to remove the remaining ones.

I did not read the petition until after it was served. One glaring insult remained. Regarding evidence against the defendants, the petition compared Pollack to the three monkeys who "see no evil, speak no evil, or hear no evil." The comparison was justified, but was a serious blunder. An insult against the judge would anger the judges passing on the petition.

When I confronted Harnes, she said she wanted to take out the reference to monkeys but John refused. What mother can control her son? John had no right to overrule his mother and me. The petition was denied on the ground that we could present the unresolved issue in an amended complaint at which time Pollack would be required to decide the issue. We filed the new complaint and Pollack called for an immediate conference. He began by asking why I should not be sanctioned for filing the new complaint. Sanctions are imposed on lawyers who file sham pleadings. If the attack is against plaintiff's pleadings, the motion is initiated by defendants and they bear a heavy burden of persuasion. The motions are disfavored and rarely granted. Prior to my case, never in the history of sanctions, had one been initiated by the judge. Moreover, the judge reversed the procedure; I had the burden to persuade him that a motion he made should not be granted by him. Of course, I lost. I was fined $15,000. I could have appealed, but decided against it. If I appealed and won, it would be a Pyrrhic victory; I would have to try a claim before a judge who believed it so frivolous that I should be fined for asserting it. There comes a time when a lawyer has to lick his wounds and pack his bags. That time had come.

The time had also come for John to find a new home. As an inducement to a firm to hire him, I agreed to pay his salary there for one year. When that firm imploded, I got John another job. When he was asked to leave that firm, I rehired him. He was married and had a child and no job. His mother had worked hard for me and deserved a favor. Maybe John had changed. He stayed with me until my firm was dissolved. Then, with another lawyer at my firm, he formed a new firm.

7
AFFIRMATIVE ACTIONS

MOST OF MY WORK was on a contingent fee basis, which means that I got paid only if I won. The economics did not mesh with reality. Although I worked hard each year, some years I made nothing or very little, and other years, I made too much. However, unlike revenues, the office expenses did not vary. In fact, they increased as we added lawyers and staff. In the dry years, I used borrowed funds to meet expenses, but only if a fee had been awarded and would shortly be paid. Otherwise, I raised capital by selling stock.

Chemical Bank, with a branch in our office building, was our bank. When I deemed a loan appropriate, I explained to the bank officer, "Look, here is an agreement. It provides for a fee to my firm of X dollars. I will certainly get it. It is ordered by the judge and the payer is a large solvent company. It will take time because of a technicality. The fee does not have to be paid until the order becomes final. That means no party can appeal. No party can appeal because all have consented. It will take about sixty days before the fee is paid. I need to borrow half of X now. When I receive the fee, I will repay the loan."

Bank officers are not the brightest bulbs; in branches they are even dimmer. It took time and patience to get the first loan, but after it had been repaid, the next transaction was easy. However, there was a nagging problem. The people handling my account never stayed very long. Each change meant that I had to reeducate the new officer.

One day, I received a call from a man named Herman Taitt, who said he was new at the branch and had been assigned my account. He asked if he could come to my office. Before our meeting, I got out the papers from the most recent loan. Although I did not then need a loan and none was outstanding, I anticipated I would be back at the bank and could use the meeting to my advantage. Taitt was handsome, smart, and black. He said he had studied my account and was aware that I borrowed against future fees. When I next needed a loan, I should just call. He would prepare the loan agreement, send it to me by hand, and when it was returned, he would deposit the proceeds into my account. Although lending money is the business of a bank, only Taitt made me feel I was doing the bank a favor.

Taitt stayed put for two years. One day he called and invited me to lunch at the famous 21. "I'm leaving the branch but not the bank. I've been reassigned to headquarters and the change represents a step up the corporate ladder. The rumor is that the bank wants to advance blacks. It's about time. I met my replacement and told him about your lending pattern. He's a good guy and you should get along." I was happy for Taitt and said, "I would not be surprised at all if you become the president of the bank."

I did not hear from Taitt for two years. When he called again, he asked if I remembered him. "Of course, you're the president of the Chemical Bank." "No. No. I've made no progress, been put in dead-end areas and denied promotion. Several black officers had brought an employment discrimination case. I am in sympathy with their complaint but not them. I would like you to meet with my group and chart a course." I agreed to meet, but told Taitt I had no experience in discrimination cases.

Taitt and about a dozen other black officers came to my office. They said they were denied promotions they deserved, and that there was out and out discrimination against blacks. There were times when they were asked to train new white officers. Before long, the new officers received promotion after promotion, while the black officers who had trained them remained in place. In time, a black officer found himself reporting to the officer he had trained. The frustration level was high because they knew they were better bankers than the white officers who had moved up while they hadn't.

Banks had been the province of the white male until Congress passed a law outlawing discrimination by companies doing business with the government. Banks serving such companies were also considered to be doing business with the government. The banks began actively recruiting blacks. Since so many jobs in banks and elsewhere had been closed to blacks, the available pool was large and overflowing with talent. One of the black officers, Henry Williams, who came that evening to my office was a Rhodes scholar, summa cum laude from Princeton and a graduate of Harvard Law School. He attended the bank's six month course on credit. At the end, the instructor flunked the Rhodes scholar, Harvard lawyer and required him to spend an additional three months studying credit. The guy was so smart and the subject so ridiculously easy that the instructor had to be biased. I asked Williams, "Why, in heaven's name, did you join the bank? There are so many better opportunities. I'll bet there are no white Rhodes scholars at the bank or even ones who graduated with distinction." He replied, "In my neighborhood, banks represent the establishment. They stand in contrast to the fly by night businesses that have 'going out of business' signs every other week. Banks are forever and a job there means security for my family and me. That's why I chose Chemical."

A pattern of discrimination against black officers up for promotion had sparked a lawsuit by four officers against the bank. The group meeting with me was upset over a proposed settlement of the case. They showed me the agreement. The four named plaintiffs were declared representatives of all black officers and were given preferential treatment. They received cash and promotions; all others in that category got nothing. Worse, as part of the settlement, they released the claims of all other black officers. Since the settlement compromised the rights of the class, a hearing and court approval were needed before the settlement could take effect. A notice was sent to the black officers describing the complaint and the settlement and giving class members the right to object to the settlement.

There was only one woman at the meeting. She asked to meet separately with me. "Don't include black women," she said. "We are not discriminated against. The white officers flirt with us and frankly we get good jobs and promotions. The white bank officers compete against the black men, not against us."

The men who had come to see me claimed that a class action settlement benefiting only the plaintiffs was not only unfair but unlawful. I prepared the objections which accused the plaintiffs and their lawyers of a sellout. I gave them to Taitt and asked him to get as many black male officers as possible to sign. Taitt did his job. He collected signatures from a majority of the class. The judge, of course, rejected the settlement.

Subsequently, Taitt's group and the original complainants entered into a joint agreement with the bank. It received the support of the court and the class. The joint agreement provided for cash payment for all class members based on their years at the bank and the appointment of Williams, the Rhodes Scholar, to serve as an ombudsman. Black officers who believed they were discriminated against could go directly to Williams and, if he believed the claim had merit, he could bypass the chain of command and go directly to the president of the bank. The black officers unanimously approved the settlement. I received, however, several anonymous hate letters. One called me a "nigger lover." Another claimed I was having affairs with my clients. I really liked my black clients, but denied there was any impropriety; they were all males and I am heterosexual to a fault.

Taitt had taken the lead in opposing the settlement and in the negotiations that led to the revised agreement. The agreement became final sixty days after it was approved by the judge. On the sixty-first day, Taitt was fired.

Under the Civil Rights Act, adverse job action cannot be taken against an employee because he asserted his civil rights. I agreed to take Herman's case. We sued the bank.

Before trial, I read a treatise on how to try a retaliation case. The authors said that a prima facie case was made by putting in evidence the facts that the employee had asserted his civil rights, and that thereafter the employer fired or demoted him. The burden then shifts to the employer to show the adverse job action was the result of poor performance. After the employer testifies, the employee is given the opportunity to rebut the employer's evidence that he performed poorly.

The case was tried before a jury. The presiding judge was Robert Carter. He was formerly the general counsel of the NAACP, the architect of the federal civil rights law, and clearly the perfect judge for our case. If I had been given the right to select a judge from the available pool, I would have chosen Carter.

I followed the treatise. Taitt testified about the promotion discrimination case, his prominent role in opposing the initial settlement and negotiating the second agreement, and the fact that he was fired shortly after the agreement became final. The bank's lawyer, Ronald Greene, was a leading employment lawyer. He was skillful and, what we called in the 1950s, smooth, immaculately groomed. Looking at and listening to him, one would never guess his origins from a poor Brooklyn family. Greene's firm sponsored semiannual forums on discrimination in the workplace and the general counsels of major corporations were invited to attend. Greene was the featured speaker. He discussed recent decisions and advised on strategy. When a corporation was sued, it turned to Greene; he was the preeminent defense lawyer in discrimination cases.

In cross-examining Taitt, Greene was gentle but expertly laid the foundation for the bank's defense. He claimed that Taitt was dismissed because of poor performance and not as retaliation. He showed Taitt written evaluations of his performance and asked whether the reports had been read by Taitt at or about the time they were written, and whether he had been provided copies of the reports. Taitt answered both questions in the affirmative. Greene then asked Taitt to read the penultimate paragraph of a report on him which gave him the right to object, in writing or orally, to any part of the report. He asked whether Taitt had voiced any objection. When Taitt said no, Greene ended his cross and began the bank's defense.

He called the officers who wrote the reports. They testified that they liked Taitt, thought he had the makings of a good bank officer, tried their best to motivate him, and give him opportunities to shine. However, referring to the performance reports, they noted Taitt was late to work, failed to call meetings with his staff, was in charge of the bank's Christmas party that flopped, and was unsuccessful in attracting new business when he was made the new-business officer. They denied their evaluations were related in any way to Taitt's assertion of his civil rights.

Judge Carter was protective of the civil rights law. He wanted them used for the purposes intended and not by an undeserving black to extract money from his employer. By the time Taitt returned to rebut the evidence, the judge's mind was made up: Taitt was attempting to use the civil rights laws to cover his poor performance and to extort money from the bank. Taitt's rebuttal testimony annoyed the judge. At the conclusion of the case, he ruled that our evidence was insufficient to allow the case to go to the jury. He dismissed the case and discharged the jury.

I took an appeal even though I had little confidence that the court would reverse Carter. He had an outstanding reputation for fairness, was a leading advocate for civil rights, and had decided that another black man had no case. At argument, the appeals court appeared to be sympathetic. Nevertheless, I was astonished when the court reversed and remanded the case for a new trial. At the second trial, I changed tactics and ignored the treatise. At the first trial, I put in only the technical evidence that Taitt had asserted his civil rights and was fired. This time I put all the evidence in our direct case, holding nothing back for rebuttal.

After Taitt testified about his role in the discrimination case and the subsequent firing, I asked him to enumerate what he considered his strengths as a bank officer. He said that he had a thorough knowledge of credit, worked well with customers and fellow bank officers, and was loyal to the bank. He said the president of the bank had come to Taitt's office to present him with a letter commending his work. After the letter was received in evidence, I asked whether he was aware of any other officers receiving a similar letter hand delivered by the president. Taitt said he was not.

I then asked Taitt to discuss what he perceived to be his weaknesses as a bank office. Taitt said, "I have no weaknesses." This answer led directly into Taitt's rebuttal testimony which at the first trial had only served to annoy the judge. Now it was coming in before the bank's witnesses could put on their carefully rehearsed dog and pony show.

I asked, "You say that you have no weaknesses, yet the most recent report on your performance states that last year you were late for work on five occasions. How, if at all, do you explain your tardiness?" Taitt answered that he lived in Queens and had to take a bus and two subways to work. The trip took about an hour and ten minutes when the transit system was on time. He allowed an extra thirty minutes to guard against breakdowns. Most days, he arrived at work early. Occasionally, the extra minutes were not enough. Of the five late days, several were only by five or ten minutes. One day, on a bitter cold morning, the bus broke down and he walked three miles, in a snowstorm, to the subway station. Both trains were unusually slow and he arrived at work fifty minutes late.

I then referred to the bank's Christmas party. "You were in charge and the party was a flop. Did that not reflect a weakness on your part as a bank officer?" Taitt said, "I am not Perle Mesta and have had very little experience in throwing parties. I tried but faced several obstacles." To my question what were the obstacles, Taitt testified that, "the bank officers were to provide me with names and addresses of their customers and my task was to make sure they received invitations. The officers did not consider the party a top priority item, resented my nagging, and were late in turning over the names of their customers. Some who might have come if they had received timely notice declined because of other engagements. It was Christmas and it is a busy season. The day selected for the party was also the first day of Chanukah. I appealed to the officer in charge of operations to get the date changed, pointing out that many of the bank's customers were Jewish. He refused. Finally, on the day of the party, it rained heavily and the rain turned to sleet and snow. I thought it remarkable that anyone attended but about two hundred did, more than the number who had attended the prior year."

I then turned to his role as new-business leader and asked what the job entailed. Taitt said he made cold calls on businesses in an effort to persuade them to change banks. The bank provided no inducements for a business to switch. "Nevertheless, I got two new customers, two more than my predecessor." Taitt went on to say that his work in obtaining the two new customers was the very reason the president of the bank wrote a letter commending him.

It was now Greene's turn to cross-examine Taitt. The bank's lawyer recognized that questioning Taitt would likely be a disaster for his client. If Taitt had been shown his performance reports, he would have acknowledged they were half truths and repeated his testimony, drilling it into the minds of the jury. Also, it was not Greene's style to bully a black witness before a black judge. Instead, Greene declined to cross Taitt and called the bank officers who had so effectively testified against Taitt at the first trial.

What had happened to Taitt at the first trial now hit the bank's witnesses. When one discussed Taitt's tardiness, the judge interrupted to ask where the witness lived and how he got to work. The witness said he lived in the East Sixties and walked to work. The judge also asked whether the witness were aware that Taitt came to work early most days. The witness said that when he arrived he often saw Taitt already at work. The judge asked why the late arrivals were noted and not the early ones. The witness meekly said, "A bank officer is supposed to come on time, I only marked the late arrivals." The judge shook his head in disbelief.

The judge also asked each witness when he had provided Taitt with names for the Christmas party. One said about two weeks before the party, another said one week, and a third did not remember. The judge asked each witness whether he attended the party; two said they had not.

The judge also asked each witness whether he had received a letter of commendation from the president of the bank. None had. The judge then asked whether they knew of any officer who had received such a letter. Two said they had not. The third, a wiseguy, said he knew of one: Taitt. A judge can get far more from a witness than any lawyer. The judge's questions cannot be objected to, he can interrupt testimony, and the majesty of his office intimidates witnesses.

Judge Carter did a great job of cross-examination and I did not want to muddy the waters. I said my cross would be very short, as I did not want to waste the court's or the jury's time by rehashing testimony. However, I did not want the jury to draw the inference that I accepted a witness's testimony because I did not question him, a pointed reference to Greene's failure to cross Taitt. To reinforce the point, I stared several times first at Taitt and then at Greene.

Damages were problematic. After Taitt was fired, he started his own business as a financial consultant and was doing quite well. He believed he would soon be making more money than in his old job. While the jury was deliberating, the bank's lawyer made a fair settlement offer and Taitt accepted it. We informed the judge and he discharged the jury. The settlement was placed under seal, so I am not at liberty to disclose the amount.

I met members of the jury in the hallway and questioned them. One was an executive for IBM. I thought she would be against us, but she said she was for us. She also said the one black woman on the jury was hostile towards Taitt. I asked Taitt why a black woman would be unsympathetic. He said, "Black men have a bad habit of leaving their women and some black women take it out on all black men. Who knows? I may have reminded her of a deserter of a husband or one who abandoned a family member or friend."

I had wanted to exclude the white woman from IBM from the jury but was out of peremptory challenges. Each side can excuse, at will, a prospective juror, but has a limited number of challenges. The bank would probably have removed the black woman if it had not used up its challenges. Relying on stereotypes in selecting a jury may be a mistake. A person's prejudice may differ from the stereotypical view. Who really knows why one person is prejudiced against another, or whether prejudice is even the cause of hostility.

8
MY OPPONENT
BECOMES A JUDGE

THE CORPORATE DEFENSE BAR was a bastion of male dominance. Not only were the lead lawyers men but, as near as I can recall, so were all the assistants. I did not encounter a woman opponent until Susan Getzendanner. I represented the minority shareholders of Transocean Oil and Gas, and she represented Esmark, the owner of a majority of Transocean's stock. She was a partner in the Chicago firm of Mayer, Brown, and Platt. Although Getzendanner was trial counsel, Leo Hertzl, a corporate lawyer and senior partner in Mayer Brown, attended every court proceeding, deposition, and meeting. Conference calls were held even on mundane matters to allow Hertzl to participate. Esmark was his client and, although he did not litigate, he controlled the defense of the case.

Transocean's directors were also defendants. The company was incorporated in Delaware and based in Texas. Two Texas law firms represented them. One represented the affiliated directors (those who were officers of either Transocean or Esmark), and the other represented the non-affiliated or independent directors (those who were not employed by either company). The Texas lawyers were virtually inactive; Hertzl and Getzendanner controlled the defense.

Esmark wanted to increase its majority stake in Transocean to 100 percent ownership and it wanted to do so on the cheap. The first step was a cash tender offer to the minority stockholders at $12 per share. It was unlikely that Esmark would acquire all the outstanding stock in the tender offer—there are always holdouts—but the offer would be successful if Esmark raised its stake to 90 percent. As the owner of at least 90 percent, Esmark could embark on the second step, a short-form merger which allows the super majority shareholder to acquire the minority's stock without a vote. The minority has only one right: to dissent to the merger and seek fair value through an appraisal proceeding. The proceeding is disadvantageous for the dissenting stockholder. It can only be brought as an individual action, is expensive, and technical rules impede a true determination of fair value.

Transocean, a small oil and gas company, held a unique position in the vast natural resources industry. The company partnered with major companies in bidding on leases on offshore property in the Gulf of Mexico. Before bidding, Transocean was asked by its partners to review the data and advise as to which leases should be bid for and the amount of the bid. Why was Transocean selected? Its president, Stormy Smith, was the only geologist to chart the potential oil and gas fields in the Gulf. In deference to Smith's expertise, the consortium also designated Transocean as the operator of the leases. As operator, Transocean decided which leases should be explored first, supervised the exploration activity, and oversaw production. Transocean and its partners made a perfect team. Transocean lacked the capital to bid on its own; the others lacked the expertise.

The minority stockholders of Transocean were mostly large, sophisticated institutional investors. They included the Ford Foundation, the trust department of the Morgan Guaranty Trust Company, and General American Investors. They knew Transocean was a rare company with enormous potential.

I got the case through Harold Kingsberg, an officer of General American. Kingsberg was a graduate of Harvard Business School and an excellent securities analyst. He also managed money as an accommodation for friends. At least one of them owned Transocean and she became my client and the plaintiff in the lawsuit. General American itself would not sue. Institutional investors rely on the goodwill of the management of companies whose stock they own. A lawsuit against one management might make the institution an unwelcome investor in other companies. Kingsberg's client was the cat's paw.

The case was strong on the merits. The $12 offer was much too low, but there was a serious legal problem. The tender offer was voluntary. Stockholders had an effective remedy against a low-ball price: don't tender. But did they have that choice? The circular describing the tender offer disclosed Esmark's intentions should the tender offer succeed. Transocean would become a private company and the remaining stockholders would receive no financial information, have no market in which to sell their stock, and be forced out in a short form merger at a price which might be lower than the $12 tender price. Our claim was that the offer only appeared to be voluntary. In fact, the consequences to non-tendering shareholders were so adverse that tendering was the only viable option. If shareholders had no choice, Esmark, as the parent, owed a fiduciary duty to the minority stockholders to offer a fair price. In its defense, Esmark claimed they were required under the rules of the SEC to make the disclosures we claimed were coercive, and moreover, the tender price of $12 was fair.

In litigation, contentions must be supported by facts, not conjecture. I needed evidence that stockholders were pressured to tender their stock. When Kingsberg told me that the institutional shareholders had tendered because they could not take the chance of being locked into a private company, I had potentially powerful evidence. To turn the potential into actual evidence, I served subpoenas on the institutions requiring them to appear at my office for depositions.

Their testimony was damning for Esmark. The institutions claimed that they treasured Transocean stock and tendered only because of the possibility of adverse consequences if they did not. The Ford Foundation was helpful on more than the coercion issue. Its representative described Transocean as a "company in incubation, snatched away by Esmark, before its true value could be realized." He said when the dust settled and Esmark acquired less than 90 percent, the foundation purchased as much Transocean stock as it could in the thin market following the tender offer. It paid more than $12 but was able to buy only a tiny fraction of what it had tendered.

The officer appearing for Morgan Guaranty, William Shea, was even more helpful. He was an oil and gas analyst. He said Transocean's oil and gas assets (that is, proven reserves, probable reserves, and exploration property) were worth more than $20 per share. He advised against tendering the 500.000 shares held in various trust accounts but was overruled by the legal department. It said the trust accounts would be seriously disadvantaged if the offer were successful. The Morgan Guaranty bank should not put trust assets at risk. After his deposition, I asked him to meet privately with me.

We considered how the bank could help at the trial. I needed expert witnesses to testify on fair price. Experts are expensive but Shea suggested a way to get them for free. The bank generates a vast amount of commissions on securities transactions. Brokerage firms employ experts in industries such as oil and gas to provide research and advice to clients. Shea believed that a request to brokerage firms to make available their oil and gas gurus as expert witnesses would be readily granted. The firm would know that Morgan Guaranty would return the favor with brokerage business. Before Shea, of Morgan Guaranty, acted on the plan, he wanted the bank's lawyer to speak with me.

Hazard Gillespie, a senior partner at Davis Polk, called. His firm represented the bank. He said the bank was eager to help but wanted assurance that the case would not be settled without its consent. I agreed and shortly thereafter was flooded with calls from potential expert witnesses. The calls began the same way: "The bank [none mentioned the name] suggested I call." I met with four experts and chose John Chalsty of Donaldson, Lufkin and Jenrette, and Geoffrey Hertel of Rotan Mosle, a boutique oil and gas brokerage firm based in Houston, Texas.

Chalsty was South African, a graduate of Wittwatersand University and Harvard Business School. He was tall, handsome, smart, and knowledgeable. He was right out of central casting. Having previously served as chief oil and gas analyst at Donaldson, Chalsty was then head of investment banking for the firm. He came to the interview with Otto Wolfe, who was currently the firm's oil and gas analyst. Together they made a presentation on Transocean based on public documents. Chalsty assured me that once they received internal documents, their presentation would be much better.

I have a simple test to pick an expert: you must be an expert. Many witnesses professing to be experts flunk that test. Not Chalsty, and not my second expert, Jeff Hertel. He lived and breathed oil and gas, and when he slept, I am sure he dreamed about oil and gas. Hertel spent all his time studying financials of oil and gas companies, meeting with their principal operating officers, and dining with his firm's clients, advising them on investments. *Institutional Investors*, a publication geared to institutions, had named Hertel oil and gas analyst of the year for two years running. While Chalsty and Wolfe were good at crunching numbers, Hertel excelled at evaluating prospects. I had two highly qualified experts for free.

In addition to the support of the institutional shareholders, I had another ally, Smith, the president of Transocean. The documents produced by Transocean came directly from Smith. He underlined facts helpful towards establishing the true worth of Transocean and also wrote notes to make sure I did not overlook anything of importance. In the usual case, the company's documents are first given to its lawyers for review and then sent to me by the lawyers.

The most critical document was one created especially for the litigation. Smith had asked Edward Harrell, the chief financial officer, to prepare a "what if" study based on assumptions furnished by Smith. The study showed a value for Transocean's oil and gas assets ranging from $16 to $20.

The case was too good to be true. It was a stockholder's lawyer's fantasy.

The fantasy, however, was threatened by a call from Hertzl, requesting a settlement meeting. I had spent many hours being tutored by Chalsty and Hertel and reading books they suggested. I understood models valuing proved, probable, and possible reserves. I learned to read seismographs and interpret logging reports on exploration wells, appreciated the significance of anticlinal slopes and inferences drawn by geologists on fluids, porosity, and permeability. I wanted to try the case, not settle it. That decision, however, would rest with Morgan Guaranty, not with me. I was honor bound to defer to the bank.

The settlement meeting took place over breakfast at the St. Regis where Hertzl and his wife were spending the weekend. Although Hertzl was present at every stage of the litigation, he had not spoken a word. Now it was his turn. Hertzl rhapsodized over the importance of stock market price. He subscribed to the efficient market theory, popular among academicians, particularly at the University of Chicago. The theory claims that all relevant information is incorporated into the price. Since Transocean's price before the tender was $10, the tender price of $12 represented not only a premium over market value, but also over fair value. To Hertzl and the strict form-efficient market theorists, there is no such animal as an undervalued or overvalued marketable security. Esmark's experts were two of the theory's leading proponents.

Although Hertzl said he was convinced Esmark was overpaying, it was prepared to pay an additional $2, raising the tender price to $14. As part of the settlement, Hertzl insisted that non-tendering stockholders be required to sell at $14. Hertzl advised me not to waste time making a counteroffer; Esmark would not pay a penny more. The offer was nonnegotiable.

I waited impatiently for Monday morning to arrive. My first call was to Gillespie. I relayed the offer and the substance of Hertzl's argument. A few hours later he called back. The bank rejected the offer. He called it "an insult and grossly inadequate."

My case was easy to present. Shea testified both as to coercion, and fair value. He valued Transocean at $20, an estimate confirmed by the "what if" study. Chalsty's and Hertel's testimony was letter perfect. I put into evidence the depositions of General American and the Ford Foundation, the "what if" report, and other relevant documents. There was only one thing wrong—the judge, Chancellor Marvel, was not paying attention.

He was also not very smart. Milton Gould, an outstanding New York trial lawyer, coined a nickname for Marvel: schmatta head.

Marvel was a widower in his early sixties. Getzendanner is tall, blonde, and strikingly attractive. Marvel stared at her while my witnesses were testifying. I even caught him smiling and winking at her. I tried hard to get his attention. I instructed witnesses to look at the judge, not me, and address their answers to him. It did not matter. Marvel was interested only in Susan Getzendanner, who encouraged his interest by smiling and winking back.

Marvel's attitude changed when it was Getzendanner's turn. He was absorbed in what her witnesses were saying; he took notes. He took no notes during my presentation. When the first efficient market expert said no one can consistently beat the market because the stock price incorporates all relevant information, Marvel said, "That's comforting."

The defendants did not call Smith as a witness. Instead they called Harrell to explain the "what if" study. He called the study a game that he and Smith played on a whim and branded it speculative. Marvel observed that "something speculative should not be disclosed, as stockholders could be misled." Harrell was a loyal Transocean company man but to his credit he replied, "I do not know whether it should be disclosed. That is a matter for the lawyers. Smith showed it to the lawyers."

Although my case was powerful, I was worried about the judge. After trial, Hertzl asked if I was now ready to reconsider his $2 offer. I said no but I would consider a higher offer. Hertzl shook his head and said, "Two dollars is as high as I will go." I was amazed that there was no movement, but I soon learned the reason.

At the time my action was started, Peter Rosen, a lawyer in Chicago, also brought a lawsuit challenging the tender offer in the federal court in Chicago. The lawyer took no action to advance his case. After the trial, but before the decision, Hertzl and Rosen attempted to settle this case in Chicago on the very terms I had rejected. I wrote to Hubert Will, the federal judge in Chicago assigned to Rosen's case. I said the issues before him for settlement had been tried in Delaware. I had rejected the $2 offer both before and after trial. Judge Will replied that the settlement would be deferred pending the result in Delaware.

Marvel took a long time to decide even routine matters, and then typically dashed off a short, poorly written opinion. A year passed without a peep from him. Esmark was edgy and urged Will, the judge on the Chicago case, to process the settlement that had been agreed to. Instead, Will wrote to Marvel telling the Delaware judge that another shareholder and his lawyer supported a settlement of the very action tried before him at an additional $2 per share. Will said he had refused to process the settlement because the lawyer who had tried the case had rejected an identical offer before the case was tried and again after trial. Will asked Marvel to advise when his decision would issue. Marvel telephoned Will and said a decision would issue promptly.

It did. Marvel found the tender offer voluntary, the closing price of $10 before the tender was announced represented fair value, and the tender offer at $12 was more than fair. He ruled the "what if" study was not only speculative but wrong, and that it did not have to be disclosed.

I sent Will a copy of the decision, my reasons for believing it was seriously flawed, and told him an appeal had been noticed. I asked him to await the decision on appeal before processing the settlement. In reply Will said, "You told me you were going to win much more than $2. You had your turn at bat. I will not wait for the appeal. Esmark advised that it would not withdraw the settlement, which it had every right to do. The settlement hearing will go forward."

Judge Will was a hardworking judge, fair and brilliant. He asked the parties to present witnesses on the fairness of the settlement. The settlement was a retrial of the Delaware case. Will became so engrossed in the proceeding that the last trial day did not end until 11:00 PM. At the end of the trial, he rejected the settlement. His final words to me were, "You had better win on appeal. Otherwise, we have both hurt the stockholders."

I wanted the appeal heard as soon as possible and so did Esmark. Deals are like eggs. If they stand around for too long, they give off an odor. Esmark's proposed takeover was now almost three years old.

The Supreme Court of Delaware reversed Marvel. It ruled the tender offer was false because it omitted the "what if" study. If Esmark believed the study was speculative it still had a duty to disclose it with a caveat expressing this belief. The court remanded the case for a new trial and ruled that, on the issue of fairness, asset value should take precedent over stock market price.

Esmark wanted a deal, not another trial, and agreed to increase the offer to $20. A stunned Marvel approved the settlement and awarded my firm the very large fee Esmark had agreed to pay.

Transocean was a hard-fought case with touches of bitterness and very little goodwill. I never expected to hear from Getzendanner again. I was wrong. She called to relate good news for her: "I have been nominated to the federal bench in Chicago." To my congratulations, she responded defensively: "There are many better qualified candidates, but I was selected because I am a woman. I will be the first female judge on the Illinois federal bench." I assured her she would make an excellent judge, and said, "Don't assume all the male judges were appointed on merit. You're a lot smarter than most."

She then got to the purpose of her call. She had to name the attorneys against whom she had tried cases. She laughed, "Sidney, you're it."

The Chicago Bar Association rates nominees for the federal bench highly qualified, qualified, or not qualified. The rating is an important criterion considered by the Senate in determining whether to approve a nomination. As part of its process, the association interviews a nominated judge's trial opponents and colleagues. I knew the association's representative had already talked to the other lawyers because he said, "The Texas lawyers claimed I will get the full story from you."

The Texas lawyers disliked Getzendanner and I knew the reason. After a day in court, they played poker. Getzendanner, like most good trial lawyers, worked at night to prepare for the next day. She marched into their poker game, demanded they work, and used four-letter expletives to reinforce the importance of trial preparation. They did not like her choice of words and thought she was a harpy. They were certain I shared their view; they were wrong.

The extra-judicial maneuvering—the attempt to settle my case with another—was a shoddy practice, but Hertzl, not Getzendanner, was to blame. Flattering the judge by responding to his flirtatious conduct reflected poorly on the judge, less so on Getzendanner. It is common practice for lawyers to ingratiate themselves with judges. For example, when a judge cracks a joke, no matter how bad it is, the lawyers will roar with laughter. One day, after a judge had told a really stupid joke and we had obligingly laughed, my opponent asked for time to make a note of the joke. Getzendanner's smile and wink were no worse than other forms of false flattery.

The association heard only praise from me. "She is a talented trial lawyer and one whose word could be trusted. She will make an excellent federal judge. I wish she were sitting in my home court." Her rating: "highly qualified."

The *Chicago Tribune* did a feature story on Getzendanner in its Sunday supplement. I knew the article was coming because the reporter had called me. Getzendanner sent the article to me with a note: "You are mentioned more often than I."

9
ITT MAKES ME RICH

THE PAYOFF FOR A lawyer in a contingent fee case can be many times more than the fees of the highest-priced hourly lawyer. The reason: contingent fee lawyers get nothing if they lose, carry the case for years without compensation, and deserve a handsome prize when they win. I lost many cases and, as one says, "ate" my time, but the cases I won more than made up for them. Overall, I earned a lot of money, much more than I was worth. It was not, however, until the ITT case that I became rich.

Corporations have traditionally purchased businesses in their industry or a related one. In the 1970s, it became the rage to buy unrelated businesses. ITT, formerly International Telephone and Telegraph, led by its CEO, Harold Genneen, made so many deals in diverse businesses that this formerly staid telephone company defied classification. A new word had to be invented: conglomerate. ITT's most celebrated purchase was Hartford Fire and Casualty Company.

Genneen was a shrewd deal maker. Once he selected a target, he quietly purchased as many shares as possible in the open market, always careful not to inflate the stock price. By acquiring a large position, he gained access to the board and clout with management. He followed that course with Hartford. Before approaching its board, he purchased about 20 percent of its stock (the "Hartford Block"). It made ITT Hartford's largest stockholder and gave it influence. It also discouraged competing bidders. It is not unusual for one offer to attract another. In fact, once an offer is announced, Wall Street declares the company in play, and teams of investment bankers seek competitive bids. The Hartford Block would discourage a competing bidder, who would know the largest shareholder would oppose and probably sway the board.

Although from a business prospective, ITT's purchase of the Hartford block made sense, it caused tax problems. The sale of stock, whether in exchange for stock of another company or for cash, is a taxable transaction. In a cash transaction, sellers can use the proceeds to pay taxes. But, if the sellers receive stock, they must either sell stock or dig into their cash reserves to pay Uncle Sam. There is an exception in the tax code. If a company buys all the stock of another company "solely for stock," the transaction is tax-free. The rationale is that the seller's stockholders have exchanged "like property for like property," not sold their stock. The exemption is strictly construed and the exemption is lost if the acquirer purchases any shares for cash.

ITT could not afford to purchase Hartford for cash and proposed an exchange of stock. The offer had to be tax-free, but there was an impediment. ITT had purchased the Hartford Block for cash and an offer for the remaining 80 percent would not qualify as an acquisition "solely for stock." The tax experts advised ITT to sell the Hartford Block and then make the exchange offer for 100 percent of Hartford. The advice was untested. There was concern that the IRS might claim the divestiture did not reform the transaction to make it tax-free.

When ITT asked its investment banker, Lazard Freres, to find a buyer, it came up with Mediobanca, an Italian bank. Hartford's lawyers, however, were uncertain as to the curative effects of the sale and refused to let the matter rest. They asked ITT to obtain a favorable ruling from the IRS as a condition of Hartford's board's approval. The IRS will assist taxpayers by issuing rulings on important tax issues. The taxpayer may rely on the ruling provided the material facts have been fully disclosed. ITT applied for a ruling and IRS issued a favorable one.

There was a lot of noise about the ITT–Hartford merger. Hartford was valued at just under a billion dollars. The deal set a new high watermark for the acquisition of a company. Charles Rosenthal, a lawyer, called me and said he had a disgruntled client, Hilda Herbst, who owned Hartford stock. She opposed the acquisition and wanted Hartford to remain independent. Rosenthal specialized in trusts and estates, but he knew a lot about corporate litigation. He liked the idea of attacking this largest of mergers, but we could not figure out a cause of action. A few days later, a smart and agitated lawyer pointed the way.

I was invited to substitute for a player in a regular tennis doubles game on a Wednesday night in an indoor tennis court near Yankee Stadium. The missing player was away on business. Our games were judged to be about the same. The other players were a corporate lawyer, Leonard Lyman; Ray Troubh, a partner at Lazard, and my good friend Harold Kingsberg, the person who invited me. We played for two hours from seven o'clock to nine o'clock. During the game, Troubh made some questionable calls on Lyman's serves and returns which decided the match. Lyman was angry. On the ride back he teased the banker, "My tax partner was astonished to see the IRS ruling allowing ITT to get the benefit of a stock-for-stock exchange by selling the block to Mediobanca. He said the deal was tainted when ITT assembled the block and the stain was a permanent one. What did you do, bribe the service?" A frown crossed Troubh's face, and he said, "Your partners are not deal friendly. That's why we do not use them. Our lawyers did not even think it necessary to apply for a ruling. They were prepared to issue a tax letter." (A lawyer's tax letter protects a taxpayer against a claim of fraud. It imposes a heavy responsibility on the lawyer.) The good-natured teasing made Lyman even angrier, so angry that he accused Lazard, ITT, and their lawyers of fraud; "Of course you did not want a ruling. Your lawyers were compelled to make false statements. I've had deals with foreign banks. Mediobanca is small. It would not tie up about $200 million in a U.S. insurance company about which it knew nothing. And the deal closed in three days! There had to be a guarantee against loss and a put [an option to resell the stock]. That was no sale; ITT parked the block."

The next morning I called Rosenthal. I told him what I had learned, and added, "Tell Hilda Herbst, if she agrees, I am ready to go."

ITT's offer was described in a prospectus mailed to the insurance company's stockholders. It stated unequivocally that: "Hartford stockholders who exchange their stock will not incur any tax liability as a result of the exchange."

In stockholder actions, the substantive allegations are based on "information and belief," not personal knowledge. Was the chitchat in the car enough information to allege fraud? Probably not, but my gut instinct told me to take a chance. The pertinent allegation stated: "ITT made false and misleading statements to the IRS. It failed to disclose the side agreements protecting Mediobanca against loss and the nature and extent of ITT's continuing control over the Hartford Block. If ITT had fully disclosed all the terms, the IRS would not have issued the ruling." The complaint sought recision and money damages.

If we proved the IRS was deceived, the ruling would be revoked and the Hartford stockholders would be required to pay tax. We would be shooting our own clients in the foot. If we did not claim that ITT had misled the IRS, we had no case.

I had a choice between the federal court in Hartford where the insurance company was based or the court in New York where ITT was headquartered. I chose Hartford. There, the acquisition was unpopular. Many residents feared headquarters would be moved to New York and jobs and support facilities lost.

John Schaefer was ITT's lawyer. He was a partner in Covington and Burling, a prominent Washington DC law firm. He was tall and upright. There was not a bend or stoop in his entire body. His posture was reflective of his personality—he was a straight arrow.

At our first meeting, he told me what he thought of the case. He said, "Stockholder suits serve a purpose. The threat of a suit can discourage overreaching and, if it occurs, protect the stockholders. Your suit hurts the stockholders. Drop the case." Perhaps I should have but I had gone too far. If, however, we lost the motion on class action status, Schaefer's wish would have been granted.

My client's stake was too small to justify a lawsuit. The case was viable only as a class action in which all Hartford stockholders would be deemed to be represented in Herbst's action. Class actions promote efficiency by trying at one time all similar claims and further the interests of justice by allowing a claim, too small to be pursued on its own, to go forward when combined with many identical ones. Class actions work only if common questions of law and fact predominate, and commonality was problematic. Many of the stockholders were tax-exempt institutions and did not care whether the exchange offer was taxable. Still others sold ITT stock promptly after it was received, and paid approximately the same amount of tax as if the exchange were taxable.

In addition to common questions of law and fact, the attorneys representing the class member must be qualified in order to insure that the interests of absent class members who had no say in the selection of counsel are protected. I had been found competent in many cases and was confident that the federal judge assigned to the case, Joseph Blumenfeld, would not deny class action status on that issue. It was the other criteria that were troubling.

At oral argument on the class action motion, Schaefer began with the wrong issue: my competency. He argued, "Hartford should be represented by a prominent law firm, not by an undistinguished, small New York firm. If the stockholders had a vote they certainly would not choose Sidney Silverman."

The judge interrupted and asked whether Schaefer's firm accepted contingent fee cases. He said no. The judge mused about his own career in a two man law firm. He and his law partner, Senator Tom Dodd, the father of the present Senator Chris Dodd, accepted contingent fee cases but only ones in which damages were vast or liability was certain. "We might have accepted Ms. Herbst's case, but the law firm of Dodd and Blumenfeld was not national. We were based in Hartford, a few blocks from this courthouse. Were we worthy to represent the Hartford stockholders? On your standards, probably not."

The judge then discussed me: "Mr. Silverman comes to court on time [a pointed reference to a time when Schaefer was late], his brief and oral argument on this motion were good." The judge was playing with Schaefer: "What is there about Mr. Silverman that, in your judgment, makes him unacceptable to the Hartford stockholders?" I do not remember what the lawyer replied, but it was too late. He had lost the motion.

Schaefer was right to raise the competency issue; his timing was wrong. He should first have discussed the flimsy merits and the potential harm to the Hartford stockholders, and then addressed my competence. An argument attacking competence might then have been attractive.

The class action determination was appealed and affirmed, and a petition to the Supreme Court denied. Depositions continued and I examined Andre Meyer, the senior partner of Lazard Freres, and the architect of the Mediobanca deal. He had a weak heart and his doctor insisted his deposition be limited to sessions of no more than three hours. It took five sessions to complete his deposition.

Meyer tried to distance himself and his firm from the Mediobanca transaction and claimed: "I was simply a messenger boy." He looked straight at me and then added, "If you can imagine the senior partner of Lazard as a messenger boy." There was a paper trail, however, that Meyer could not dodge. After five years of pushing and pulling we obtained the evidence that Lyman had prophesied that night in the car. Mediobanca had a separate deal with Lazard. Profits were guaranteed but only in an amount equivalent to interest with any excess enuring to Lazard. The Italian bank had no downside; it had an option to put the Hartford Block to Lazard if the exchange offer were not consummated. Lazard, in turn, had a handshake arrangement with ITT assuring the investment banking firm against loss and providing a generous fee for arranging the "sale." The transaction was a way for ITT to retain control over the Hartford Block and create the impression it had been sold.

The IRS, prompted by the many publicly reported decisions, requested transcripts of the depositions and our briefs. Thereafter, the IRS revoked the ruling, claiming ITT had misrepresented the facts surrounding the sale to Mediobanca and assessed taxes against the class. ITT had no defense to our charge that the prospectus was false. The case was settled. Class members were given a choice. They could accept $5 per share tendered or elect to have their tax liability paid by ITT. Class members who did not owe taxes either because they were tax-exempt institutions, or had sold the ITT shares received in the exchange and paid taxes, elected the cash supplement. Those with tax liability elected to have ITT pay their tax bill. ITT also agreed to pay my fees as awarded by the judge.

The settlement was a victory for everyone. The government collected taxes; the class got, in effect, the tax-free exchange promised; ITT acquired Hartford, which it probably would not have accomplished if it had sold and not parked the Hartford Block; and I got a humongous fee.

In class actions, the court must find the settlement fair and in the best interests of the class. That part was easy: the settlement was a 100 percent victory. The difficult part was our fee. We asked for $3.2 million, an amount unprecedented in stockholder litigation. The year was 1978 and at this point no fee in a stockholder action had been awarded in excess of $750,000.

To support our request, we submitted time records detailing our activities in the case. Computers were not yet in use and our records were transcribed by hand. The scrivener was Harnes's daughter in law, Mary Harnes, the wife of Harnes's oldest son, Mark Harnes.

She was the perfect person to transcribe our entries. Her handwriting was neat. Each letter was beautifully formed and in perfect alignment with its neighbor. Despite the good form, it was practically illegible. I suppose it could be deciphered but only if one were willing to spend countless hours.

Mary Harnes's handwriting reminded me of a lawyer named Frank Purcell. He sometimes spoke several sentences saying words that sounded like English words but were gibberish. Frank's performance was deliberate and funny; Mary's penmanship was also funny, but unintentional.

Judge Blumenfeld held a hearing on the settlement and fee award. He quickly approved the settlement. Then, he turned to the fee. He asked if ITT objected. The answer was no, an answer required by the agreement. The judge then, holding the time records, questioned me. "When were the records prepared?" I turned the question around. "We lose many cases and when that happens we get no fee. Why waste more time compiling time records? So we only record our time when we are entitled to a fee. The records you are holding were prepared after the case was settled reconstructed from contemporaneous records."

It was better practice to prepare time compilations contemporaneously and shortly thereafter that became the rule. The judge may have remembered using a similar procedure at Dodd and Blumenfeld and made no further reference to the timeliness of the records.

The fee was a multiple of our hourly rate to compensate us for the risk that, if we lost, we would get nothing. The settlement was excellent and ITT, who was to pay the fee, did not object. Nevertheless, the judge reduced the fee to $2.9 million plus our expenses.

Simon Rifkind, a former federal judge, represented Lazard Freres. He was regarded as one of, if not the, best lawyer in the country. After the IRS revoked the ruling, bad blood developed between ITT and its banker. The company insisted on excluding Lazard from the settlement and expressly reserved the right to sue Lazard. I speculated on the cause. Lazard got a generous fee from ITT for arranging the Mediobanca transaction and, probably unbeknownst to ITT, the Italian bank's excess profits when it exchanged the Hartford Block for ITT shares. Lazard, in effect, received double compensation.

There was also bad blood between Rifkind and me. He scolded me for concentrating on Lazard. He said ITT was the principal and Lazard followed orders. Great lawyers, and Rifkind was one, are intense advocates. Their clients never do anything wrong. While I respected Rifkind, I followed my instincts and concentrated on Lazard's role. Rifkind was agitated by my conduct.

Since Lazard was neither a party to the settlement nor paying the fee, Judge Rifkind was silent at the hearing. He broke his silence and evened the score with me shortly thereafter in an Op Ed piece in the *Times*. He inveighed against the practice by "some ordinary lawyers" who represent a stockholder owning very few shares and escalate the case to a major litigation through the class action device. When a class settlement is reached, they multiply their hours by a risk factor and become instant millionaires.

When asked about the column, I said: "I cried all the way to the bank."

10
THE BIG OIL
AND GAS CASES

THE MARKET WENT CRAZY in the 1980s
fueled by a buying frenzy, not of stocks, but of publicly traded companies
whose shares were selling at depressed prices, or so thought prospective
buyers. They believed if non-productive assets were sold, excess staff fired
and, in general, the business more efficiently managed, the company
would be worth far more than the price paid. The offers were usually
opposed. The target claimed an acquisition violated the antitrust laws, or
disclosure was faulty, or some other claim that did not reflect the target's
true motive. It did not care about the antitrust laws or disclosure but only
about remaining independent. To do so it had to kill the offer. Resistance,
however, was rarely successful.

The initial offer hung a "for sale" sign on the target and the risk
arbitrage departments at investment banking firms did everything possible
to bring about a deal. They purchased the target company's stock, often
paying as much or more than the initial offer, and rapidly accumulated
major positions. Their purchases were heavily financed and the interest
expense added a big burden. They needed a quick deal to make a profit
and used their influence to push for a sale. The stockholders, especially
the institutions, also leaned on management. The offer was above market
and they feared that if the deal were rejected the stock price would drop

precipitously as the arbitragers would dump their stock. A management fighting a legitimate offer was swimming against the tide.

Management also had to defend itself against stockholder litigation. A mere announcement sparked as many as fifty stockholder suits, all claiming the directors had violated their fiduciary duty by rejecting the offer.

They were brought, however, before the directors had even considered the offer. The claim of violation of duty was, therefore, premature and specious. Although the cases could easily have been dismissed and the lawyers sanctioned, the bidders and the target had a use for the suits. When a deal was made, either with the original bidder, a competitive bidder, or a white knight (a friendly bidder brought in by the target), the parties wanted a court to put its stamp of approval on the deal. The legal term for court approval is res adjudicata, and, if obtained, all pending cases are ended and future cases, based on existing facts, precluded. The banks, which put up the money, were the strongest advocates. They needed to be assured the deals would not unravel.

Here is where the stockholder lawyers served a purpose. Only an existing lawsuit could be settled. The lawyers offered to settle their cases and provide the needed res adjudicata in exchange for a fee. The fee depended on a finding that the stockholder litigation benefited the stockholders of the target company. The claim was farcical. The parties, the court and the lawyers, knew the price would have been the same regardless of the lawsuits. In order to obtain the settlement, however, the parties had to make a weak form of representation: "The stockholder cases were taken into consideration." The corporate parties obliged and the plaintiffs' attorneys were awarded fees for no work and no benefit. A new cottage industry was born.

The stockholder suits were almost always brought in Delaware. Under different circumstances, i.e., those involving actively contested actions, the Delaware Supreme Court ruled that settlements are favored. The parties used this precedent to settle the inactive stockholder cases. The courts routinely approved the bogus settlements and awarded fees to the plaintiffs' attorneys. The legal fees, agreed upon in advance of the settlement, varied with the size of the deal and ranged from a few hundred thousand dollars to many millions.

I got into the game when the son of the founder and former CEO of Shell Oil objected to a takeover bid of the company by Royal Dutch. The law firm of Coudert Brothers was his attorney but could not represent him because of a conflict. Coudert referred the client to me and I commenced a lawsuit. Our suit was filed a month after the others. The other suits were already consolidated and lead attorneys appointed. They told me my case was started too late. They would, however, let me join the consolidated action but as a tagalong. I opposed. My client owned more stock than the other suing shareholders, knew the company inside out, and acted only when the terms were finalized. We, not they, should be in control of the action.

The dispute was placed before the judge. The other stockholder attorneys argued their activities would be duplicated and the efficient management of the case undermined unless my action was stayed. They informed the court that I had turned down an offer to join the team.

I took off the gloves. I said the lawyers typically do nothing and it is hard to duplicate nothing. I detected a smile on the judge's face and was encouraged. I pointed out that my client owned more stock then the forty other plaintiff stockholders combined. Moreover, my client's father built the company and the son was duty bound to protect the stockholders. I further told the court, before committing to a lawsuit, that my client asked about the adequacy of the other attorneys to represent his father's company. I told him they were not adequate and were interested only in fees. I urged the court that this very important case should not be entrusted to sell-out artists. The motion to stay my action was denied.

As it turned out, I did not make a difference. An independent committee of directors and their lawyers and financial advisors did all the work. Before announcing the new terms, one of the directors, who knew my client, called him and obtained his support for the new deal. I learned this from my client's personal attorney, William Rand, a senior partner and litigator with Coudert Brothers.

The lead attorneys were advised that the terms had been substantially approved and agreed to by the independent directors. For going along with the merger, they were offered a large fee. They were not told, however, that my client had also agreed. Anxious about my position, they offered me $1.5 million for going along. I accepted.

When Rand learned about my fee, he called to congratulate me. He made it clear that he had no claim to the fee but that he would be interested in actively participating with me in other stockholder litigation. He said trusts in Coudert's trust department held large positions in many different companies. If the right case came along, he was sure his firm and their clients would take part.

I did not keep Rand and Coudert waiting very long.

British Petroleum announced an offer for Standard Oil of Ohio; it was at $35 billion, the largest deal ever. Five plaintiff law firms had anticipated British Petroleum's offer (I don't know how) and before the offer was announced drafted a complaint on behalf of several stockholders claiming the unannounced offer was unfair. They gave a copy of a draft complaint to a Cleveland law firm and waited for the announcement. Within five minutes of the news, the lawsuit was started and by the end of the day, the five lawyers, the very same fellows who were lead counsel in the Royal Dutch–Shell Oil case, secured an order from a judge in Cleveland appointing them lead counsel.

Ten days later, Rand and I filed our complaint in the same court. We represented a charitable foundation and, through Coudert's connections, retained a very savvy Cleveland law firm. We moved to be added as lead counsel and the judge promptly scheduled argument on the motion. Rand argued.

He said we did our homework before drafting our complaint, reviewed it with our client and its general counsel, obtained their approval and only then commenced a lawsuit. Although we put all other matters aside, the process of preparation and client review took ten days. Rand pointed out that since the lead attorneys filed within five minutes of the announcement, it was impossible for them to have acted in a responsible manner. He urged the court to add us as lead counsel to ensure that the stockholders were represented by responsible attorneys. He also stated that his firm had offices in London, the home base of British Petroleum, as well as offices in other major European capitals where stockholders may also reside.

Our opponents were thrown for a loss. They had anticipated I would make the argument. They were prepared to replay my argument in the Royal Dutch–Shell Oil case, and then claim I made no contribution but picked their pockets. That argument, which might have carried the day, could not be made since Rand was not involved in the other case.

The judge was impressed by Rand and we were added as lead counsel.

Several weeks later, British Petroleum's lawyers asked the lead attorneys to meet with them as the directors of the two companies had agreed on new and improved terms. Our approval was made a condition of the new proposal.

I had a chip on my shoulder over the Royal Dutch–Shell Oil case. I had not earned my fee. I wanted a big fee in this case but I also wanted to create a significant benefit for the Standard Oil stockholders. But how could that be done? Under the present structure, we were doing nothing more than approving the work done by the directors and their advisers.

I searched for a way to oppose the new agreement and found a basis in a disclosure in the draft proxy statement. It said that Standard Oil had drilled a discovery well on land abutting the Alaskan National Wilderness Refuge (ANWR), but disclosed nothing about the results. There could be no deal until I learned all about the discovery well.

British Petroleum's lawyer said he anticipated my objection and I could examine, under oath, the oil company's chief petroleum engineer who had knowledge of the well. The testimony, however, was highly confidential; no copies of the deposition would be made, the original would reside in the lawyer's safe and only the witness, British Petroleum's lawyer and I would be present. Further, I had to sign a confidentiality order prohibiting me from disclosing information obtained to anyone at any time. I agreed to all the conditions except one: I insisted Rand also be present.

A lawyer can effectively examine an oil and gas expert, indeed any expert, provided the lawyer has enough expertise in the field to ask the right questions and understand the answers. The Transocean case prepared me for my new role. I knew where I was going: what did the one well drilled in the area adjacent to ANWR say about the potential of the area?

When the deposition was over, I was satisfied I knew the approximate value of the Standard Oil property surrounding the development well. Twenty years have passed since that deposition was taken. To date, there has been no drilling in ANWR. Environmentalists think their efforts have preserved the wilderness area. I know better, but must remain silent.

After the deposition, I agreed to the settlement. The agreement recited that the parties took into consideration the pending lawsuits in arriving at the price to be paid for Standard Oil, and also disclosed that the stockholder lawyers were seeking legal fees in the amount of $35 million.

The press was all over the settlement. The merger terms were given high marks but the legal fee was a red flag. The fee was the largest ever sought in stockholder litigation and attracted too much attention from the media for the good of the plaintiff lawyers. Many stockholders wrote to the judge expressing outrage. The judge did not remain quiescent; he spoke to the press. "The work done by the lawyers was not worth anything like $35 million. They can ask for whatever they want, but they get only what I approve."

The settlement agreement bound all Standard Oil stockholders to the merger. Before the agreement could become effective, however, the judge had to conduct an evidentiary hearing and find the terms fair to Standard Oil's stockholders. At the hearing, Standard Oil stockholders had the right to appear and oppose the settlement.

We anticipated some stockholders would file objections to the settlement. We did not, however, anticipate the extent.

The California state pension fund, known as Calpers, was Standard Oil's largest stockholder. Calpers and other state pension funds were regarded as passive stockholders; if they did not like a merger, they sold their stock but did not sue. In Standard Oil, Calpers came out of the closet and filed an objection. Its objection put the settlement in jeopardy.

The companies' lawyers suggested that it would help if we agreed to cut our fee. We disagreed. A cut was an admission we had overreached; it was better if the judge did the cutting, which we believed he would do even if we had voluntarily reduced our fee request.

I felt bad for Rand. It was his first stockholder case; not only might there be no compensation, but the possibility of dishonor loomed.

A joint proxy statement and notice of settlement was mailed to the company's stockholders. A critical disclosure was the values placed on Standard Oil's assets, i.e., its reserves of oil and gas, by Standard Oil and BP. (Neither party placed a value on the ANWR exploration property, although the proxy disclosed the drilling of a well). The two valuations differed greatly. Standard Oil valued its assets at more than the per share merger price; BP valued the same assets at less.

Valuations of oil and gas assets are subjective and, in this case, the subjectivity was influenced by the conflicting interests of the two parties. Standard Oil wanted a high valuation to discourage BP and, if not, to obtain the highest possible price for its stockholders. Its valuation was skewed on the upside. BP wanted to make its offer appear generous; it lowballed the assets.

The judge scheduled an evidentiary hearing. The most immediate issue was to reconcile the conflict between the different valuations. Our expert undertook that task. I examined him. I liked him but not his report. He used Standard Oil's estimates of oil and gas reserves but applied his own economic data to reach a value. His result: a valuation exceeding even Standard Oil's expert's. Together, we developed a simple and disarmingly honest approach to demonstrate the unreliability of oil and gas valuations.

I showed him his report and asked whether he believed it was accurate. He said no and gave his reasons. He was sure that Standard Oil's reserves were either more or less than he had assumed. He said until the last barrel of oil was extracted—in some cases twenty-five years from now—you could not be certain of the amount of reserves. He further said his assumptions on prices were also wrong. He projected oil and gas prices would rise by 6 percent each year and thus would double every twelve years. The then price of a barrel of oil was $40. He doubted that our economy could tolerate a price of $80, twelve years hence and $160 in twenty-four years. I asked him why he used an escalation rate of 6 percent, and he replied that without a crystal ball that was as good a number as any other.

The valuation projected revenue over a long period. The present value of future revenues is obtained by applying a discount rate to the income stream. A rate that is too high penalizes value; a rate that is too low inflates value. Using charts, our expert showed the dramatic change in result if the discount rate was raised or lowered by even one percentage point. Since a principal component of the discount rate was an estimate of the rate of inflation, he testified that the rate selected was a pure guess as no one could accurately predict inflation.

I showed the witness the reports prepared by the experts for Standard Oil and British Petroleum and asked him whether they were accurate. He said, "I am certain they are wrong. Like me they had to make assumptions on the future prices of oil and gas, the quantities of reserves and the rate of inflation. Predicting the future was as difficult and fraught with errors for them as for me." He then discussed valuations of oil and gas properties made by him five years earlier. He said that assumptions used in those reports were consistently used by his firm at that time; he also believed other firms used similar assumptions. He then showed that every one of his assumptions turned out to be wrong--some by a wide margin.

I asked how many analyses of oil and gas assets he had made and he answered upward of a thousand. I then asked how many of them had turned out to be right and he said none, and then volunteered, "If any turned out to be right, I would suspect a manipulation." I asked, "Are you aware of any analysis made by a petroleum engineer that turned out to be correct?" "I have reviewed thousands of appraisals and none have ever been accurate," he said.

I glanced at the judge and detected a puzzled look on his face and decided that it was time to let him know where I was going.

I asked my expert, "How could the directors of Standard Oil and ultimately the court find the merger fair if the valuation reports are wrong?" He answered, "The reports provide a range of values. Since the price proposed to be paid by British Petroleum fell within a range of plus or minus 15 percent, the directors and the court could find the price to be fair even though it might ultimately turn out to be too high or too low."

The judge then questioned the witness. He asked whether he could approve the settlement if he accepted Standard Oil's valuation of its own assets. The witness said no, for the reason that the valuation exceeded the merger price. The judge then asked if he could find the merger fair if he accepted British Petroleum's valuation. The witness said yes, as the judge's concern was fairness to the Standard Oil stockholders. Since the merger price was in excess of British Petroleum's valuation, the merger was certainly fair to Standard Oil stockholders if that valuation turned out to be right. "I get it," said the judge. "We are dealing with reports that are wrong but nevertheless provide a reliable range of values." The witness agreed with the judge—always a good policy.

The defendants had intended to call their experts but wisely decided not to do so. Instead, the proponents of the settlement, the defendants and the plaintiffs, rested and turned the case over to Calpers. Its attorney informed the judge that Calpers had retained an expert who reached a different result, and asked the court to consider the report. We knew the new report would not register with the judge when he said, "I'll read the report carefully but I am not surprised that it provides a different answer. Given the mind-boggling assumptions that have to be made, I doubt whether any two honest experts could ever reach the same result."

The lawyer then raised the issue concerning the exploration well in Alaska. He said experts may differ on the value of oil and gas properties, but all properties have to be valued. If exploration property owned by Standard Oil was not valued then its stockholders were cheated. He produced a report issued by a federal agency estimating millions of barrels of oil in that area.

BP's lawyer asked for a conference, known as a bench conference, and the judge agreed. The lawyer told the judge that the plaintiffs' lawyers had raised the same issue. They insisted on examining the company's exploration expert on the well and BP agreed. The information obtained was highly confidential and only an original of the transcript was made. The transcript was in a safe in the New York office of BP lawyers. The lawyer offered to bring the transcript to court the next day and review it with the court and Calpers' attorney. The judge agreed and the hearing was adjourned. A young lawyer was dispatched to New York to bring the transcript to Cleveland.

We met the next morning in the judge's chambers. Present were the lawyers who attended the deposition, the Calpers' attorney, and, of course, the judge. The floor belonged to me, and I milked it. I reviewed each substantive question and my reason for asking the question. I read the answers and explained their significance. At the end of the conference, the Calpers' attorney was satisfied that nothing had been overlooked. More important was the impression made on the judge; he believed the plaintiffs' lawyers were thorough and knowledgeable. Later that day, the judge approved the settlement and awarded the full fee requested, $35 million, at the time the largest fee awarded in stockholder litigation.

I levitated, not walked, out of the courtroom.

11

My Neighbors the Fishermen and the Case of the Poisoned Fish

In 1967, we bought a summer home in Amagansett, a neighbor to the fashionable and glitzy East Hampton. Irene, a journalist, had stopped work six years earlier when Emily, our first child, was born. She was eager to return to work and found a job as a reporter for the local newspaper, the *East Hampton Star*. She was famous for her feature stories and rose to associate editor. The working folk and the summer crowd courted her. Irene was a true Hamptons insider.

Believe me, I did not mean to intrude into Irene's world when I took on the fishermen's case; it just happened that way. The East Hampton fishermen stood in sharp contrast to the summer people. The fishermen worked the bays and ocean in which the summer people played. The fishermen, poor to begin with, became even poorer, as the years passed and their number declined. The summer community grew rapidly as hordes of rich New Yorkers and Europeans migrated to the Hamptons. The increase in population and seemingly endless construction of new homes along the shoreline caused waste water and other pollutants to run off into the bays. The contaminants made their way into the clam and scallop beds; at least two lucrative fishing areas were done for. The death knell for commercial fishing sounded when striped bass became contaminated by polychlorinated bi-phenyls (PCBs), and, for health reasons, the bass fishery was closed. The striped bass was the money fish, providing the fishermen with their small profit; the other catches only covered overhead.

General Electric was the cause of the contamination. It operated several plants adjacent to the Hudson River in upstate New York The plants manufactured transformers and capacitors used in the transmission of electricity. PCBs are a chemically stable, non-flammable fluid used to insulate transformers and capacitors. In handling this chemical, GE was sloppy to the point of recklessness. PCBs spilled onto the floor of the factories and when the plants were hosed down at night, the waste PCBs were discharged into the Hudson.

Striped bass spend the winter in the fresh water of rivers, such as the Hudson, and there they cast their spawn. In the spring, summer, and fall, they migrate from the Hudson River through the bays and oceans surrounding Long Island and New York City The fish feed only in winter (while in the Hudson) and never while migrating. Newborn fish remain in the river for several years before they are large enough to leave. While in the Hudson, the stripers ingest PCBs by feeding on fish lower in the food chain. PCBs are non-biodegradable and remain for years in the lipid fats of the stripers. PCBs are a suspected carcinogen. Their concentration in fish is monitored by federal and state agencies. Over time, the accumulation of PCBs in the striped bass reached unhealthy levels and, in 1987, a ban was imposed on harvesting the species. The local fishermen were devastated; they could not survive without striped bass.

At a July fourth party held on the beach of the editor of Irene's paper, I met Arnold Leo, a member and secretary of the East Hampton Baymen's Association, one of several associations formed by fishermen working the waters in Long Island, New York Harbor, and the upper reaches of the Hudson. Arnold was not your typical fisherman. He was college-educated. He had worked in advertising. In his early forties, he left Madison Avenue, moved to East Hampton, and became a full-time fisherman. Leo complained to me about the loss of the striped bass fishery and asked if the fishermen could sue GE.

I researched the issues, concluded that the fishermen had a good case against GE, and offered to represent them on a contingent fee basis, provided that the fishing associations and their officers joined as plaintiffs. It was important that all join. Many class actions are perceived as "lawyers' cases" and bear a stigma which can overshadow the merits. I wanted this case to be perceived as the fishermen's case. Fishermen are hardworking, self-employed, and risk their lives on the high seas. Sir Walter Scott captured their essence in *The Antiquary* (Chapter 11): "It's no fish ye're buying, it's men's lives." I wanted the romance to rub off on the case.

Leo solicited the officers of the associations. All agreed. It was a good deal; free representation and a chance to hit back at GE for destroying their livelihood..

The New York State Department of Environmental Conservation had ten years earlier sued GE, contending that it had discharged PCBs in the Hudson, contaminated its waters, and damaged fish and wildlife living in and near the water. The case was tried before Abraham D. Sofaer, a professor of law at Columbia who was designated by the parties to decide the dispute. The proceeding addressed the issues of liability: did GE intentionally or acting with gross negligence discharge PCBs into the Hudson, and were its discharges the cause of PCB contamination of the Hudson? Sofaer's decision was a powerful indictment of GE. He found that the company knew, as early as the mid-1930s, that PCBs were a suspected carcinogen. He also found that Monsanto, the manufacturer of the chemical, had warned GE to take every precaution to prevent PCBs from entering the environment, and urged that waste and spent PCBs should be returned to Monsanto for destruction at an incinerator maintained by the manufacturer. Sofaer concluded that GE alone was responsible for the accumulation of PCBs in the Hudson, all other sources contributing negligible amounts.

GE and the state department agreed upon the remedy. GE would cease discharging PCBs, pay a fine to the state, and conduct an extensive study to determine the best method to rid the Hudson of PCBs. They have a half life of fifty years. That means their toxicity is only half dissipated after fifty years. GE, of course, knew this but the company's study cynically concluded that doing nothing was the most effective way to rid the river of the toxic chemical.

Sofaer's opinion served as a blueprint for all stages of the case. It was attached as an exhibit to the fishermen's complaint, and its allegations accusing GE of polluting the river were derived from the earlier decision. GE made several motions aimed at getting rid of our claim; none were successful. GE failed because we quoted from and gave the court copies of the Sofaer decision. How could we lose? We had a well-documented decision, finding that GE, with knowledge that PCBs were a carcinogen, recklessly and negligently discharged them into the Hudson. Or, as I said in court, "GE treated our beautiful Hudson River as though it were the company's private cesspool."

In preparation for trial, GE examined many of the fishermen. They testified about work they did when they were forced to give up fishing; mostly mowing lawns and banging nails. Ironically, this evidence was devastating to the fishermen's claim for money damages. They earned very little from their chosen work, more from the substitute odd jobs. From a strictly financial point of view, the fishermen were better off not fishing. GE argued that any claim for loss of earnings due to the closure of the striped bass fishery had to be offset by money earned from other jobs. The company also argued that the fishermen had depleted the stock of striped bass and even if the fish had not been contaminated, conservation rules would have restricted the catch and virtually closed the fishery. This argument was supported by size and catch limitations placed on striped bass in areas unaffected by PCB contamination.

I got copies of the testimony of the witnesses and all documents submitted in the state's case against GE. When it was my turn to examine GE, I made good use of that record. If a witness had testified in the earlier case, I read selectively, picking out important facts that helped our case. I then asked whether he had testified truthfully. I did not care whether he answered yes or no. If he said yes, as most did, the facts became uncontested. If he answered that his testimony was inaccurate, as several witnesses did, his credibility was impeached. Some witnesses had died or were otherwise no longer available. In their place, I examined their successors and asked whether their colleagues had a reputation for telling the truth. As good company men, they invariably answered yes. I then read the testimony I wanted into the record. I also made extensive use of documents to fill in holes.

The case was strong on liability but weak on damages. After working on the case, on and off for five years, the best I could see was a Pyrrhic victory. GE would be bloodied but the fishermen would collect very little in damages.

Riverhead is the county seat for the East End of Long Island. The case was pending there, and when discovery was concluded, I wanted a jury trial as soon as possible. The trial calendar was jammed; a trial would be years away. Cases, however, can be advanced for good cause. I moved for an expedited trial on the ground the fishermen were both old and poor. My motion was granted; the case was set for an immediate trial. I contacted the television program *Court TV*, whose producers agreed to televise the trial. In addition, prominent local politicians promised to attend and sit with me at counsel table. Would their presence have an effect on the jury? It could not hurt.

At a pre-trial conference, the judge asked how long my opening would take. "Your honor, it will take a full day for me to describe to the jury the extent of GE's wanton and grossly negligent conduct, and its devastating effect upon the men who sell not just fish but their lives." GE knew what was coming—and on national TV!

Jack Welch, the CEO of GE, had a policy when it came to PCB litigation: never settle a case. But he changed that policy. A week before the trial was to begin, his attorney proposed a settlement. GE's lawyer said the ban on striped bass lasted for five years and was augmented by limitations imposed in the interest of conservation. "The company perhaps could be found liable for the health ban but not the conservation restrictions." GE's lawyer pointed out that a New York State agency's records showed that in the five years prior to the ban, the aggregate value of the catch to the fishermen was $7 million. The lawyer offered to settle the case for $7 million, to be distributed under any method approved by the court. GE also agreed to pay the costs and expenses of the litigation, including my fee. The offer was a favorable one. In return for giving up the right to tarnish GE's slogan, "We bring good things to life," the fishermen divided the approximate value of the catch as if no health ban had been imposed and without offset for money earned in lieu of fishing. The fishing associations and its members unanimously endorsed the proposed settlement and GE agreed to pay my fee of $2.5 million.

The case was extensively covered by the *East Hampton Star*. Every preliminary decision was a front page story. Praise was heaped upon yours truly. Nothing, however, compared to the announcement of the settlement. It was the lead story, entitled, "Fishermen Win a $7 Million Dollar Recovery." I was the subject of a glowing editorial that began, "One man...."

That weekend, there was a benefit performance for the East Hampton fishermen of Joe Pintauro's play, *Men's Lives*, based on Peter Mathiessen's book, followed by a gala party. At the party, a newspaper tracking the celebrities in the Hamptons photographed Leo and me; the picture appeared in the center of the rotogravure page.

Several weeks later, when the settlement papers were filed, my fee became public. It was not a front page story, but still got a lot of attention. Apparently the community thought I was representing the fishermen out of the goodness of my heart. They were shocked by the fee. I explained to anyone who would listen that the fishermen paid no part of the fee; they received a full recovery. What possible difference could it make to the fishermen that GE voluntarily paid my fee? But it did make a difference. My wife expressed the view of the community: "You do not need the money. Add it to the fishermen's pot."

The fishermen were no longer poor. If I had wanted to give my fee to charity, I would not give it to a group of strong, healthy men. I had planned to take a week off and spend it basking in glory. Instead, I spent it sweating away in New York, hiding out.

12
A ROCKEFELLER'S MONEY

IN THE 1970S, NEW York City's economy collapsed; the city just barely avoided bankruptcy. The recession hit commercial real estate hard. Rents fell, vacancies rose, and new construction stalled. In the early 1980s, prosperity returned. The lack of new construction during the past decade and the needs of businesses to expand caused rents to rise rapidly. The cyclical real estate industry was on the move again and this time it was booming. I had first-hand experience with this. In 1975, my law firm moved from One Rockefeller Center to larger and better space at 75 Rockefeller Center. The space was a sublet at $7 per square foot from Warner Brothers, which agreed to remake the space to our specifications and, to boot, give us a six-month rent concession. In 1980, when our lease was up, Warner offered to re-let for an additional five years at $25 per square foot. I asked instead for a one-year extension so that I could find new quarters. At the end of the year, the space was re-offered to me at $35 per square foot. In the interim, I purchased a brownstone at the corner of Thirty-sixth Street and Lexington Avenue. If our firm had to pay a high rent, it would pay it to me.

Rockefeller Center was a first class commercial property, perhaps the best in the city. Smart people sell when the market is hot and the Rockefeller family, the owner of the center, was smart. In 1985, the family began the process of packaging the center for sale. The buildings stood on land owned by Columbia University and leased to the Rockefeller Group, the family's holding company. The initial Columbia lease, entered into in 1934, expired in 1994, but could be renewed for additional periods of twenty years at rental terms established by experts. Columbia and the Rockefellers were willing sellers and buyers. Columbia was eager to cash in on the ground lease and the Rockefellers wanted to consolidated their ownership and eliminate the uncertainties surrounding the lease. As a first step in preparing the property for sale, the family purchased the ground lease. The next two steps showed why the Rockefellers are still the Rockefellers.

They formed a real estate investment trust, known by the acronym REIT. A REIT distributes its income to its stockholders and, unlike an ordinary corporation, pays no taxes; its stockholders do. The REIT raised $1.3 billion through a public offering of its stock. Although the REIT was named Rockefeller Center Properties, it owned not even a tiny chip of the Rock. Instead, it loaned the proceeds of the public offering ($1.3 billion) to the Rockefellers and took back a mortgage secured by Rockefeller Center. Once one got past the fine print, the family owned 100 percent of the center plus the mortgage proceeds of $1.3 billion. What did the REIT own? A low interest, high risk mortgage. Although the interest rate was only 5 percent, the aggregate interest payment was more than the center's cash flow. The mortgage was risky because it was secured only by the center; the Rockefeller family assumed no liability to the REIT. In the event of a default, the REIT could look only to the property and, based on current rents, it was worth less than $1.3 billion.

The stockholders were told that their prospects would improve. The center's rental income was bound to soar, increasing on average by at least 6 percent per annum. In that event, the interest rate would also increase to a rate in excess of market, and the value of the center would equal or exceed the amount of the loan. But what would happen if rents failed to rise by 6 percent, or stayed the same, or, worse, declined? The REIT's stockholders alone would suffer. It was a classic case of a one-way deal: the public assumed all the risks and if the property prospered, received only a small share of the rewards. For the Rockefellers, the deal could not have been improved upon. Mortgage proceeds, i.e., the cash received by the mortgagor, is a loan and therefore not taxable. The Rockefellers, who took out a mortgage on the center, paid no taxes on the $1.3 billion received from the REIT. If rents increased, the Rockefellers as the owner of the center received almost all the benefits. If rents did not increase, then the Rockefellers mortgaged the property for more than it was worth and the stockholders of the REIT were left holding the bag.

Bad deals like this one should not happen. Investment banking firms, who represent the prospective stockholders, should either refuse to participate in such one-sided deals or require that they be renegotiated. The magic of the Rockefeller name must have blinded the banking firms. The deal, as initially structured for the family, was unchanged. The investment banking firms competed for the privilege of selling the greatest number of shares to the public.

Phillip Pruitt was a successful entrepreneur. He knew how to evaluate an investment. He purchased shares in the REIT, however, without any analysis, and based on his broker's inaccurate statement that the company owned Rockefeller Center. As is typical in public offerings, he did not receive the prospectus, the document describing the investment, until after he had purchased stock. When he read the prospectus and learned what a bad deal he and others had made, he wanted only one thing: to sue the Rockefellers and the investment banks.

Pruitt was the ideal plaintiff. He was committed, intelligent, sophisticated, and black. What difference did his race make? A lot. I brought the case in the state court in New York County and requested a jury trial. The juries in New York County are and continue to be mainly black. Now imagine the trial. The deal is a swindle and the jury is black. On one side is the victim, a polished black man; on the other side is the Rockefellers, accused of overreaching innocent investors. I could not have invented a better script.

Then, a dramatic and unexpected event occurred and the case fell from top drawer to bottom. In the mid-1980s, the Japanese entered the U.S. commercial real estate market. They wanted only the very best and were willing to pay prices far in excess of market value. On the foreign currency market, the yen was strong and the dollar weak. The dollar prices expressed in yen were bargains, as compared with prices when the dollar was strong and the yen weak. To Americans owning trophy real estate, the price in dollars was too attractive to turn down. At one point, it looked like Japan would own all the best properties in America.

Rockefeller Center was the quintessential trophy property, but it was burdened by a $1.3 billion mortgage. Would even a Japanese company bite? The answer was yes. The Rockefellers and the largest Japanese real estate company announced an agreement: the Japanese company would purchase Rockefeller Center for cash of $1.8 billion. Since the property was burdened by the REIT's $1.3 billion mortgage, the purchase price valued Rockefeller Center at $3.1 billion. Our contention that the center was worth less than the mortgage was refuted by the strongest form of evidence, an arm's length sale placing a value on the property of $3.1 billion. To me, the Rockefellers had sold the property twice, to two different suckers. The public loaned more than the property was worth and a Japanese company purchased the worthless equity above the debt for $1.8 billion. Regardless of what I thought, our claim was weak. I lost interest and made no effort to push the case. I did not know time was on my side.

The escalation in New York office rents continued and reached a high of about $75 per square foot. Then, during 1989–1990, the bubble burst. Rents did not fall as low as $7 per square foot, but for $20 to $25, one had a choice among many first class buildings. What did this mean for our Rockefeller case? It became top drawer again.

I began my preparation by examining all relevant documents. I dispatched my number-one man, Jai Chandrasakkar, the most brilliant young man I had ever met, to make an initial search. I got Jai through our son, David. They roomed together at Exeter and again at Yale. David made no bones about it. In their crowd of very smart students, Jai stood head and shoulders above the rest. One day, David said Jai was interested in going to law school, but wanted to test his interest by working as a paralegal. Jai was having a tough time getting a job. He needed a salary of $400 per week to live in New York, and asked if I could help.

I called Jai and told him there was no need for an interview as he was well known to me. A job at my firm was available, but not at $400—we would pay him $600. For the first and only time in our relationship, Jai was speechless. When he recovered his composure, he thanked me and agreed to start work the following day. Jai stayed for four years. He quickly learned how to research the law and write briefs and complaints. I preferred Jai over the lawyers in the firm and worked exclusively with him. Through his extraordinary work, we won case after case and each year Jai received a huge bonus. In his last two years, Jai's overall compensation was second only to mine. Although he was pleased, I felt that he was cheated; he deserved more than I. When he left my employ for Yale Law School, I assuaged my conscience by giving him a bonus to cover his tuition, room, and board.

Jai worked well on the fishermen's case and on several stock appraisal cases that I tried and won, mainly because of his work. But it was not until the Rockefeller Center case that he achieved superstar status within the firm. The defendants produced tens of thousands of documents and placed them in one large room. For three weeks, while Jai was examining the documents, I heard not a peep from him. Finally, he emerged from that large room with three sets of documents. One set he marked with his notes and gave to me; the other sets, unmarked, were for use at depositions. Jai spent a week with me reviewing the documents he selected and explaining their significance. Jai had put the documents in order so that they told the whole story. And what a story they told.

The Rockefeller Group, the owner of the center, was in turn owned by a trust headed by David Rockefeller. He considered the property to be a Rockefeller monument, not a money machine; he opposed a sale. The younger generation of Rockefellers, referred to as the cousins, pressed for a sale. They were beneficiaries under the trust and although they were rich in assets, many were short of cash. This was because the center was conservatively managed. Instead of distributing cash flow to the trust and ultimately to the beneficiaries, the cousins, income was plowed back to upgrade the buildings and the public space. The cousins argued that the return on the property, as a percentage of fair market value, was very low. "Why not sell the property and buy high-yield investments?" The trust's advisers sided with the cousins. They understood that the commercial real estate market was cyclical. Based on experts' reports, the advisers believed that the market was at a peak and bound to decline within the next few years. They concluded that it was a good time to sell.

As a compromise between David Rockefeller's resistance to a sale and the cousins' need for liquidity, the advisers suggested placing a mortgage on the center. In that way, the Rockefellers would own the property and obtain cash at least equal to its fair market value, a practice called mortgaging out. The advisers suggested that the best mortgage terms could be obtained from a newly formed real estate investment trust, controlled by representatives of the Rockefellers.

Initially, the advisers thought that the property could support a mortgage of $800 million. Then the investment bankers got into the act. They hired real estate appraisers who placed unrealistically high values on the property based on improbable assumptions. They assumed that the market was not cyclical and that the then current rate of $75 per square foot, would increase at a compound rate of 6 percent per year and, like a ratchet, move in only one direction, upward.

The rule of seventy-two measures the number of years it will take for a principal sum to double, based on the average rate of growth. All you do is divide the average return, in this case 6 percent, into seventy-two. The rent of $75 per square foot in 1985 would double in twelve years and reach the unprecedented, unimaginable rate of $150.

The trust's advisers and David Rockefeller believed the new appraisal reports to be inflated, but went along with the investment bankers' suggestion to increase the loan from $800 million to $1.3 billion. The investment bankers' job was to sell the REIT's securities to the investing public, their clients. By increasing the amount of the mortgage, they increased the risk, to the detriment of their clients. On the other hand, since the investment bankers received a generous commission on each share of the REITs' stock sold to the public, as the size of the REIT increased, they benefited. Never mind that all an investor got was the privilege of making a loan to the Rockefellers. The name was magic; the public offering was oversubscribed.

In addition to documents that showed without any doubt that the Rockefellers and their advisers did not believe the appraisals described in the prospectus, Jai uncovered earlier appraisal reports valuing the property at much lower than $1.3 billion; one was at $500 million. I now had hard evidence and was ready to examine the defendants.

I prefer to examine the low level people before taking on the chiefs. The former know the details. Often, after examining them, the pieces of the puzzle start to come together. Then, when I examine the head of the investment banking team, the trust's chief adviser, and finally, David Rockefeller, the whole puzzle would appear before me. Jai's documents identified those having a role in the management of the center, the valuation reports, and in the planning for the REIT. I got through several rounds of depositions and then circumstances changed dramatically, and I did not finish.

By 1990, new leases were made at $20 plus concessions, and the vacancy rate was high. A cash reserve, initially established to enable the center to meet interest payments in the early years until rising rents made up the shortfall, was almost depleted; foreclosure and bankruptcy seemed likely. At that point, the Rockefellers made a settlement offer. They offered to add $300 million to the reserve fund, thereby insuring interest payments would be met for the next few years.

The offer was more than fair if the REIT's stockholders were limited to money damages. Under the controlling statute, our damages could not exceed the difference between the per share public offering price of $27, and the market price at the time we discovered the wrong, the day we brought our action. On that day, the price was $24. The aggregate amount of our damages, $3 per share on fifty million shares, was half the settlement offered to us. There was a possibility that we could get recision, i.e., return the mortgage for $1.3 billion, but because of the many changes in circumstances, including the purchase of the property by the Japanese buyer, that remedy was unlikely. I accepted the offer, but regretted that the case would never come to trial.

13

A TANGO WITH
A TEXAS BILLIONAIRE

ALAN KAHN MANAGED OTHER people's money with a twist. When he purchased stock for an account, he purchased the same stock for himself. He then told his accounts, "You are protected against fraud and self-dealing. I own what I buy for you. If any of our companies engage in fraudulent conduct, I will sue." When he did sue, Kahn sent bulletins to his accounts describing the lawsuits and kept them posted on developments. He used litigation to promote his investment advisory business. I was his litigation attorney.

Kahn came from a fine old New York family, but you would never know that listening to him speak. He used words depicting sexual acts to describe corporate wrongs, and almost everything else. I urged him before speaking to ask himself one question: "Would David Rockefeller say that?" His reply was, "Fuck David Rockefeller. Now his brother Nelson, that's a different story." I tried a different tack. In reporting to him on a case, I used scatological language. At first, he laughed. Soon thereafter, he said, "What a terrible way for a lawyer to report to his client." It worked; he stopped using foul language.

One of Kahn's cases involved Harold Simmons, a billionaire Texan who controlled a corporate empire consisting of Valhi Corp, NL Industries, and Tremont. Simmons owned a majority of Valhi's stock. It in turn owned large blocks of stock in both NL and Tremont. Simmons nominated the directors of all three companies and his slate ran unopposed.

Valhi borrowed from banks to purchase control of NL and Tremont, and secured the loans with shares of the acquired companies. A credit crunch developed when the stock price of NL fell substantially and the banks demanded that their loans be paid off or reduced. Valhi lacked the funds to comply. Tremont, however, was awash in cash which it planned to use to purchase companies in complementary businesses. Valhi's need for cash, however, trumped Tremont's plans. Simmons proposed that Tremont use its surplus cash to purchase NL stock owned by Valhi.

For Tremont, the proposal made no business sense. It was an operating company, not an investment company; for Tremont, the acquired NL stock would be an investment only. Further, NL was a poor investment; it was losing money and would soon eliminate its dividend. For Simmons, the proposal met a pressing need. Valhi would get the cash to pay off loans and Simmons would retain majority control of NL through his control of Tremont.

The Tremont directors, with strong ties to Simmons and none to the other Tremont stockholders, approved the proposal. It was a classic stockholder derivative case. In such cases, the injury affects the corporation directly and the stockholders indirectly through their stake in the corporation. A shareholder is allowed to bring an action on behalf of the corporation, i.e., derivatively, provided a majority of the directors are the wrongdoers, or employees or affiliates of the wrongdoer (as was the case in Tremont).

Kahn and his clients owned stock in Tremont. We brought suit in Delaware, where Tremont was incorporated. The case was assigned to William Allen Jr., the chancellor of the Chancery Court, a legal scholar and a recognized authority on corporate governance. Although his decisions on preliminary motions imposed high moral and ethical standards upon directors, during the twelve years he served as chancellor, he never decided a case for the plaintiff stockholder. Was he biased? No. He was conservative and the cases fit a pattern. In every one, independent directors (directors having no economic interest in the challenged transaction) approved the deal. The chancellor, employing a rule requiring a judge to defer to the business judgment of the directors, called appropriately the business judgment rule, dismissed the cases. Four of Tremont's seven directors were affiliated with Simmons and three were independent. The independent directors formed a committee and recommended the transaction; the board ratified the committee's recommendation. If the board had considered and approved the transaction, the business judgment rule would not apply. Would board approval based on a recommendation by a minority of independent directors make the rule applicable? Our case would test the extent of the chancellor's adherence to the business judgment rule.

The defendant's attorneys were well aware of the chancellor's judicial philosophy and moved to dismiss Kahn's case, contending that the recommendation by the independent directors invoked the business judgment rule. At the time of the oral argument, about a year after the challenged deal, NL had cut its dividend and its stock price was about half of what Tremont had paid. Had the stock price not declined, the chancellor might have bought the defendants' argument and dismissed the case. Instead, the defendants' argument irritated the chancellor. The independent directors were not only fallible, but appeared to be corrupt. He asked, "How could independent directors approve such an obviously bad deal?" I think, if he could have, he would have awarded us judgment then and there. He could not do so until after trial but did everything within his power to advance the case.

He ordered the defendants to produce documents without any delay and to promptly arrange for witnesses to be examined. He addressed me, "Mr. Silverman, inform me as soon as discovery is completed. I will then assign the case for trial peremptorily. There will be no adjournments of the trial date."

As soon as discovery ended, I informed the chancellor and the trial was scheduled to begin on a Monday in late May. A trial, however, seemed unlikely. Good cases settle, and this was a good one. Therefore, I did not waste time preparing for trial. I was wrong. No offer to settle was made. I learned later that Simmons rejected his lawyer's advice to settle. He told them, "I do not pay you top fees to settle cases."

On the Thursday before trial, I began my preparation. Counting the weekend, I had four days for trial preparation. In fact, I had only one day. Our son's graduation from Exeter and related festivities began early on the Friday of the weekend before the trial, with a six hour drive to New Hampshire, and continued through Sunday at noon. Although preparation time was short, I was not worried.

Before a trial begins, it is customary for the parties to exchange batting orders, that is, a list of witnesses and the order they will be called, and to provide each other and the court with an estimate of the time each witness will take. The defendant's list began with the three independent directors, then the experts the directors relied on, and finally Simmons. According to the estimate, Simmons would not be reached until the second week.

The plaintiff's evidence comes first. It is his task to present a prima facie case strong enough to win, if unrebutted. The burden then shifts to defendants and at the end of their case, the plaintiff has the last shot by calling a rebuttal witness. My direct case consisted of documents and selections from deposition transcripts. My only witness, an expert, was reserved for rebuttal. The plaintiff's direct case would take no more than thirty minutes and I needed a minimum of preparation.

On Thursday, I selected the material needed to cross-examine the first week's witnesses. I worked late on Thursday. On Friday, Irene drove and I continued my preparation in the car. On Saturday and Sunday, I arose early and, so as not to wake my wife, worked in the bathroom. Again on Sunday, Irene drove to New York and I worked in the car as I did later that night on the train to Delaware. I was prepared for the first week.

At the opening of the trial, defendants announced that Simmons, listed as the last witness, would be called first. I protested: "What good does a batting order serve if a party can reverse the order before the trial begins? I'm prepared for the directors and the experts, not Simmons." My opponent replied that Simmons had urgent business to attend to later this week and next on behalf of his companies, including Tremont. In Delaware, business outranks every other consideration. The chancellor permitted the change but said that when Simmons's direct testimony was over, he would call a recess for an hour to allow me to prepare cross.

The change in order was not a trick. It is always good to end a case on a high note. Simmons was an excellent witness and, for the good of the case, should have testified last. But, a CEO is a king and kings do not want to be kept waiting.

Donald Scott was the lead attorney for the defendants. He had all the good qualities of a trial lawyer and none of the bad. He was smart, thoroughly prepared, personable, low-keyed, and had so much charm that judges and juries loved him. Many trial lawyers delight in speaking and never turn down an opportunity. Scott confined his courtroom comments to the essentials, never repeated what he had earlier said, and if asked by the judge to reply to an argument he had advanced and the other side had answered, as often as not, declined, saying that he had nothing to add. He was a perfect gentleman, and yet the toughest adversary I had ever faced.

Simmons told how he started as a pharmacist with one little store in a dusty suburb of Dallas. Within a few years, while still in his twenties, he owned a chain of stores throughout Texas. He sold the chain and then used the cash, plus borrowed funds, to buy operating companies. Some of his acquisitions were friendly, others hostile, and from time to time, Simmons augmented his cash reserves by accepting greenmail.

Greenmail arises when a well-heeled wheeler-dealer purchases a large block of stock in a company, makes a hostile offer to buy the company, and then gets bought out by the company at a substantial premium over both his cost and the market. Under Scott's skillful questioning, Simmons made greenmail seem socially desirable. He said he purchased large blocks of stock of companies he deemed undervalued, then attempted to buy the company at a premium over its stock price. On occasion, management of the company persuaded him that his offer was too low compared to the true value of the company. Simmons said that he did not want to cheat the company's stockholders by paying too low a price. Therefore, if he were unwilling to offer the fair value, he resold the shares to the company, at fair value, a price always above market and his cost.

Simmons described each of the companies he owned or controlled. He called NL the jewel in his crown as its cash flow was $200 million per year, by far the leader in his empire. Tremont paid $14 a share for NL. At the time of the trial, NL stock had advanced from $7 to $16. Simmons said he believed NL was greatly undervalued at $16 and claimed it was worth about $40. Scott then showed Simmons several brokerage reports on NL and directed his attention to pages reflecting future prices. Several suggested possible prices of $25 to $30. Simmons dismissed those reports as too conservative. One analyst projected a price over three to five years of $40. Simmons said that fellow was probably right.

Simmons then addressed the challenged transaction. He testified that the deals under consideration by Tremont's management were, in his opinion, unattractive. He described the negative aspects of each potential deal. He told the other Tremont directors that an investment in NL would provide a better return then any of the other deals. He offered to sell NL at $16.

A committee of the independent directors was formed, consulted with experts, and offered $12, $4 less than Simmons had asked. A compromise of $14 was reached. Simmons said he reluctantly agreed to the compromise. He believed the committee got the much better end of the bargain. He was pleased Tremont made an attractive purchase; after all, he owned indirectly about one-third of the company's stock.

Scott and Simmons painted a compelling picture of good faith and fair dealing. Simmons, their story ran, rose from a humble beginning to become a compassionate billionaire who hurt himself in order to help Tremont make a fine investment. A deal that made no business sense was made to seem not only a plausible investment, but a good one.

When it was my turn, not being well prepared, I began with a frontal attack and hammered away. It is more effective to develop slowly, but that method takes a lot of preparation and I was not well prepared. I began with Valhi's balance sheet and the dangerously high ratio of debt to equity. After showing Simmons financial statements and credit reports, I extracted the annual amount needed to service Valhi's debt, to pay interest, and amortization. I put the number on the blackboard. From the same documents, I got Valhi's annual cash flow and forced Simmons to admit that that was the cash flow. It was far less than the amount needed to service the debt. It took several hours to get Simmons to concede the obvious: Valhi was insolvent.

I then scrutinized Valhi's efforts to sell NL stock to others. Simmons maintained that Valhi did not offer NL stock to others and claimed he would never sell NL stock to anyone other than one of his controlled companies. When I showed him several letters offering the stock, he said the offers were unauthorized and made without his approval. I then showed him Valhi board minutes discussing attempts to sell NL stock. Although Simmons was present at the meeting, the minutes made no mention of his opposition to a sale of NL stock to unrelated third parties.

Simmons refused to admit that Valhi had to sell assets in order to repay debt. Although there were documents to that effect and Valhi used the proceeds of the sale to Tremont to repay debt, Simmons said he was confident the banks would refinance Valhi's debt. I showed him letters from the lead bank insisting that the loans must be paid down and would not be renewed. Simmons claimed the letters were written by junior officers. His friends were at the top echelons of the banks. They had worked with him during other tough times and he was confident that they would help him again.

I showed him letters from companies refusing to consider a purchase of NL stock and an offer from an investment banking firm willing to buy the stock but at $8 per share, a price much lower than the $14 paid by Tremont. Simmons held fast; Tremont got a bargain. He would not have agreed to sell the stock for less than $14.

My assessment was that Simmons came out ahead, but only because NL's stock at the time of the trial was above the price Tremont paid.

The next witnesses were Tremont directors and their experts. They were ineffective. At the conclusion of the trial, the chancellor met with the lawyers. He said that the case was a close one and until he began to write his decision, he did not know how he would decide.

The chancellor wrote a long and detailed decision. He criticized severely the Tremont directors and their experts and found the $14 price at the very bottom of the range of fairness. The case, he said, turned on burden of proof. Because a committee of independent directors approved the transaction, the plaintiff had the burden of proof. In this close case, the plaintiff had failed to prove unfair dealing by a preponderance of the evidence. Accordingly, he dismissed the complaint and entered judgment for the defendants.

We appealed to the Supreme Court of Delaware. On the day before oral argument, NL's stock closed at $10 per share, $4 below the price paid by Tremont. Although the Supreme Court never mentioned market price (I sure in hell did), I believe that if the price had stayed above $14, the chancellor's decision would have been affirmed.

The Supreme Court reversed on burden of proof and found it rested on defendants, not on Kahn. This case made history in Delaware. It was the only case decided on burden of proof and reversed on burden of proof. The victory on appeal was important because it gave me a second chance. The chancellor resigned before the second trial; he accepted a professorship at the New York University Law School and an executive position with a think tank affiliated with the university.

The case was retried before a newly appointed vice-chancellor. I had plenty of time to prepare for Simmons. I got documents from his bankers demanding that the loans be repaid. I also caught Simmons manipulating the price of NL through repurchases. The judge had worked in enforcement at the SEC and was angry. At the end of the first day, the judge called the lawyers to his chambers. He said, "I do not believe Simmons." Addressing Simmons' lawyer, he said: "You would be wise to speak to Mr. Silverman." When a judge says that, you settle quickly. That night we settled the case.

My opponents are usually enemies, not friends. On occasion, an opponent becomes a friend. After the first trial, but before the decision, I received a letter from Scott. He said he has a high when he wins and a low when he loses. This time, if he wins, his high will be lower, and if he loses, his low will be higher. What a nice man! We became friends.

14
THE MAXXAM CASE:
SIMMONS AND SCOTT REDUX

I WAS ONE OF SEVERAL lead attorneys in a derivative action against Charles Hurwitz, known as Chainsaw Charley because of his devastation of a redwood forest. The case involved not timber but a real estate development in Palm Springs, California. Hurwitz controlled Maxxam and borrowed money from it to develop a luxury community in the Rancho Mirage section of Palm Springs. When it seemed likely that the development would fail, Hurwitz sold the development to the company in cancellation of the debt, plus cash and a profit participation. The case was quickly settled by my colleagues; the corporation received very little. The lawyers' fees were generous. I did not participate in the settlement negotiations.

Simmons was a large Maxxam stockholder. At one time, he and Hurwitz were friendly. Then, Hurwitz reneged on a promised contribution to one of Simmons' pet charities. Simmons decided to punish Hurwitz by objecting to the settlement and putting Scott on the case. Scott did an excellent job and the court rejected the settlement. Simmons and Scott controlled the case and it was theirs to try.

We had just finished the trial of the Tremont case when Scott asked me to work with him on Maxxam. We worked well together. Scott was the lead. He made the opening argument and cross-examined the directors, including the principal defendant, Hurwitz. I examined our two experts and cross-examined the defendants' experts. It was a relaxing trial; for the first time in my career, I shared responsibility of the trial with another lawyer. The result was a complete victory. Defendants threatened to appeal and to avoid an appeal we settled. The new settlement was heard by the judge, who rejected the earlier one and presided over the subsequent trial. Approval of the settlement was certain, as it was a vast improvement over the rejected one, but I anticipated a problem persuading the judge to award the huge fee we were requesting. Judges receive modest salaries for long hours of hard and difficult work. Many judges resent the fees obtained by plaintiff lawyers. The Maxxam judge was one of those. I believed he would choke on our fee, as he could not amass in fifty years of service on the court what we were seeking for less than a year's work.

I urged Scott to address only the fairness of the settlement and let me make the fee application. As expected, the judge approved the settlement from the bench and complimented both Scott and me on the conduct of the trial and the fairness of the settlement. The judge said even he could not have done a better job. Scott thanked the judge for comparing us to him. I had to restrain myself from laughing. The judge had been a fair trial lawyer. Before becoming a judge, he assisted me in a trial. He was no Don Scott; he was not even a Sidney Silverman!

I then presented the fee petition. I said the plaintiffs' bar was short on excellent litigators and it was important to attract attorneys of the caliber of Donald Scott. Awarding a large fee is a way to attract him to serve again. The argument must have appealed to the judge because, without the slightest hesitation, he granted our request.

Scott's and his firm's appetite were whetted. He wanted another stockholder's case and a chance to earn another huge fee. He said, "Keep me in mind on the next big case."

Shortly thereafter, the press reported on a major stock fraud. The publicity generated over thirty cases, all pending in a federal court in New Jersey. To manage the litigation, the judge consolidated the actions and proposed an unusual procedure for the appointment of lead counsel. He asked those plaintiff lawyers who wanted to be lead to submit written proposals stating their qualifications and their fees based on a percentage of the recovery. The judge said that the attorney representing the largest stockholder would have an option to accept the lowest fee; otherwise, lead would go to the low bidder.

Scott and I decided to bid even though we had not filed a complaint and did not represent a client-stockholder. Clients are an essential component of a lawsuit. Could we end-run the requirement? Scott arranged for a leading New Jersey firm to join with us. A lawyer from the firm called the judge's chambers and asked whether we could bid even though we did not represent a stockholder. The judge's clerk called the next day and said we could submit a proposal.

Since the New Jersey firm was well known to the judge, our proposal touted Scott's firm and mine. A national legal magazine ranked Scott and his firm among the nation's top ten trial lawyers. A copy of the article was attached. A compendium of the stockholder cases I had tried was also attached, and the claim made that I had tried more stockholders' cases, for the plaintiff, than had any other lawyer. Our fee proposal began at 5 percent of the first $100 million of recovery, and increased by 5 percent for each additional $100 million. It was the reverse of the usual fee proposal which scales down the percentage as the recovery increases. The rationale for our *sui generis* proposal was that it provided an incentive to obtain the largest possible settlement and to discourage acceptance of a small settlement, a point we emphatically made in the proposal itself. We asked the court to regard the fact we did not have a client as a mere technicality.

The New Jersey lawyer and Scott attended the court session. The judge said one group submitted a knock-out proposal but did not represent a stockholder. He wanted to grant lead to that group but was constrained by the recently adopted law that mandated lead be assigned to the stockholder having the largest stake in the lawsuit, provided that the stockholder's lawyer was qualified. While he did not believe he had to automatically crown the largest stockholder, he interpreted the law as requiring that the stockholder, not his lawyer, must be designated as lead. Since the best qualified team of lawyers did not represent a stockholder, he could not name them.

The case was settled for $500 million. The attorney for the lead plaintiff was one of the law students who had worked for me that hot summer of 1970.

15
U.S. SUGAR AND THE SWEETEST WITNESS

U.S. SUGAR CORPORATION, A farming company, was run as efficiently as industrial giants such as General Motors in its heyday. And there are good reasons for this analogy.

Charles Stewart Mott, one of the founders of GM, was raised on a farm. After retiring from the automobile company, he returned to farming. In 1931, Mott purchased 120,000 acres of muck land in Palm Beach County, Florida, lying south of Lake Okeechobee. Muck is nitrogen-rich land, formed millions of years ago from the decomposition of vegetation. It is so rich in nutrients that crops raised there have no need for additional fertilizers. Lake Okeechobee, the second largest fresh water lake in the country, moderates the extremes in weather. Land lying south of the lake, as was Mott's land, is milder in winter and cooler in summer, ideal conditions for farming. Mott converted the land into a vast sugar plantation. He named his new venture the United States Sugar Corporation.

Sugar cane consists of a large fibrous stalk, called bagasse, and a tip containing raw sugar. At harvest time, the plants are cut and transported to mills where the tip is ground to produce raw sugar. U.S. Sugar's mills made use of the entire plant. The bagasse provided fuel for the mills' furnaces; no fossil fuels were used. Long before the term came into vogue, U.S. Sugar was "green."

Railroad tracks connected the mills with the land. Mott built specially designed railroad cars to haul the cane to the mills. When the cars reached their destination, they tilted, dumping their contents at the mill entrance. All other sugar cane farms transported cane by truck. At harvest time, the trucks were often stuck in traffic, involved in accidents, and otherwise delayed. To obtain the maximum sugar content, it is important that the cane be ground as soon as possible after harvest. The highly mechanized procedure used on Mott's plantation extracted the maximum amount of raw sugar. U.S. Sugar was so efficient that it was the lowest cost producer in the United States. The company, however, was subject to foreign competition.

The governments of underdeveloped nations, particularly in South America, subsidized sugar cane farms to the extent that the crop far exceeded demand, causing the price of sugar to fall to very low levels. Rather than reduce supply, the governments continued to support raising sugar because it provided a living for poor workers at less cost than welfare payments.

Imports of cheap foreign sugar threatened America's sugar producers. In order to protect them, tariffs on imported sugar were set at prices affording a profit to the highest cost producers. Raw sugar, regardless of its origin, was sold to U.S. refineries at the tariff price, not the much lower world price. U.S. Sugar, as the lowest cost producer, profited from federal protection. As long as Congress imposed a tariff, U.S. Sugar would be profitable.

At his death, Mott left his holdings to the Mott Foundation, a charity based in Flint, Michigan. The foundation, managed by members of the Mott family, owned 72 percent of U.S. Sugar; the public owned the remaining 28 percent. The foundation and Mott's descendants were dedicated to maintaining the company as a shrine to their ancestor.

Although the company produced only sugar, it had potential in other areas. If federal protection of sugar ended, the company could switch to ranching and growing other products, such as citrus and vegetables. And there was always the prospect of developing some or all of the 120,000 acres situated in Palm Beach County, one of the fastest growing counties in southeastern Florida.

Many investors follow a strategy of value investing. They seek stock of companies whose net assets, when divided by the number of shares outstanding, greatly exceed the market price of the common shares. In September 1983, U.S. Sugar's stock was selling at $60 per share. At that time, its land was appraised at $408 million or $100.50 per share. The replacement value of the company's assets (fixed assets and land) was appraised at $631 million or $130 per share. On the assumption of a forced sale of the assets at foreclosure, the most pessimistic of assumptions, the assets were valued at $369 million or $75 per share. In effect, the value investors were paying as little as $0.40 for each dollar of assets. Many value investors owned common stock of U.S. Sugar.

The value investors are patient, willing to wait for the sale or conversion of the assets to a more productive use. If however, the asset-rich company makes obtaining asset value unlikely, the value investor sells. A change occurred in U.S. Sugar that made asset realization improbable. It was caused, in part, by an unlikely agent, the attorney general of the State of Michigan.

The state attorneys general exercise oversight of charities based in their states. The Mott Foundation is located in Flint, Michigan. Its stated purpose is to benefit the citizens of that city. As the domestic automobile industry declined, Flint became a depressed city. The Michigan attorney general prodded the foundation to do more for the poor of Flint. He also objected to the concentration of the foundation's stock in U.S. Sugar and believed that diversification into higher-yielding securities would enable the foundation to better serve the community.

The foundation and U.S. Sugar devised a plan that would satisfy the attorney general and still allow the foundation to retain a large interest in U.S. Sugar. Under the plan, the foundation would sell 3.6 million shares, or 75 percent, of its holdings in U.S. Sugar at $68 per share to the company for an aggregate price of about $245 million. The cash proceeds would then be invested in high-yield securities, providing the foundation with more income with which to help the Flint community. To create an aura of fairness, the company gave the public stockholders the right to sell any and all shares owned by them back to the company at $68. As a final step, the company created an employees stock option plan, an ESOP, and sold one million shares, approximately 35 percent of the stock purchased from the foundation, to the ESOP at $68 per share. The ESOP paid for the stock by borrowing $68 million from U.S. Sugar. Over time, the balance of the repurchased shares will be transferred to the ESOP in lieu of employees' pensions and other benefits.

U.S. Sugar did not have the money to fund the plan. In order to obtain funds, the company borrowed $300 million. The loan proceeds were sufficient to enable the company to buy 75 percent of the foundation's holdings, all stock held by the public, and lend $68 million to the ESOP.

In September 1983, U.S. Sugar made a tender offer to its outside stockholders offering to purchase any and all shares at $68 per share. Although the price was above the $60 market price, and was exactly the same as the foundation received for its stock, the value investors considered the price to be below fair market value. Their real grievance, however, was not price, but the $300 million loan.

The loan changed U.S. Sugar from a debt-free company to a highly leveraged one. More important, the loan proceeds were not earmarked for business purposes, such as acquisitions, enhancement of the company's operations, or the reduction of outstanding stock. Rather, the loan had a single purpose. It was designed solely to enable the transfer of the outstanding shares to the ESOP. Further, the loan was secured by the company's assets. This meant that proceeds from the sale of assets would be applied against the loan and not passed on to the stockholders. The loan agreement also restricted the company from paying dividends; the stockholders would no longer receive a return on their investment. They turned to litigation as a means to obtain fair value for their stock. I was retained.

Since U.S. Sugar was incorporated in Delaware, our action was brought in the Chancery Court in Delaware. We contended that the tender offer coupled with the loan was coercive. Tendering shares was our only economically viable option. If the offer were coercive, the company had a fiduciary duty to offer a fair price. My clients believed a fair price was substantially above $68.

The Hartford Insurance Company, the very same company acquired by ITT and involved in my lawsuit attacking that acquisition, held a large position in U.S. Sugar. Its chief financial officer, Paul Buchanan, heard about our lawsuit and he and the insurance company's general counsel asked to meet with me. I was skeptical. Hartford was owned by ITT, my enemy in over five years of bitter litigation. I doubted that Hartford would join the lawsuit on our side. Nevertheless, I attended the meeting.

At the meeting, I said my clients felt compelled to tender. Holding U.S. Sugar stock without a return and with no prospect of realizing on asset value destroyed the nature of the investment. I further stated that if the court found the offer was coercive, the company had a duty to offer a fair price. While the asset value of $130 per share was an unrealistic goal, the present offer was much too low. Buchanan left to caucus with the Hartford's general counsel. When they returned, Buchanan said, "We purchased U.S. Sugar based on asset value. The loan altered the playing field. The asset value which we had hoped to realize over time now goes to the employees. The workers will get a taste, but most of the stock in the ESOP will go the top officers. That is the way ESOPs are structured. This is an outrageous deal designed to look democratic. The foundation sells U.S. Sugar's stock to be able to bestow more benefits on the poor people of Flint. The company's heart bleeds for the workers in Florida. It turns the repurchased stock over to them. Nonsense. The real purpose: to enrich the executives. The rest is camouflage. We have no objection to Sugar purchasing the foundation's stock and then retiring it. We would then own a higher percentage of the assets. But to turn the stock over to the executives is gross self-dealing. We will tender our stock and join your lawsuit."

The Hartford's attorney then spelled out the level of the insurance company's support. "I talked to a Harvard law school classmate of mine practicing in Delaware. He agreed to represent the Hartford and assist you. His name is Jack Jacobs. The Hartford will foot the expenses. If you win, you will pay us back." I expressed appreciation for Hartford's financial support and, more importantly for Jack Jacobs. "Jack is a good lawyer. We will work well together."

Hartford intervened in the action. The case was certified as a class action without opposition. Documents were produced. The next step was depositions.

Steve Rothschild, one of Delaware's most able trial lawyers, represented U.S. Sugar. He called to discuss a schedule for depositions: "I propose all depositions be taken in Miami. The company's Miami lawyers will make their offices available to us. The only drawback they say is traffic. The roads are congested during the morning and evening rush hours. They suggest we meet at their offices at two o'clock and depositions begin then. It would be nice if you stopped at seven o'clock, but you can go longer if you need to. I figure five days should be enough. We can start on Monday and take a late plane home on Friday. And, by the way, since you play golf, they suggest you stay at the Doral Country Club. On the grounds are three championship golf courses. Assuming no traffic, the Doral is less than a fifteen minute drive from their offices." I agreed to the deposition schedule. Jacobs and I both booked rooms at the Doral.

I knew how I would spend my mornings at the Doral. It would not be preparing for depositions. I therefore devoted the week before the depositions to preparation. I prepared outlines of the examinations for each witness, and keyed in relevant documents for use during the examinations. I sent my outlines and copies of the documents to Jacobs. Over the weekend, I received his comments. On Sunday, I departed for Miami. Jacobs and I agreed to meet at 1:30 PM in the lobby of the Doral for the drive to the offices of the Miami law firm.

On Monday morning, I arose early, ate a light breakfast, played eighteen holes of golf, swam, and met Jacobs on time. I started my examination promptly at two o'clock and ended before seven o'clock. Jacobs and I discussed the deposition over dinner in a Cuban restaurant recommended by the local lawyers. I returned to my room at about 9:30

PM and went directly to bed. I swam every day, but played golf on alternate days, Wednesday and Friday. On Tuesday and Thursday, I stayed at the pool with Jacobs. We discussed the case some, but mainly our different careers and lives. Jacobs told me he was a candidate for a judgeship in the Chancery court. In fact, he said, "The next appointment is mine, unless we do a lousy job in this case." I reassured him, "We may lose the case; it is a tough one. But we will not disgrace ourselves." When Jacobs saw me spending my mornings not on preparation, but at golf and swimming, he was not so sure.

Discovery revealed both the strengths and the weaknesses of our case. On the plus side, valuations of the company in excess of the tender price were not disclosed or were buried in footnotes at the back of the tender offer. Contrary to disclosures made therein, the price was set based on what the company and the ESOP could afford to pay. Fair price can be determined many different ways. I did not believe that the highest price U.S. Sugar and the ESOP could afford to pay were legitimate factors in such a determination.

On the negative side, the company's executives discussed the environmentally sensitive nature of the land. Growing sugar was tolerated only because the land had been long used for that purpose. Conversion to a higher use, such as a residential development, was unthinkable. The necessary approvals, local, state, and federal, would never be obtained. The only permissible use was for agriculture. Sugar was the best cash crop. This testimony meant the land had no independent value; its worth was strictly a function of the cash flow generated from the sugar crop. There was yet another factor that weighed against our case.

Most stockholder cases involve an element of corporate greed. In this case, a good social purpose was present: the foundation was selling stock to help the poor of Flint. The transfer of stock to the ESOP also had a positive side. It sounded a populist note; the employees would eventually own the fruits of their labor.

The case was close. It could go either way. I thought it would be settled. I was unaware at the time of an edict issued from on high. Rothschild, the defendants' principal trial attorney, was a member of a very large firm. Headquartered in New York, it had branches in Boston, Washington, Chicago, San Francisco, Los Angeles, and Wilmington, Delaware. The powers in the firm decided that too many stockholder cases were being settled. More should be tried. The U.S. Sugar case was designated for trial.

The trial was a battle between experts. I had two experts. One was James Walter, a professor at the Wharton School, the business school at the University of Pennsylvania. He held a chair, the Saul Steinberg Professor of

Business. I regarded this chair as a lucky omen. In the Leasco-Reliance case, I had prevailed over Saul Steinberg. Now I hoped the object of Steinberg's generosity would help me win the Sugar case.

Walter relied on cash flow. He took the company's average five-year cash flow. He analyzed other publicly-traded agricultural companies and extracted the multipliers applied to reach the market price of the other companies. In a few cases, in which companies had been sold, the multipliers used to reach acquisition price. He found U.S. Sugar to be the best agricultural company in the country. Accordingly, he selected the highest multiplier and applied it to U.S. Sugar's cash flow. He then added a plus factor of 10 percent for the excess value of the assets over their use to produce sugar to arrive at a price of $78. Walter held up well in cross-examination. Not so my next witness.

Hartford retained an agricultural consulting firm based in Connecticut. It spent two weeks on U.S. Sugar's land at harvest time. It took many photographs. At trial, the heavy curtains adorning the large courtroom's windows were drawn to exclude daylight. The lights were dimmed. The experts presented a slide show. The slides first showed fields just before harvest; then the workers cutting the cane by hand using machetes, the box cars on the rails loaded with cane, a box car dumping its cargo at a mill, the use of bagasse to run the mill, and the mill in operation. The slides brought U.S. Sugar into the courtroom. The witness was impressive in every respect except one: he misdescribed the land. He included adjacent land belonging to another owner as U.S. Sugar's property. He also attributed muckland that contained no muck to U.S. Sugar. These mistakes undercut his opinion of value. He could not be saved from these errors. He had fatally wounded himself.

The plaintiffs' expert was not the only wounded witness. Testimony from First Boston and Bear Stearns did not help the defendants. First Boston conceded that the initial tender offer price of $70 was based on how much U.S. Sugar could afford, not on the intrinsic value of the stock. The banker reduced the price to $68 because the ESOP could not afford to pay more. Market value is defined as the highest price in dollars that a property can bring when freely and unconditionally exposed to sale over a reasonable period of time. By equating market value with the highest price one party can afford to pay, the banker skewed the classic definition. In addition, both bankers admitted that the public stockholders had no outside representative bargaining for them.

In its report, First Boston wrote that the tender price was fair "from a financial point of view." This phrase is always found in so-called fairness opinions. In the past, I tried to extract a meaning for this term.

I was unsuccessful until this case. The First Boston banker said, "Fair from a financial point of view means the price is above market." I asked no follow-up question. First Boston was paid $650,000 to make the determination that $68 was more than $60? I knew I would have fun with that answer in the brief.

As the trial drew to a close, Rothschild complained to the judge that I refused to identify my rebuttal witness, the last witness. I told the judge, "Plaintiffs cannot know what they will have to rebut until all the defendants' evidence is heard. As soon as Mr. Rothschild says the magic words, 'defendants rest,' I will identify the plaintiff's rebuttal witness." Although my position was technically correct, it departed from the usual practice. In past trials, I had identified a rebuttal witness at the beginning of the trial. The judge considered the delay whimsical on my part. He ruled, "You are within your rights to name your witness at the close of the defendants' case. But as soon as the defendants close, you will be required to name your witness."

I delayed naming my rebuttal witness for a tactical reason. I planned to call one of the defendants' expert witnesses, William Schaffer, as my rebuttal witness. The parties had called seven experts to testify on the value of U.S. Sugar. Only Schaffer had devoted his entire career to the sugar industry. He had inspected and performed appraisals for almost all the companies engaged in growing and refining sugar in the U.S. He had also worked for many foreign companies. He was the defendants' last witness.

Schaffer valued U.S. Sugar at $52, the lowest expert opinion of value in the case. There was, however, something missing in his testimony, an estimate of the condition and worth of U.S. Sugar's appurtenant assets. These included the internal railroad used to transport the harvested cane, the energy-efficient mills, the company's superior farm equipment, irrigation, ditches, canals, roadways, and housing for migrant workers. I believed these elements of value could be better developed through Schaffer as a rebuttal witness than through cross examination.

When Schaffer's testimony was over late on Friday, Rothschild announced in a loud voice, "Defendants rest." I then revealed that Schaffer was my rebuttal witness. I asked the court to instruct Schaffer to return to Delaware on the following Tuesday, the day set aside for my rebuttal witness. Rothschild protested, "It is against the rules of litigation for one party to call another party's expert. Mr. Schaffer is planning to return home to Florida. He may have other plans for Tuesday. Further, if the court allows this ploy, Mr. Silverman must pay for Mr. Schaffer's travel expenses and court time. Mr. Silverman must also agree to be bound by Mr. Schaffer's testimony." The judge said he knew of no rule prohibiting a party from calling as his own witness, an opponent's witness. He then asked Schaffer whether he was available on Tuesday, and, if not, when it would be convenient for him to return to Delaware. Schaffer replied he was free on Tuesday. The judge cautioned that I would not be allowed to reject Schaffer's testimony on redirect, and required to pay for his time in court and his travel expenses. I responded with one caveat: "He can't travel first class." The judge laughed and said, "Mr. Schaffer, you may travel first class but Mr. Silverman will reimburse you only for tourist fare."

I believed Schaffer would be helpful provided he was kept on a tight leash. I began with questions about the internal railroad. He testified that it reached all areas of the plantation. The tracks and cars he said were in excellent condition. Transporting the cane by rail was more efficient and cheaper than using trucks. He testified that U.S. Sugar was the only producer in the United Stated using rails and, with prodding, extended that claim to the world. He called U.S. Sugar's two mills "world class" and its farming equipment "superior." He credited U.S. Sugar's clean, migrant housing and fair farm store as one reason for attracting the best migrant workers at harvest time. He said, "U.S. Sugar has the pick of the class." He then discussed the importance of the ditches, canals, and irrigation system in raising cane. I then turned to the ultimate questions.

"Did you assign a dollar value to U.S. Sugar's unique operating system? Kindly answer yes or no." The witness said no. I then turned to his valuation of $52 per share. "Did you extract the average multiplier of cash flow for publicly traded agricultural companies as measured by their stock market price, yes or no?" He answered yes. My final question was, "Did you apply the industry average multiplier to Sugar's cash flow in reaching your opinion that a share of U.S. Sugar was worth $52?" He had no wiggle room and said yes. I concluded with four words, "Thank you, Mr. Schaffer."

After trial, both sides submitted extensive briefs. Jacobs said, "Hartford insists I write the first draft of our brief since you hogged most of the trial work." Jacobs wrote an excellent brief.

While we were waiting for a decision, Jacobs's appointment to the Chancery Court came through. He invited me to his induction ceremony and to a party given by his former law firm. Jacobs had realized his dream. I was happy for him. Two weeks later, I was happy for both of us. The judge decided the case for us.

In an opening paragraph, the judge wrote: "I find from all the properly admitted evidence that there was a breach of fiduciary duty by the defendants because the disclosures made in the tender offer solicitation material did not disclose with complete candor all the material facts a stockholder needed to know to make a fully informed decision.... I also conclude that the tender offer was coercive. I also find that it would be impossible to rescind the transaction and that, therefore, an award of damages is the only possible remedy. I find the amount of damages is $4 per share."

The damage award of $4 valued the stock at $72 per share, $20 more than Schaffer's valuation. It was also a lot less than the valuation of our experts. However, a win is a win. My clients might have complained if I had settled the case for $4; none could complain about a judgment rendered after trial.

The opinion listed me as attorney for the plaintiffs, but not Jacobs. In his place were the names of two minor players from his firm. I called Jacobs and asked for an explanation. He said, "The chancellor said it looked bad to have a sitting judge's name on a decision. I'm proud of my role in the case and disappointed that I receive no credit. There is more to the story. My law firm deducted from my severance the un-reimbursed time I spent on the case. That was all my time. Now my firm will be entitled to a fee for my time. What happens to me? The managing partner claims the firm cannot pay a sitting judge." I sympathized with him and reminded him of the adage, "Be careful what you wish for; it may come true."

Two years later, Rothschild called me. He said there were less than one hundred thousand shares in the hands of the public. "It is unduly expensive to file and mail reports. The company would like to buy the stock but does not want another lawsuit. I propose you and your expert value the remaining stock. We will pay a fee and expenses. The proxy will disclose that you and your expert determined the price. Will you do it?" I said yes.

I had the financial statements sent to Walter, my financial expert at trial. He and I then spent a lovely weekend at the Clewiston Inn near U.S. Sugar's headquarters. An officer of the company gave us a tour, including the new citrus fields. The citrus fields were an experimental operation and occupied only a few acres. Each tree had its own irrigation system that dripped water only as needed, wasting not a drop. Citrus farming appeared to be as efficiently run as the sugar plantation.

The company signed off at Walter's price. The shares were acquired in a merger at the cash price set by Walter. No one sued. In 1988, the ESOP, the foundation, and the Mott family became the sole owners of U.S. Sugar.

Twenty years later, the event the value investors had hoped for came to pass. In June 2008, Charles Crist, the governor of Florida, announced an agreement in principle for the state to purchase all of U.S. Sugar's land for $1.75 billion. Their purpose was the revival and preservation of the Everglades through restoring the natural flow of water from Lake Okeechobee to the Everglades. In the general euphoria of this great environmental achievement, I doubt many people read through the release to learn how the purchase price was set. I did. It was based on the company's own land appraisal report. Based on the number of shares outstanding at the time of our lawsuit in 1983; the sale returned $350 per share.

Oh to be a value investor, to be allowed to keep one's investment, and to live long enough to profit from it!

16
PLUM CREEK:
THE ULTIMATE SETTLEMENT

THE PLUM CREEK CASE was settled in 1999, on unusual terms. The benefit to the class was contingent. It depended upon Plum Creek's performance over the next five years. If the company's earnings equaled or exceeded certain benchmarks, the class received nothing. If Plum Creek earned less, the class could receive up to $30 million. My fee, 25 percent of the amount received by the class, was subject to the same contingency. If the class got nothing, I got nothing. The circumstances of the case dictated the settlement terms. They were the only fair way to resolve the controversy.

Plum Creek owned thousands of acres of forest land in the Northwest containing prized Douglas fir trees. Lumber made from these trees sold for premium prices in the company's principal markets in Japan and other Pacific-rim countries.

Plum Creek was a limited partnership. The limited partners, many thousands in number, owned units, instead of common stock. The units were traded on the New York Stock Exchange in much the same way as common stock of other large companies. There were, however, significant differences between a limited partnership such as Plum Creek and a comparable business in a corporate form.

Under United States tax laws, a partnership, unlike a corporation, pays no taxes, as its taxable income is passed through to its partners. They

97

are responsible to pay taxes on partnership income to the extent of their interest. Timber companies, such as Plum Creek, may deduct from income certain non-cash items, such as depletion and depreciation, from their otherwise taxable income. Plum Creek took these deductions and passed them through to the partners. The non-cash deductions sheltered most of the taxable income. The partners also received cash distributions equal to the company's cash flow, as defined in the partnership agreement. These distributions far exceeded the non-sheltered partnership income.

A corporation is managed by its board of directors who are elected by the stockholders. Plum Creek was managed by its general partner, a boutique investment banking firm located in San Francisco. The general partner was not elected but instead purchased the office from the prior holder, the Burlington Northern Railroad. The general partner held absolute control over the business affairs of the partnership. The limited partners had no voting rights.

In 1998, a plan of reorganization was proposed that would convert the partnership into a real estate investment trust or REIT. In the reorganization, both the limited partners and the general partner would receive stock in place of their partnership interests, the former getting approximately 75 percent of the stock of the new corporation, the balance going to the general partner.

The general partner's share of Plum Creek's cash distributions fluctuated in accordance with a formula the parties referred to as the promote. It provided that a distribution over the fixed formula amount raised the general partner's interest in the partnership. If the dividend were cut, the general partner's interest was correspondingly reduced. The reorganization purported to allocate the interests of the limiteds and general partner pursuant to their respective right to distributions. At the time of the reorganization, the general partner's share of the distribution was 22 percent. Nevertheless, the general partner was assigned a 25 percent interest in the REIT.

The general partner justified the increase based on the company's five-year projections. It reflected an increase in distributions which, if Plum Creek remained a limited partnership, would raise the general partner's interest to above 25 percent. The general partner was willing to go along with the conversion into a REIT provided it received the value now of its potential interest five years hence.

The forecast was prepared by persons under the control of the general partner. The underlying forecast appeared unduly optimistic, thus favoring the general partner. For example, it assumed distributions would rise based on purchases by Plum Creek of other timber companies at bargain prices. If no purchases were made, or if purchases were made at fair market value, the amount of Plum Creek's distributions would not increase. It is unheard of to base a forecast on fortuitous deals, neither identified nor identifiable.

The forecast was speculative in other respects. Although Plum Creek's earnings had recently declined, reflecting the then general economic malaise in the Japanese economy, the projection predicted a quick turnaround for Japan and increased sales by Plum Creek into that market. The projection ignored the long and slow recovery predicted by independent experts.

There was a further reason to believe the forecast was inflated. I obtained from an independent, private research group a five year forecast for the entire timber industry. The study, consisting only of fifteen pages, was expensive. It cost $10,000. It was sold only to the industry and to brokerage firms. I got the report through the good offices of a friendly firm. It showed that companies such as Plum Creek would continue to suffer from increased competition from Canadian companies and a further deterioration in the Japanese economy.

The reorganization benefited the general partner in a second respect. Its interest, unlike that of the limiteds, was not listed or traded on any public market. While it could be sold privately, the partnership agreement barred fractional sales, requiring the general partner to dispose of all or nothing. After the reorganization, the general partner's interest would be converted into the corporation's common stock. The stock would be listed and traded on the New York Stock Exchange. Non-marketable securities, when a buyer can be found, sell at a discount. No discount was assessed against the general partner's interest.

There also appeared to be manipulation in fixing the general partner's interest as high as 22 percent. In 1997, Plum Creek's distribution to its partners should have been reduced, reflecting lower earnings. Inexplicably, the distribution was increased. Under the promote, the general partners' interest rose from 20 percent to 22 percent. If dividends had been cut, as they should have been, the general partners' interest might have been reduced to18 percent.

The reorganization was a classic type of self-dealing. The general partner held, by virtue of its office, absolute control over the partnership. It proposed the terms of the conversion to a REIT which benefited the controlling party at the expense of its *cestui que trust* (literally, he who trusts), the limited partners. The case was on its face a very strong one.

Jerry Sonet was a Plum Creek limited partner. He and my father-in-law were partners in the law firm of Levy and Sonet until 1979, when my father-in-law died. Sonet, a graduate of Harvard Law School, specialized in real estate and tax. Over the years, Sonet referred litigation to me. When Plum Creek announced the reorganization, Sonet called me. He said, "In the past, you ran the cases I gave you. I stayed on the sidelines; you had all the fun. In this case, I want to work with you. I know real estate. I can make a real contribution." I readily agreed.

In attacking a corporate transaction, it is good practice to wait for the proxy statement to be mailed to the stockholders before bringing an action. The proxy provides all the details and is sent out only after all the terms have been finalized. Until the proxy was issued, all I had to go on was a press release by Plum Creek describing the deal. I had, however, a good reason for not waiting before starting a lawsuit. I wanted to examine Plum Creek's documents and witnesses before the proxy statement was issued in order to be better positioned for the major assault, the attack on the proxy itself. In order to do so, I had to file a complaint initiating the action, move for a preliminary injunction, and seek discovery in connection with the preliminary injunction motion. The action was filed in Delaware. The motion and discovery request was heard by the chancellor, William Chandler.

I presented the facts in all their gory details and then said, "A wrong this egregious should be stopped at the earliest possible time. It is difficult and costly to unwind a corporate transaction after it has been completed. It is easy to do so now. Doing so would spare the partnership the costs and expenses of a proxy solicitation and further litigation."

The defendants argued that the action was premature. "If the plaintiff had waited for the proxy statement, he would have learned that the general partner granted the limiteds a right to vote. Moreover, the reorganization is subject to the exclusive vote of the limited partners. Only they, not the general partner, will vote. If the deal is as bad as described by Mr. Silverman, it will be rejected. This case should be resolved in the meeting room, not in the courtroom. Discovery should not be ordered. It is costly and unnecessary. We intend to move to dismiss the complaint and are confident our motion will be granted."

The defendants should have prevailed. They did, but only in part. The chancellor denied the preliminary injunction on the ground that monetary damages were adequate. He said, "If I determine that the general partner took unfair advantage of the limiteds, I can assess damages. A legal remedy is adequate. There is no reason to enjoin the reorganization."

The chancellor decided in my favor on discovery. He ruled, "Defendants should comply with the plaintiff's discovery requests. They can make their motion to dismiss, but should not seek a delay in discovery pending determination of the motion. No delay will be tolerated."

Defendants produced four large boxes of documents. They also agreed to gather the witnesses, who resided in different states, for examination in San Francisco. I arranged for the documents to be copied and sent a set to Sonet. After we reviewed the documents, I traveled to San Francisco to spend five days examining witnesses.

I arrived in my hotel room in San Francisco at about 8:00 PM local time, 11:00 PM my time. I unpacked and looked at my notes. I was tired. Within an hour, I was asleep. I awoke at 3:00 AM and began my preparation. I worked until 7:00, ordered breakfast in my room, and at 9:00 began examining a witness. By 5:00 PM, I was tired, but we had agreed to end the day at that time. I went for a swim, had an early dinner, sitting at the bar of an excellent fish restaurant near my hotel. I went back to my room. I thought I would prepare for the next day and digest today's deposition, but I was too tired. I went to sleep at 9:00 PM and awoke at 3 AM. The second, third, fourth, and fifth days replicated my first day's schedule.

On the plane back to New York, I thought about my career. I had failed in an important respect. I had not developed anyone in the firm to undertake the burden of preparing a case for trial. I liked trial work, but as I aged, the strain of the intense, nonstop work affected my efficiency. In 1998, I was sixty-six. I doubted I had enough strength for many more years of trial work. For the first time, I thought about what I would do when the time came to stop lawyering. No ready alternative appeared.

While discovery was going on, the defendants made their motion to dismiss. The motion was briefed and argued before discovery was completed. I thought they would win, but apparently they had doubts. On my last day in San Francisco, they discussed a possible settlement. The defendants offered $10 million to be paid to the limiteds in complete settlement of the case. I could not accept this. If the projection was inflated, the defendant's gain amounted to $30 million. If the projection turned out to be accurate, the payment of $10 million fell into the category of a strike suit settlement. I rejected their offer and made a counterproposal. "I don't know how I can justify to the judge a $10 million settlement as fair. I would have the same difficulty sponsoring a settlement for $12 or $8 million. I suggest holding the value of the general partner's increased interest, $30 million, in escrow. If Plum Creek meets or exceeds the projection, the escrow is returned. If the company fails to do this, then the escrow sum is paid to the limiteds based on the percentage of the shortfall. For example, if actual results are 50 percent less than the projected ones, then $15 million is paid to the limiteds and the balance to the general partner." The attorneys for the defendants were not enthusiastic about my proposal. When I suggested we alert the chancellor that we were in negotiation to spare him the work of deciding the motion, the attorneys declined. They did not believe we were close enough to reaching agreement.

Shortly after I returned to New York, the chancellor issued his decision. He agreed with the defendants. Since approval of the reorganization was exclusively in the hands of the limiteds, the court would not interfere with or replace their business judgment with his own. The chancellor, however, announced a new principle of law favorable to the limiteds. Because the vote was the limiteds' sole remedy, the disclosures made in the proxy statement would be examined under a "heightened standard of scrutiny."

The defendants' principal litigation lawyer was Robert Sacks, the head of the Los Angeles office of one of New York's most celebrated law firms, Sullivan and Cromwell. Sacks was an excellent litigator. I was sure he understood every nuance of the case. Unfortunately for the defendants, neither Sacks nor his firm was asked to work on the proxy. Rather, it was prepared by corporate lawyers at another firm. They were oblivious to the evidence I had obtained from Plum Creek's officers, experts and representatives of the general partner. They even ignored damaging evidence from documents provided to me from Plum Creek. Among the evidence overlooked was the following:

Plum Creek's earnings had declined severely in 1997, to the point where it had insufficient cash on hand to pay the 1997 distribution. The company borrowed money and used the borrowed funds to pay the distribution. This was a shoddy business practice, designed to conceal Plum Creek's financial plight. Documents revealed and witnesses corroborated the fact that the tax consequences for stockholders of a REIT were less advantageous than the limiteds enjoyed from the present form, a limited partnership. My discovery also uncovered a motive on the part of the general partner for favoring the conversion.

When the investment banking firm purchased the general partnership from the Burlington Railroad, it used funds from accounts managed by it. These accounts received shares in the general partner, a closely held corporation. Some of the investors wanted to sell but, because of the restriction on a sale of a part of the general partner, the investors were locked in. The general partner advised its clients that after the conversion to a REIT, they would receive shares of the REIT and be able to sell the shares on the New York Stock Exchange.

When I read the proxy statement, I knew Sonet and I had an excellent new complaint. The proxy was filled with representations disputed by Plum Creek's witnesses and documents. I drafted a second complaint.

Most complaints state facts, not evidence. The new Plum Creek complaint alleged both. After setting forth a statement contained in the proxy and alleging it was false, the complaint quoted from testimony and documents showing that the statement was false or misleading, or both. At the same time the complaint was filed, I served a motion to enjoin the meeting, contending that the proxy solicitation material was false. In my motion papers, I stated that plaintiff relied on the evidence set forth in his complaint. The defendants served their answering papers, the plaintiff replied, and the motion was set down for argument.

At the argument, I stressed the importance of the proxy statement: "The vote is the only remedy available to the limiteds. Votes will be cast based upon the disclosures made in the proxy statement. A vote based on a false proxy statement is meaningless." I concluded by reminding the court that the proxy statement must be examined "under a heightened standard of scrutiny," and said, "this proxy statement even flunks the ordinary standards."

The court granted our motion and enjoined the meeting. It was, I believe, the first time a billion dollar transaction was stopped by a holder of shares worth only a few thousand dollars. In his decision, Vice-Chancellor Jacobs (the chancellor reassigned the case) directed the parties to work together to correct the proxy statement.

The defendants prepared a short supplement and proposed to send it and a copy of the judge's decision to the limiteds. They proposed that limiteds could change their vote but unless they did, their prior vote would count. They sent their material to me for review. They asked, in accordance with the judge's decision, that I comment on their material. I refused. "Only the SEC can approve proxy material. Your false proxy is a poisoned tree. The votes are the fruit from a poisoned tree. You must begin the process all over again."

At a hastily arranged conference before the vice-chancellor, given on such short notice that I could not attend, he was told that I had violated a term of his decision by refusing to review the supplemental disclosure. The judge was angry. He found the supplement, together with his decision, cured the defective proxy statement and allowed the defendants to make the contemplated new mailing.

As soon as I heard about the court's ruling, I called the SEC attorney in charge of Plum Creek's filings. I told him a Delaware court had enjoined the meeting because the proxy statement was false. I then summarized the reasons it was found to be false and said, "Plum Creek proposes to mail a supplemental proxy statement to the limiteds, retain their vote unless cancelled, and bypass SEC rules requiring all proxy material to be reviewed by your agency. I intend to enjoin the supplement if issued. I expect the SEC to join in my new action." I then advised the defendants' attorneys by e-mail that if the material were mailed, as contemplated, my client would move for injunctive relief in the federal court in Seattle, where Plum Creek was headquartered.

The defendants backed down and the SEC moved in. It requested transcripts of the depositions, the documents supplied to me, and other disclosures. Four weeks later, a new statement cleared the SEC. It disclosed everything that had previously been concealed, and more. It was an exemplar of full disclosure. There was only one thing wrong. The SEC allowed defendants to use the votes obtained on the false solicitation unless a limited took affirmative action and cancelled a prior vote.

I called several large institutional investors. They agreed the general partner had acted egregiously. Yet, all said they were voting in favor of the plan. Their reason: if the plan is defeated, the morale of the general partner will suffer and the limiteds may lose more than if the deal were completed. It was better to appease the bully than fight him.

Approval by the limiteds was obtained, but the litigation was not over. I prepared a third complaint for filing in the federal court in Seattle. The gist of it was that the prior votes can not lawfully be counted; the voting had to start anew. As background material, the draft complaint recited all the statements in the initial complaint that were false, why they were false, and a summary of the vice-chancellor's decision.

I provided defendants with a draft of the complaint. After reviewing it, the general partner, under the threat that the reorganization might be rescinded, elected to settle rather than risk the deal. In transactional cases, and this was one, certainty is very important. Certainty means the end of litigation.

The defendant's lawyer, Sacks, called and asked if my earlier offer to place the value of the general partner's increased interest of 3 percent in escrow was still available. I said yes and we entered into an agreement. It provided that the general partner would receive 25 percent of the stock of the REIT. However, the fair market value of the disputed 3 percent, $30 million, would be placed in escrow. If the REIT performed as projected, the escrow sum would be returned to the general partner. If not, the percentage by which it missed would be distributed to the limiteds. The only remaining item was my fee.

The general partner offered to pay legal fees based on the theory that the settlement provided a contingent benefit, the chance that the limiteds might receive up to $30 million . The general partner also offered to pay me a separate fee for the improved disclosure, a benefit compensable under Delaware law. I accepted the fee based on the improved disclosure, but rejected a fee for creating a contingent benefit. Instead, I said a second fee should be paid but only if the limiteds receive compensation. If they did, the fee should be 25 percent of the benefits.

Settlements of class action, including the award of attorneys' fees, must be approved by the court at a hearing, after notice is mailed to class members and an opportunity given to them to object. The procedure is designed to protect the class from attorneys who might be tempted by large legal fees to negotiate settlements that shortchange the class.

At the settlement hearing, the vice-chancellor asked only one question: "The class receives a benefit only if the company fails to meet the performance parameters of the five year forecast, is that right?" The answer was no, but I have learned never to tell a judge that he is wrong. So, I answered, "Your honor is right. The class does not get any money if the company meets its performance requirements. However, if the company meets those requirements, the class benefits through excellent operating results which will translate into stock market appreciation and enhanced distributions. These benefits may exceed the escrow amount of $30 million. In short, the class cannot lose. Either it gets performance or cash. The only losers are the poor attorneys for the class. If the five-year projection is met or exceeded, they get nothing."

The settlement and the fees were approved.

Plum Creek's performance fell short of the projection. In 2004, the class received $18 million; I received a fee of $4.5 million. What a wonderful pension for a retiree to receive!

My joy turned to anguish when two years later, four of my former colleagues claimed they were entitled to share in the fee. They were wrong. Profits are split only among equity partners. None were. Three, John Harnes, Gregory Keller, and Adam Prussin, received W-2s, a tax form given to employees. Joan Harnes was formerly an equity partner, but in1992, at sixty-five, she accepted "of counsel" status and her equity interest was converted into a flat salary of $200,000. In return, her work week was shortened to four days. From 1992 through 2000, the firm's tax returns listed Joan Harnes as a partner but assigned her profit and ownership interests in the firm at 0.0000 percent. The same returns listed me as the owner of 100 percent of the firm and entitled to 100 percent of the profits.

The dispute evolved into a lawsuit. I needed a lawyer. I chose Mark Elliot, a young partner in the New York office of Bingham and Dana. Elliot, when he was still an associate, opposed me in a trial of a small case. He won. I was impressed with this young man's skills.

He did a great job in my case. His examination of my former colleagues cut through their threadbare claim. When discovery was concluded, he made a motion for summary judgment. This is a tool used to decide cases in which the facts are not disputed. If granted, a costly and time-consuming trial is avoided. It was granted, and my former colleagues, now foes, were denied any recovery. The judge called their claim frivolous. The decision was reviewed on the front page of the *New York Law Journal*, the lawyer's newspaper of record. I was vindicated; they were spanked in public.

I was sad that a long-term working relationship had ended in acrimony. I did, however, have a consolation prize of $4.5 million.

17
GOLDBERG VARIATIONS

THE HILTON HOTELS CORPORATION was founded in 1919 by Conrad Hilton, and headed by Hiltons until 1996 when Steven Bollenbach became CEO. His mission was to jump start a stagnant company, lift its depressed stock price, and massage the ego of the Hilton he replaced as CEO.

Arthur Goldberg headed the Bally Corporation. He was a lawyer, but shortly after he passed the bar, his father became ill and Goldberg took over the management of the family's trucking business. The business was floundering; Goldberg saved it. His success started him on a new career: buying distressed companies and turning them around.

Bally was Goldberg's greatest turnaround triumph. In 1990, the company was on the verge of bankruptcy. Its stock was trading at about $2 per share. Goldberg purchased a ton of stock, became Bally's largest stockholder, and persuaded the board to let him take over. Bally was in two businesses. One owned and operated casino hotels in Atlantic City and Las Vegas; the other manufactured slot machines. Goldberg sold the manufacturing business and used the proceeds to enhance the casino operations.

Fads are a habitual Wall Street addiction. In 1996, gaming companies were the rage. Bally, a pure play in gaming, became a Wall Street favorite. Its stock traded at over $40.

Upscale casino hotels seek to create an atmosphere of glamour and excitement by replicating exotic foreign places. One Las Vegas hotel recreates Venice with canals and gondolas coursing through its lobby. Another, in Atlantic City, duplicates the Taj Mahal. Not so with Bally's casinos; they lacked pizzazz. The key to their success was that they gave the customer the best chance of winning, by maintaining odds more favorable to the bettor. Bally's image as a lunch pail casino, however, was about to change.

The company owned a building site in Las Vegas in the heart of the Strip, on which Goldberg planned to build the Paris Hotel, complete with a replica of the Eiffel Tower and wall-to-wall five star French restaurants. The hotel was estimated to cost about $1 billion. Raising the money meant hocking the company. If the new hotel flopped, Bally would be back in the tank. Goldberg liked sure things, not high stakes. He decided to bail out and let another company take the $1 billion risk. He discreetly let out the word that Bally was for sale. His timing was excellent. Bally's steady earnings, its excellent balance sheet, and the prospect of a glitzy new hotel made the company an attractive acquisition candidate.

Hilton took the bait. In early April 1996, an agreement in principle was reached to exchange Hilton stock for Bally. The agreement was made subject to a due diligence inspection. In performing due diligence on deals involving an exchange of stock, teams consisting of bankers, accountants, and lawyers examine the confidential and non-public financial records of both companies. By mid-April, the due diligence inspections were completed and a merger announcement was anticipated. Instead, the parties said negotiations had terminated; Bally had decided to remain an independent company. It was unlikely that the inspection had turned up adverse information. Something was wrong. The transaction had gone too far for Bally to have changed its mind.

In June, negotiations resumed and a deal was made. The merger terms were almost the same as in the April agreement. Bally stockholders exchanged their high-flying stock for shares of Hilton's depressed stock. The exchange ratio valued Bally, the parvenu, as almost the equal of the world's largest chain of hotels and casinos.

Hilton's generosity towards the Bally stockholder was exceeded by the side deals made with Goldberg. He received Bally assets including options on a controlling block of Bally Fitness, a chain of exercise centers affiliated with Bally; Bally's interest in two joint ventures, one to develop a gaming casino hotel in Cancún, Mexico, and the other to buy a racetrack in Delaware, if that state were to legalize gambling; and, a golden parachute equal to three times his annual salary and bonuses, payable if he were to be terminated as a result of a sale or merger of Bally. Goldberg's parachute was unique in that it opened even though his employment was not terminated.

He was named head of the combined company's gaming operations and granted an option on a large amount of Hilton stock. Hilton also agreed to purchase Goldberg's house, which he had been unable to sell, at a price determined by an appraiser selected by Goldberg.

Alan Kahn owned Bally stock. He valued the Goldberg package at $300 million. He contended the Bally stockholders would have received better terms if Goldberg had not negotiated for himself. In fairness to Goldberg, he negotiated a great deal for the Bally stockholders as well as for himself. I tackled this dilemma early in the case in an argument before the newly appointed chancellor, William Chandler of the Chancery Court of Delaware. Reasoning by analogy, I said, "Let's assume, Chancellor Chandler, that you owned ten undeveloped acres in a resort area in Delaware. Assume further that you asked me to serve as your agent and negotiate a sale of the land for at least $1.5 million. A few weeks later, I inform you, 'I have an offer for $2 million. Further, the buyer liked me so much he said I could keep one acre, free of charge, the one bordering the lake, the most valuable site.' You would undoubtedly congratulate me on the deal, but require the return of the gifted acre to you." The chancellor smiled and said, "Suppose I did not ask you to return the acre, approved the sale, and shortly thereafter died. Could my estate sue you for the return of the acre?"

Implicit in the chancellor's revision was his opinion that if he had knowledge and did not object, his heirs would be precluded. By extension, if Bally's directors were aware of the Goldberg package and did not object, the stockholders, like the chancellor's heirs, were precluded. He dismissed the case. He ruled that since a majority of the Bally directors were independent and approved the merger with knowledge of the Goldberg package, it could not be attacked by stockholders. The business judgment of the directors prevailed.

I thought the chancellor was wrong. Goldberg negotiated for Bally and its stockholders and owed them a duty of loyalty. He violated that duty when he, at the same time, negotiated a deal for himself. Hilton was willing to pay more for Bally and Goldberg took the more for himself. A fiduciary cannot profit from a breach of duty and should turn over his profit to the Bally stockholders. I maintained that directors could not approve a violation of the duty of loyalty owed by an officer to the corporation.

John Harnes worked with me on the case. He said it was usual in mergers for the CEO of the acquired company to negotiate a new position or retirement benefits, and no court had held the practice to be unlawful. He was right on both counts. I had no legal precedents for my position and CEOs typically bargain for themselves. However, there were no decisions saying it was right to do so. To me, it seemed clear: an honest CEO should first complete the merger negotiations before negotiating for himself. My legal position depended on an issue of fact: did Goldberg withhold approval of the merger until Hilton approved his package?

John proposed a different theory. The Goldberg package was a waste of corporate assets, and corporate waste could not be ratified by an independent board. There was support for this position, but the cases imposed an impossibly high standard to prove waste. The standard was that no rational person could approve the transaction. The Bally directors believed Goldberg deserved the package. One might disagree with their decision, but it could not be labeled irrational. I did not want to win on appeal and have the case remanded for trial on an impossible issue to prove.

Our dispute was much more than an argument about a point of law. John was hostile and I knew the reason. Shortly before, I had offended him by criticizing his trial work. My comment reflected my honest belief. I should not, however, have undermined John's confidence. My career was coming to an end and, after spending years in the background assisting me, John was about to emerge on his own. Previously, he had regarded me as his mentor. Now, I was his enemy.

I turned to Joan. She and I always got along. She had been with me for almost thirty years. We sometimes disagreed but our disputes were always resolved in a friendly manner. Not so this time. Joan not only took John's side but attacked me. We reached an angry and uneasy compromise: both points would be briefed and argued. Joan would write the brief and John would argue the appeal.

John argued the appeal before a panel of three judges of the Supreme Court of Delaware. Shortly after the argument, John received notice that the court would re-hear argument. The court has five sitting judges. By law, all decisions must be supported by a majority of the court. If one member of the panel dissents, the case is scheduled for en banc argument, i.e., before all five members. At least one judge and possibly two had disagreed with John's argument.

We got a transcript of the oral argument and I read it along with the briefs. The compromise we reached was barely observed. My point came last in the brief and was poorly made. Further, John had not mentioned it in his oral argument. Before re-argument, I decided that we needed an impartial arbiter. I had the perfect candidate.

Drew Moore was a former judge on the Delaware Supreme Court and its most influential member. His decisions defined the law of corporate governance and were cited and relied upon by courts throughout the country. He was tough on lawyers, including prominent Delaware lawyers.

One lawyer, whom Moore had offended, was close to the governor and persuaded him not to reappoint Moore, who then joined a New York investment banking firm. We met as panelists at a continuing education program for Delaware lawyers sponsored by Tulane Law School. I liked him and when he told me he spent several days a week in New York, we agreed to meet for dinner. We both liked to eat, drink, and talk, and our dinners lasted for hours.

I told Moore about the dispute and requested his assistance. He agreed and asked for the briefs, the transcript of the oral argument, and the decision below. After reading the material, we met in my office. John argued the appeal with Moore serving as the panel of judges.

Moore lost no time in attacking John's position. Waste, he said, was a concept in derivative cases only, ones on behalf of corporations, and had limited application to our action brought on behalf of the Bally stockholders. Was John contending that the merger ratio was so grossly unfair that it amounted to waste? John answered that he could not make that contention. Moore then told him to forget waste.

Moore's questions made clear, if Goldberg negotiated for himself at the same time as he was negotiating for Bally, he violated his duty of loyalty, and the directors could not ratify a breach of loyalty. For support, he cited one of his own decisions. There, a director who did not participate in the negotiations received a special benefit. Moore ruled that if the director had participated in the negotiations, the deal would have been suspect and beyond the power of the board to ratify. Joan sprang to the defense of her son. She said the statement was dictum, that is, not part of the court's ruling, since the director had not participated. Moore dismissed Joan's comment. While dictum was not binding, it was persuasive.

John reargued and this time stuck to my point. He won the appeal without any dissent. The new argument persuaded the dissenting judge or judges to change their position. The case was remanded for trial. In appreciation, I sent Moore a case of very fine French wine and promised him a deed to the vineyard after we won the case.

John and I prepared the case for trial. Hilton and Bally produced documents and we examined the bankers, lawyers, officers, and directors. Our focus was on whether Goldberg delayed approval of the merger until Hilton agreed on his package.

Steven Bollenbach, CEO of Hilton, and Goldberg met two times, once in April and again in June. There were no witnesses present at either meeting. No banker, lawyer, officer, or director had even secondhand knowledge of the meetings; at least, that is what they claimed. Neither

Goldberg nor Bollenbach prepared memos about these meetings. We had to depend on their oral testimony.

The April meeting took place at the same time Bally was conducting its due diligence inspection of Hilton's records. Goldberg, whose offices were in New Jersey, accompanied his experts to California. The trip was both unnecessary and unusual. Goldberg did not intend to nor did he participate in the due diligence sessions. Several weeks earlier, Hilton's team inspected Bally's records at its offices in New Jersey. Bollenbach did not attend. Why did Goldberg appear? Bollenbach, in his deposition, provided the answer. Goldberg wanted to head the gaming operations of the combined companies and wanted assurance that the job was his. Bollenbach refused to commit, and said that as CEO, he would make that decision after the merger closed.

The message came through loud and clear. Goldberg was out and so was the merger. Like the little boy who owns the only baseball and the team will not let him pitch, if Goldberg could not head gaming, there would be no merger.

Goldberg, in his deposition, told a different story about the April meeting. He denied he asked about his future employment. In fact, he said he planned to retire and devote his time to managing his charitable foundation. He claimed the purpose of his visit was to introduce Bally's executives to Bollenbach. Further, Goldberg said he called off the merger because he thought Bally had more potential as an independent company.

Although the parties stopped negotiating, the investment bankers continued to talk. They had a big incentive to revive the deal. The bankers get large fees, but only for done deals. They thought that if Hilton gave Bally better terms, the merger could be accomplished. Apparently, they did not know that Hilton had only to improve the terms for Goldberg. Since Bollenbach knew he had a deal based on the April terms, he was unwilling to pay more, but he was willing to provide a non-cash benefit in the form of "price protection" to the Bally stockholders. The new provision provided that if at the closing Hilton's stock declined by 10 percent or more below the price on the day agreement was reached, the Bally stockholders would receive additional Hilton stock to make up for the decline. The closing occurs after the boards and stockholders approve, a process that begins after a final agreement is reached and takes many months to complete.

Goldberg interpreted the new provision as a sign that Bollenbach was ready to confront the real remaining issue: satisfying Goldberg.

When Goldberg told his banker he would reconsider the improved offer from Hilton, Bollenbach arranged for the second meeting, this time on Goldberg's turf. The meeting took place on a Sunday afternoon in a restaurant in a hotel in the Newark Airport—a great place for a secret meeting.

At Bollenbach's deposition, I asked him about the clandestine airport meeting. Bollenbach recalled that Goldberg appeared in his golf clothes and described his just-completed round of golf and nothing else. I was sure the Goldberg package was the subject of the meeting; all other terms were agreed to. What else could they be discussing? No matter what form the question took, Bollenbach answered, "I do not remember." He made that same answer forty-three times.

Goldberg, in his deposition, claimed to have a complete recollection of the meeting. He played golf before the meeting and described his game, especially his birdie on the fifteenth hole. He told Bollenbach that Bally had other options to a deal with Hilton, which he was still considering. He denied that his package or employment were discussed.

In his deposition, Goldberg further testified that after the merger terms had been agreed to, Hilton insisted, as a condition of the merger, that Goldberg accept the package and agree to head the gaming operations. Although he did not want the Goldberg package, he reluctantly accepted in order to allow the Bally stockholders to reap the benefits of the merger.

I took the depositions of the Bally officers who had worked on formalizing the merger terms. They testified that on the Monday or Tuesday following the Sunday meeting, after all the details had been ironed out, Hilton's lawyer initiated the terms of the package and insisted that Goldberg accept them as a condition of the merger. The Bally officers claimed they called Goldberg and he said that if he had to accept the Goldberg package to insure the merger then he would.

I also took the deposition of the Hilton lawyer who allegedly imposed the package on Goldberg. He testified that he had no recollection of initiating the terms. Discovery was completed and the case was set down for trial.

At the trial, I put in our evidence. In addition to documents and pages from the depositions, I called two witnesses, a valuation expert and Hilton's lawyer. The expert valued the Goldberg package at the merger date, at $50 million. While $50 million is substantial, it paled in comparison to Goldberg's stock interest in Bally. It was unlikely that Goldberg would have sold out the Bally stockholders—he was the largest stockholder—for $50 million. Our expert also testified that Bally stockholders did not get a fair share of the pie.

He could not base his opinion on current earnings, cash flow, stock price, or asset value. These showed that Hilton grossly overpaid for Bally. Instead, he used five-year cash flow projections prepared by Bally and

Hilton. Bally's projections were aggressive. They assumed that the Paris Hotel would be in operation in two years and outgross every other Vegas hotel. Hilton's projections were conservative. We tested the projections, made three years earlier, against actual results. The Paris Hotel was not operational and consuming, not generating cash flow. Hilton actual performance exceeded its projections. Our expert rejected hindsight and accepted the projections at face value. Based on the projections, Bally's contribution, over five years, to the combined cash flow was greater than the percentage assigned to it in the merger. Based on the projections, he concluded the exchange ratio to Bally stockholders was unfair.

Hilton's lawyer was my second witness. He was not out to help me beat his client. He testified that he did not remember suggesting that Goldberg get the package and an employment contract, but claimed that it was possible that he had made the suggestion. I told him that anything was possible and his testimony was not helpful to the court. After much prodding, and with my repeated references to his deposition testimony, he said it was not likely that he made the suggestions attributed to him, but he could not exclude the possibility.

The plaintiff's direct case was over. It was the defendants' turn. Their first witnesses were the Bally officers. They testified as they did in their depositions. They contradicted Hilton's lawyer's testimony and said he urged that Goldberg take the package, as it contained assets that Hilton did not want. They further testified that they had to persuade Goldberg to accept the package and agree to work for Hilton.

When the officers finished testifying, Bally's lawyer asked to meet with the judge. He said that Goldberg was the next witness. He was dying of cancer and had only a few weeks to live. He asked that recesses be called as necessary. I suggested that Goldberg's deposition be received in evidence and that he be excused from testifying. I told the court that I did not want to cross-examine a dying man. Bally's lawyer said Goldberg insisted upon testifying and the judge ruled that he might testify.

The hearsay rule excludes from evidence statements made outside the court and not under oath. There are many exceptions based on the presumed reliability of the utterance. A dying declaration is one. The law presumes a person who will shortly meet his maker will not lie, for fear of damnation.

Before he contracted cancer, Goldberg was a model of physical strength. He was a former boxer, a weight lifter, and a physical fitness nut. No more. Goldberg was barely alive when he took the stand. He was bald from chemotherapy, pale, and very frail. He had shrunk; he looked like he weighed less than one hundred pounds. Here was a dying man about to testify. Plainly his testimony would be credited by the court.

Goldberg testified that he did not ask for any benefits for himself over and above those he received as Bally's largest stockholder. He said he was told by several Bally officers that Hilton did not want certain assets and, to effect the merger, he had to take them. Further, he said he planned to retire, not work for Hilton, and neither sought nor wanted a position after the merger. It was then my turn to cross-examine.

I asked whether he believed each of the assets in the Goldberg package—they consisted of options—had value at the time he acquired them. Could he give us a single, logical reason why Hilton would prefer to give them away rather than sell them? He suggested that I ask that question of Hilton. I questioned him about the residence he was trying to sell, the one that Hilton purchased at appraised value after an appraisal done by an expert selected by Goldberg himself. "Did Hilton ask to buy your house?" "No," he said, but then added that shortly after buying it, the company resold the house at a profit. I asked to strike his answer as not responsive and the judge, with a pained look and expressing sympathy for the witness and hostility towards me, struck the answer. Goldberg's body was failing but evidently not his mind.

The decision was a foregone conclusion. The complaint was dismissed and judgment entered for the defendants. We appealed, but to no avail. The Supreme Court affirmed the chancellor's decision.

This was my last trial. It ended, like my first, in defeat. I knew that the critical issue was whether the merger terms were fair to Bally. The chancellor, however, was not likely to award damages based on speculative projections that did not materialize. My alternative theory that Goldberg received the package in violation of his fiduciary duty failed for lack of proof. The judge believed Goldberg. Dying men tell no tales.

18
JOE AND ANN AND CAROL

W<small>E SPENT OUR SUMMERS</small> in Amagansett, an ocean-side resort on the east end of Long Island. When our children were young, they played on the beach with other children their age. The parents of our children's friends became our friends; Joe and Ann Weisberg, for instance. He was a psychoanalyst and she a restaurant critic. They were good tennis players, especially Ann. She won all the tournaments, even when she got old and was a grandmother. In doubles, Ann partnered with her husband. Only teams of two strong male players were competitive.

We talked with Joe and Ann on the beach and sometimes played tennis with them. They came to our parties and we went to theirs. One summer, Joe's shoulder was out of whack and he stopped playing tennis and took up golf. We played together and Ann joined us. She played only to keep Joe company, but hit many wonderful shots. Joe's shoulder mended and he and Ann went back to tennis.

Later on, Joe and Ann separated. They occupied their Amagansett home on alternate weekends. They dated others, gave parties, and invited us. At one beach party, Joe was with a woman. It was difficult for me to see Joe without Ann, and apparently even more difficult for Joe. He kept calling his date Ann. She kept correcting him and finally left in disgust. I thought that Joe and Ann would soon get back together and they did.

Years later, when I swam at the Ninety-second Street Y, I met Ann.

She went there to play basketball. In her early sixties, she was a star of a women's team.

One summer, Ann had a stroke and died. It was a surprise. She was fit and strong.

Ann's funeral was in New York. I went and a few days later paid a condolence call. Joe said, "I have had serious health problems, including surgery for prostrate cancer. Ann has never been sick for a day. I never thought I would survive her."

Several months later, we invited Joe to a cocktail party. Also invited was Irene's close friend Carol Wheeler. She saw Joe and knew that he was a widower, but did not speak to him. The next day, Carol told Irene that she would like to meet Joe. Irene issued orders: "Call Joe. Tell him how great Carol is, give him her number, and make sure that he calls her. You will be doing Joe a great favor."

I called Joe. He said he was lonely. I told him about Carol. "If she is a friend of Irene's, she must be worthwhile. Please give me her number. I will call her." Weeks passed and no call.

Joe is passionate about opera. He holds tickets to the new opera productions at the Met, is a member of the Wagner Society, and has attended Ring Cycles at Bayreuth, Germany. He is also an accomplished pianist.

I also had tickets to new productions and usually met Joe at intermissions. On one occasion, I reminded Joe about Carol, and said, "I hope that when we meet in two weeks you will have called Carol. She is expecting your call."

Joe called. They went out and clicked in a way that baffled Joe's doctors. Some six years earlier, he contracted prostate cancer and his gland was surgically removed. The doctors told him he was impotent. Joe, age sixty-eight, explained his situation to Carol, age sixty-five.

One day, after lunch at Carol's apartment, they embraced and without any expectation that more would follow, succeeded in making love. Joe said that on his way home, "Everybody in the bus knew what had happened."

The trips to her apartment soon ended as Carol moved in with Joe. They were happy, together all the time, and very much in love. Their union was the envy of all their friends. One day, Carol told Irene to hold a Sunday in November free from any date as she and Joe were getting married on that day. She said, "Joe is always asking me to marry him and I always say we are married and do not need a formal ceremony. Joe is concerned; how does he explain our relationship to his grandchildren? So, we are going to celebrate our union with a civil ceremony and a champagne party." We attended the wedding. Just short of nine months later, Joe died.

Carol is a freelance writer and scratches out a living. She has no money of her own. Joe was a successful analyst and had a respectable sandpile. In a prenuptial agreement, Joe made provision for Carol's financial security in the event that he predeceased her. They lived in a rent-controlled apartment and, under rent control law, Carol would inherit the apartment. Joe and Carol believed that she would succeed to Joe's Social Security payments of $1,800 per month and that, plus interest on a fixed sum of money he was carving out of his estate, should enable her to maintain a reasonable standard of living.

After Joe's death, Carol applied for his Social Security benefits as his widow. Her application was denied. The law defines a widow as one married to the insured for at least nine months. Joe's death occurred just six days short of nine months from the date of their marriage, Carol was not Joe's widow under Social Security.

The adverse determination hurt Carol personally, as well as financially. She was devoted to Joe in life and cherished his memory. She refused to accept the verdict that she was not Joe's widow and asked me to help. Although I had been retired for several years, I agreed to help her. I read the law and some cases and could see no hope for Carol. The nine-month rule was a classic case of line drawing which can produce arbitrary and unfair results. Nevertheless, the side of the line determines one's rights.

For example, if an eighteen-year-old girl marries a ninety-year-old man and he stays alive for nine months, the young woman is his widow regardless of whether they cohabited or even lived under the same roof. On the other hand, Carol, who loved Joe and lived with him for three and a half years, fell on the wrong side of the line. She was out of luck and all the facts and feelings, the history of their relationship counted for nothing.

I returned to Carol's case when a mutual friend mentioned common law marriage to me. Common law marriage has its roots in the ecclesiastical law of England. The requirements were minimal. Under English common law, if a man and a woman declare a present intention to marry and, thereafter, cohabit, they are as much married as if the bonds were celebrated in a formal church service.

After the American Revolution, several states adopted the English common law wholesale, including common law marriage. The English common law remained the law of the state unless repealed by statute. New York and most other states repealed common law marriage. The District of Columbia, Florida, and Pennsylvania were among a small minority that did not. Although New York did not recognize a common law marriage within its borders, it gave full faith and credit to a common law marriage between New Yorkers contracted in a state recognizing common law marriage.

In fact, commentators pointed out that New York courts interpreted the requirements of common law marriage more liberally than the contracting states.

Fifteen months before Joe died, he and Carol had attended a meeting of the American Association of Psychoanalysts. The conference, a three day affair, was held in Washington DC. As the past president of the association, Joe was honored as the man of the year. Carol and Joe spent two nights in a Washington hotel room, cohabited, and exchanged marriage vows declaring then, there, and thereafter, that they were married. Anything less, say a mere intention to marry, would have been inadequate. The District's common law marriage requirements required strict adherence to a rigid formula.

The law of the state of the deceased governs the validity of a marriage for the purpose of the law controlling Social Security benefits. Since New York recognizes common law marriages contracted in the District of Columbia, Carol and Joe were married for fifteen months before his death and she was his widow.

The order denying Carol's initial application expressly permitted her to file an amended application if she disagreed with the commission's determination. She filed an extensive and moving amendment.

Carol is a professional writer; her copy is always very good. This time, her prose came from her heart. She described her relationship with Joe, the highlights of their time together, and the three-day stay in Washington. She attached affidavits from three psychoanalysts who swore that Joe and she held themselves out as husband and wife. She also attached affidavits from Joe's three children, affirming that Joe and Carol were married long before the civil ceremony. The amended application recounted Joe's habit of proposing to Carol and her response, "Of course, I accept. I am your wife."

In her initial application for Joe's benefits, she mentioned the civil marriage service but not the pre-existing common law marriage. She explained the omission, "When I filed my initial application, I thought married was married. I was unaware of the nine-month rule and did not think it necessary to mention the earlier common law marriage." The truth made her case less than perfect. Initially, she claimed she was married less than nine months to Joe; her new position claimed she was married to Joe for more than one year. Inconsistent statements on a critical issue weakened her claim. Her explanation was honest and logical, but it could not erase the inconsistency.

Carol's application was again denied. The agency claimed that New York does not recognize common law marriages by New York residents in states that do. The department did not cite New York law but attached a decision from an Illinois court.

The reference to Illinois law misled Carol, but not me. I had researched the law. I knew that a federal court in New York had upheld a widow's right to her husband's Social Security payments based on a common law marriage in Pennsylvania. Illinois, unlike New York, did not recognize common law marriage. Social Security could be forgiven for overlooking the controlling New York case, but not for citing an inapplicable decision from a federal court interpreting the law of Illinois.

The agency advised Carol that she was entitled to a hearing before an administrative judge. She filed for the hearing. This time she set forth New York law on common law marriage as well as the evidentiary facts. She also complained that Social Security had attempted to mislead her by attaching the Illinois decision and concealing relevant law.

I went with Carol to the hearing. I brought with me a letter written by her and published in the *New York Times*. In her letter, she criticized an Op Ed piece that advised older women not to remarry and take on the task of caring for an old man, including doing his laundry. She wrote that at sixty-five she met the love of her life and urged women to follow their hearts, and wash the laundry. I did not know how I could put the letter in evidence. I did not have to worry; the judge did it for me.

Judge Hecht was the administrative judge. He began the proceedings by asking Carol if she was the author of a letter signed Carol Wheeler. She acknowledged that she was. The judge then read the letter into the record and marked it as an exhibit. The judge next turned to the law. He said New York law controls; it recognizes common law marriages between its citizens validly contracted in other jurisdictions.

In a trial, the lawyers question the witnesses, so I came prepared to question Carol. I never got a chance. Instead, the judge questioned her. It was painful for Carol to discuss aspects of her life with Joe, but she answered all questions fully and honestly. The judge liked her and was a compassionate man. His demeanor and character induced Carol to be forthcoming.

I generally work hard at a trial but, at this one, there was nothing for me to do. I was silent throughout the hearing. On the way home, Carol said, "I got a fair hearing and if I lose that's it. I do not want to discuss my life with Joe again."

A few months later, we got the judge's decision: Carol would never have to testify again. He found all the facts in her favor, referred to her as a "very credible" witness, and held that she was Joe's widow entitled to his Social Security benefits. However, he did so on a ground other than common law marriage. He interpreted a section of the law never before referred to in any reported case. He ruled, based on that provision, that the nine-month requirement did not apply to Carol. I read the provision over and over again. Some times I got it; most times I did not. I think Judge Hecht wanted to decide in favor of Carol and believed that Joe and Carol had a pre-existing common law marriage. He did not, however, want to decide for Carol on that ground. It might open Pandora's Box to false claims by spouses married less than nine months, claims that, because of the absence of witnesses, could not be disputed.

Carol had earlier applied for Social Security benefits based on her status as the widow of her ex-husband, Tom Wheeler. That marriage had ended in divorce. Carol could, nevertheless, qualify for benefits provided she met four conditions: she and Tom were married for more than ten years; she was at least sixty-five years old; her own Social Security benefits were less than Tom's; and she had not remarried. Carol met the first and second conditions, but not the third and not the fourth if she were wed to Joe by common law. In the application, filed after Joe and Carol's stay in Washington, Carol said she had not remarried. After filing, she realized that her own benefits were greater than Tom's. She then withdrew her application but it remained in the records of Social Security.

Judge Hecht did not overlook the conflict. He questioned Carol about the inconsistency. She said, "I did not know at the time that New York recognized our District of Columbia common law marriage." The judge replied that he did not know that either until he read the New York cases cited by her.

Social Security maintains a central appeals department, called Appeals Council, to review decisions of administrative judges. In almost all cases, the rejected applicant challenges the judge's decision. It is rare for the regional office to appeal a decision against the agency. Poor Carol. The rare event occurred. The local office appealed, but did not give us a copy of the appeal or even a notice that it was appealing. Parties are forbidden from communicating with the court without providing a copy to the other side, everywhere, that is, except before Social Security.

We learned about the appeal only after the council reversed. It said the regional office had appealed and submitted a memorandum found to be persuasive. Based on the reasoning in the memo, the council rejected Judge Hecht's holding that the nine month requirement did not apply to Carol. The letter also said that the case should be reheard on an alleged conflict; it pointed out the conflict between Carol's present claim of a common law marriage and the prior filing made to collect her former husband's benefit in which she stated she was not married.

The Appeals Council said before its decision became final that Carol could submit a reply. I submitted a reply. I argued in favor of Judge Hecht's point and also urged an additional ground. The council had discretion to decide the case on a new ground based on the record. I pointed out that Judge Hecht had heard Carol's testimony, observed her demeanor, and found her to be "very credible." The council, if it held to its initial ruling that Judge Hecht's point was not sound, should decide the case on common law marriage. She was in her late sixties. The prior hearing was emotionally draining. She did not want to discuss again, before another stranger, her personal life with Joe. I urged the council to read the record and affirm Judge Hecht's decision either on the ground asserted by him or on common law marriage.

I also told the council that a new trial would be a waste of time. The case had been tried once and once was enough; Carol would stand on the record and not re-testify. I did not reveal the thought running through my mind: "If you won and the judge found your client 'very credible,' only a fool would risk a second hearing. Carol would re-testify over my dead body."

The council adhered to its initial decision that Judge Hecht was wrong. It also refused to resolve the common law issue on the record before Judge Hecht. It said that although the evidence had been recorded on a disc, it could not be found. The council hoped that the record would be found before the re-hearing.

When an appellate court remands a case, it usually returns it to the judge who tried the case. Not this time and not this agency. The council not only disapproved of Judge Hecht's legal conclusion, but also may not have like his favorable factual findings. The case was reassigned to Judge Tannenbaum.

He set a new hearing for a day when I was in St Croix, but only a week or so before my return to New York. I asked Carol to call Judge Tannenbaum's secretary, request a short adjournment, and explain that I was out of the country but would soon return. The judge answered the call. He told Carol, "You do not need a lawyer. I want to decide the case quickly and will not grant an adjournment." Carol thought the judge was impolite and hostile.

Judge Tannenbaum was also careless; his notice contained many mistakes. It said that at the hearing, he would decide Carol's claim for Disabled Widow's Insurance Benefits, and instructed her to bring her medical records to the hearing. The notice referred to "Josef Weisberg," sometimes to "Joseph Weinberg," and at other times to "Joseph Weissberg," but not ever by his correct name. The notice transposed Carol's and Joe's

Social Security numbers and in one place referred to Carol as the insured and Joe as the claimant.

In a letter to Tannenbaum, I wrote that in view of the errors, I was treating the notice as null and void. I requested that a corrected notice be issued for a later date to accommodate me, and that a pretrial conference be scheduled, not a trial. At the conference, I proposed to discuss the efforts made to find the evidentiary record, a procedure other than a retrial if the record remained elusive, and whether the case should be returned to Judge Hecht. I sent a copy of my letter to the Appeals Council.

A new notice was issued but it, too, contained a few of the old mistakes and one new one: it set the hearing time at 2:00 AM. I again wrote, pointed out the errors, but said that Carol and I would appear at 2:00 PM.

I am no stranger to hostile judges. None in my experience compared to Judge Tannenbaum.

I greeted him, "Good afternoon, Judge Tannenbaum. I am Sidney B. Silverman. I represent Carol Wheeler. I am pleased to meet you." He was a small, skinny man, bald and with a tight face, marked by years of scowling. He did not return my greeting. He ignored me and launched into poor Carol. "I run my courtroom different from Judge Hecht. I will ask questions and you will answer. Make sure your answers are responsive and do not volunteer. I am interested only in the direct answer to my question." I was watching Carol. She changed color but remained silent. I did not.

"Judge Tannenbaum, we have some preliminary matters to discuss. First, if you have not found the transcript, what efforts have you made to do so?"

Now, it was his turn to change color. "Mr. Silverman, when a decision is rendered in favor of the claimant, the transcript is placed in storage in our warehouse in Virginia. The reason for this is that favorable decisions are rarely appealed. If the decision goes against the claimant, the transcript is maintained in our office as it is likely that the decision will be appealed. Since Judge Hecht found for Mrs. Weisberg [the Judge chose to ignore the fact that Carol retained her professional name of Wheeler], the trial record was sent to Virginia. The Appeals Council and I tried to find it but we were unsuccessful." I continued, "Would you kindly detail the efforts made to locate the record? For example, was someone sent to Virginia to search for it?"

The judge exploded, "I am going to hold you in contempt of court if you say another word about the record. We tried to find it."

I did not follow the judge's instructions but made a long speech in a calm voice to contrast with the judge's loud shrieking voice. "I have lost many cases. I often wished that the record would also be lost and the case reassigned for a second trial before a new judge. But that is not the way the rules of litigation work; you get one bite of the apple. Social Security must live by the same rule. When a document is lost, courts used secondary evidence to recreate the document. We have abundant secondary evidence of the contents of the 'misplaced' record. First, there is Judge Hecht's decision. It restates Carol's testimony about the events leading up to and including her common law marriage to Joe. Judge Hecht found Carol a 'very credible' witness.

Second we have three affidavits from eminent psychiatrists who were eye witnesses to matters reported by them. Then, we have Carol's affidavit. Finally, [I could not resist] I was present at the hearing and can restate it accurately. If you have any questions, please address them to me."

The judge went through a mood change. Now he appeared friendly and tried to flatter me. "Mr. Silverman, you are an experienced trial lawyer but have limited experience in Social Security cases. You have given your client the wrong advice. Mrs. Weisberg, if you do not testify, you will suffer the consequences. It is very much in your interest to testify. Indeed, I instruct you to testify. Will you do so?"

Carol looked the judge in the face and said, "I will follow my lawyer's advice."

The judge declared the hearing over, but I still had more to say. "Before the hearing is closed, I move into evidence the exhibits submitted at the hearing before Judge Hecht and request that they retain the same numbers. I have copies for Your Honor. May I hand them to you?"

He said yes, and then angrily proposed as another exhibit the staff memo submitted ex parte to the Appeals Council. A lawyer's memo, advocating a position, is argument, not evidence. It is read by the court but it does not form part of the evidentiary record. I objected, "The staff memo is not evidence and has no place in the record." "Overruled," screamed the judge. "The hearing is closed."

As expected, the judge decided the case against us. His decision was not balanced but reflected his animus towards Carol and me. He held that Joe and Carol were not common law man and wife because the testimony that they exchanged vows was false. He rejected all the evidence to the contrary, including the affidavits filed by the three analysts. His basis was that Joe would not lie, and since Carol was not his common law wife, he would not have told the doctors that she was. Ergo, *they* must be lying. The judge's reasoning is a perfect example of a paradox: it proves nothing. It brought to mind the famous Liar's Paradox. A poet from Crete said, "All Cretans are liars."

In denying a common law marriage, the judge also rejected Carol's testimony. The judge was in a box. He did not hear Carol testify but disbelieved her. The judge who did hear her testimony found her "very credible." Further, there was no testimony contradicting Carol's and, thus, no legal basis for rejecting her testimony. For example, if the issue is whether A was drunk on Monday night and A is the only witness and testifies that he was not, a court cannot find that A was drunk by saying that it disbelieves A. There must be independent evidence that A was drunk. The opinion was irrational. I was confident we would win on appeal.

We could appeal to the Appeals Council or bypass the council and file a complaint in the federal court. A complaint in the federal court would be dynamite. What, Social Security lost the trial record? Impossible, incredible, unheard of. What, Carol loses because a judge, who did not hear her testify, disbelieves her and rejects the contrary findings of another judge that Carol was "very credible"? What, the case was not remanded to the first judge, but to a hostile one cherry-picked for the case? A federal judge would eat Social Security alive.

I chose instead to appeal to the council. The federal courts are busy. They might resent our failure to exhaust our remedies within the system. Further, they deal with large, complex cases and our case was small. If the council affirmed Judge Tannenbaum, we could still file in the federal court and I would be able to say, "I tried to avoid imposing this case on you but Social Security gave me no other alternative." Also, I believed that the circumstances were so egregious that the Appeals Council might act in our favor.

On appeal, we were allowed to add to the record. We did with another affidavit from Carol, this one attacking Judge Tannenbaum. She said he was hostile from the outset. He refused to adjourn the hearing to allow her attorney to attend, and the hearing was adjourned only because his notice was defective. She pointed out the entire litany of his errors. She said that she was emotionally disturbed after the first hearing and was calmed by her attorney's assurance she would not have to discuss her personal life again. She then recounted Judge Tannenbaum's nasty opening remarks to her and his demand that she retell her story because Social Security had lost the record of her testimony. "I could not discuss my personal life with that judge," she said. She also came to my defense. She said, "Although I disagreed with the judge, I was always respectful, and yet the judge had threatened to hold me in contempt of court."

In the appeal, I took both Judge Tannenbaum and the Appeals Council to task. I pointed out the legal and factual errors in his decision and then turned to the council. How could it not find the trial record? Why did it refuse to resolve the factual issues based on Judge Hecht's decision and avoid the cost of a second hearing? Why did it pick Judge Tannenbaum and not remand to Judge Hecht? I did not pull my punches but made it clear that if we were denied relief, the case would be heard by a federal court and the council and Social Security would be slammed. Then the staff raised a point I had overlooked.

In the week before Joe and Carol married, she called me to say they would have to postpone the wedding: "Neither Tom nor I filed the final divorce decree. Under New York law, Joe and I cannot get a marriage license because I am still married to Tom. I'm told it will take several weeks for the decree to be filed, processed, and entered. The invitations were mailed weeks ago. I don't know what to do."

Tom had died after the common law marriage, but before the civil one. Carol was free to marry. The clerk in the marriage bureau insisted that the divorce decree become final before Carol and Joe could obtain a license. There was no sense arguing with the clerk.

James Rossetti, the deputy clerk of the court, is a friend of mine. I called him, told him of the problem, and asked for his help. He said, "Tell Carol to bring the decree directly to me. I'll file it and have it entered the same day I receive it." That ended one problem, but caused another. Some eager beaver at Social Security checked on Carol's divorce. He found she was still technically married to Tom at the time of the common law marriage. A common law marriage, like a civil marriage, is not valid if one party is married to another. The uncovering of this fact destroyed our chances on appeal and effectively ended the case.

Carol moved to San Miguel de Allende, an artists' and writers' community in Mexico. It is inhabited by expats. The cost of living is low. For $75,000, Carol purchased a small house and remodeled it. Irene visited Carol and said her house was lovely and Carol had many friends. Carol is now as happy as she could be without her Joe.

PART 2
GRADUATE STUDIES

LITIGATION IS STRESSFUL--EVEN MORE
so for contingent fee lawyers. For us, a lawsuit is a battle that must be won; we feast or we die of starvation. There is nothing in between. Every day is filled with aggression and confrontation. For forty years, I lived the rough and tumble life of legal warfare. It was time to seek a new life. The new life, I decided, would begin on January 1, 2001, as I entered my sixty-ninth year. Next came the decision—what to do?

Was there a place populated by gentle people where intellectual activity reigned? I had always had the idea a university was such a place: the quiet library, the lively exchange of ideas in the classroom, the wise and compassionate professors. And learning, not winning, is the goal. Why not spend my retirement in a university? The quiet, contemplative life of a student seemed ideal.

And then there was Socrates's famous dictum: "Of this I am sure, I know nothing." He meant, of course, a wise man must live with doubt. Knowledge is uncertain, vast, and subject to change. When I applied Socrates's saying to myself, it had a different meaning. I knew nothing about philosophy, world history, literature, drama, or poetry; all the more reason to go to school.

Suddenly, retirement was not a dirty word.

The Graduate School of Liberal Arts and Sciences at Columbia University offered an interdisciplinary program leading to a master's degree. The choice of courses seemed virtually unlimited. They ranged from African Studies to Yiddish Studies with more than one hundred courses sandwiched in between. I chose Modern European Studies. I was to learn that in academia, "modern" begins with the sixteenth century and European studies include philosophy, history, literature, drama, poetry, art, music, and religion.

To me it offered the best of all academic worlds. I applied. Colgate and Columbia Law School sent my academic records from 1950–1957. I also submitted two essays; one on reasons for choosing Modern European Studies and the other, about my career in the law. Columbia accepts only 15 percent of those applying. I wondered whether I would be accepted. In March of 2000, I was. I think the fact that I was an alumnus, a retired lawyer, and a contributor to the law school might have tipped the scale in my favor. Included with the letter of acceptance was a list of courses available for the fall term. Among them were Reading German and Weimar Cinema. I enrolled for the fall term and selected those courses.

FALL 2000

THE FALL OF 2000 was a tumultuous period. I had notified the lawyers and staff that the firm would close at the end of the year. I promised the staff a year's bonus if they stayed to the end. They all did. During that year, several of the lawyers joined other firms. With my consent, they took with them cases they were working on. Two lawyers formed their own firm but remained in my offices until the end of the year. They too were given cases. There were two remaining cases which I kept. One, I thought would settle. Instead, it was tried over a three week period during late September and October.

The other case was pending in the Chancery Court in Delaware. I had retained a Delaware law firm to assist me. Together, we would be able to pursue the case. I was not sure that graduate school was the right decision. By keeping a case, I hedged my bet.

In addition to trying a case and presiding over the dissolution of my firm, I had a serious health problem. I had a rare corneal disease called Fuchs' dystrophy. It is progressive and leads inevitably to blindness. The only cure is to pluck out the corneas and replace them with tissue obtained from recently deceased donors. At the end of October, my left cornea was replaced. For almost a year, my vision in my left eye was poor. My right eye functioned, but not very well. Its cornea too would have to be replaced, but not until my left eye had fully recovered.

How did this turmoil affect my studies? Not at all. I would have done as poorly if the case had settled and my vision been unimpaired.

Reading German was limited, as the course's name implies, to translating German text. Many German words appear the same as their English equivalents. Others, by changing letters to their English equivalents, can be converted into English. A German-to-English dictionary and a good memory provide answers for all the remaining words. It should have been easy. Not for me. My language skills, never strong, became even weaker with age. I spent nine hours preparing for one class and mentioned that to the professor. She said, "That's three times longer than I would have anticipated." Even with excessive preparation, I performed poorly in class.

I used my commitment to the upcoming trial as an excuse for dropping the course. The real reason was that I could not learn a new language, not even to read it. I was both frustrated and sad.

Classes like Weimar Cinema were referred to in my college days as pipe courses, a course about as difficult as smoking a pipe. The first hour of most classes was spent discussing the reading assignment, essays and critiques of Weimar period films. Then, we watched a silent film, referred to as a photoplay, and discussed it. The films were the classics of the period: *The Cabinet of Doctor Caligari, Metropolis, Nosterafu, M,* and *The Blue Angel.* The professor, a visiting instructor from Hamburg, ran the projector. It often broke down. Even when it worked, the picture was not very clear.

The other students loved the course. They seemed to understand the subtleties of the new art form. They enthused over the direction of Fritz Lang and Ernst Lubitsch, and the production wizardry of Erich Pommer and Max Reinhardt. I'm not a film buff. Worse, I'm not even a motion picture fan. Some of my classmates would have thought me a philistine had they known the truth about me: I did not appreciate the classic silent films.

Each student was required to make an oral presentation. I made mine on how the photoplay met the psychological needs of the German people in the aftermath of World War I. My talk focused on the depressing life of most Germans after the defeat and how the photoplay provided an escape into a fantasy world. I discussed travelogues and B-grade films, not the serious films. The professor commented favorably on my presentation. I thought he was kind.

A final paper was also required. I began mine by challenging a reigning intellectual of the period, Hugo Munsterberg. He said the photoplay was "an entirely new independent art," capable of producing "a Leonardo, a Shakespeare, a Mozart." My thesis: Munsterberg was wrong. Film was more of a business than an art form. I wrote, "Since the cost of producing a film is beyond the means of the artist, financing must be obtained. The financier, whose capital is placed at risk, is usually concerned with how quickly the advance can be repaid and a profit earned. Changes may be made to the script or to the production which are designed more to ensure that the film will appeal to a wider audience rather than to enhance artistic merit."

I then threw in a reference to a Hollywood producer who said, "The picture industry is no different from the underwear business, for example. It is completely governed by the law of supply and demand."

I also wrote that a photoplay was not an individual effort but a collaborative one, involving the talents of the director, the producer, the cameraman, the actors, and the scriptwriter. In the traditional arts, great artists worked alone. I then turned to an analysis of Universum-Film AG (Ufa), the leading production studio during the Weimar Republic.

Ufa was acquired in 1926 by Alfred Hugenberg, an industrialist and media mogul with close ties to fascism. Hugenberg ran his newspapers, magazines, and book publishing operations as propaganda instruments, but not Ufa. Its films were made mainly for export. Although a few films were made for propaganda purposes, most were made for profit. My point was that the profit motive trumped politics, no less aesthetics.

Hugenberg was a virulent anti-Semite. Nevertheless, he persuaded the studio's former head of production, Erich Pommer, a Jew, to return to Germany from Hollywood. The bait was a large salary and autonomy to make three films. Similarly, Fritz Lang, also a Jew, continued to play a leading role as a director of major films for Ufa. Pommer and Lang were associated with box office hits. Ufa wanted their product. The profit motive prevailed over prejudice.

The professor liked my discussion of Ufa, calling it "an interesting historical description of Ufa." He was not as flattering about the rest. He commented, "This major part of your paper does not exactly fit your introductory and concluding question, as to whether film can be considered a legitimate form of art. As a matter of fact, I think it would have been more productive to concentrate exclusively on Ufa and drop Munsterberg's suggestion from 1916 which, in this form, does not stand in any relation to the issues pursued in film theory and history today."

At the end of the paper, the professor wrote, "Final paper: B; Class grade: B+." He must have changed his mind because on my official record, my grade for the class was B. In college, a B is an acceptable grade. In graduate school, a grade lower than a B+ is a failing one.

On reflection, my paper was flawed. I approached the issue of art in film the way a lawyer argues a disputed legal issue, A or non-A, with nothing in between. There are, of course, box office hits that are also works of art. *To Be or Not to Be, The Shop Around the Corner, Trouble in Paradise,* and *Rear Window* are just a few examples.

I was depressed. I could always go back to law. Several firms would be willing to give me a desk and a designation as "of counsel," a title applied to a lawyer who is neither an employee nor a partner. It was not what I wanted, but one had to face reality. Returning to law would be a lot better than doing nothing.

The lawsuit I had retained took an unanticipated turn. The plaintiff was Merchants National Properties, a family-controlled corporation owning and operating shopping centers and holding a portfolio of investment securities. Among the stocks owned were shares of Telxon Corporation. Merchant's president complained about a transaction between Telxon and its controlling stockholder, Robert Meyerson. Telxon financed a start-up company whose one product was developed by Telxon's engineers and scientists at Telxon's own plant. By all rights, Telxon should have owned the company; instead Meyerson did. When Telxon purchased the company from Meyerson for $25 million, we commenced a lawsuit.

Telxon was acquired in 2000 by another company, Symbol Technologies. Under the law, Merchants lost its standing as the plaintiff, as all of Telxon's stock was acquired by Symbol, who had the sole right to determine whether the action commenced by Merchants should continue. I thought the lawsuit was dead in the water. In December of 2000, Symbol's general counsel asked to meet with me. He said, "At my urging the board voted to continue the action and authorized me to retain you. If you accept, you will represent Telxon against Meyerson and the other directors."

Before accepting, I told the general counsel, "I no longer have a law firm. I will need help." He assured me that Symbol was willing "to put its outside firm on the case to assist you. Symbol will do everything it can to help you."

In view of my disappointing term in graduate school, it felt good to get back to litigation. In the winter, spring, and summer of 2001, I worked hard on the case.

The case was pending in Delaware. In the mid-1980s, I had learned to touch type and use a word processing program. I wrote drafts of legal papers, copied them to a disc, and gave them to my secretary for formatting. Working on my own, I followed the same procedure with a twist. I uploaded my drafts and sent them via e-mail to my associate counsel's office in Delaware. It then put the drafts in final form, served copies on defendants, and filed the originals with the court. I did not need Symbol's outside firm.

In the fall, I returned to Columbia. If I failed again, my college career was over.

FALL 2001

I ENROLLED IN TWO COURSES, one in history and the other in philosophy. The history class, Germany and East Central Europe, covered the period from 1815 to 1946. It was taught by Istvan Deak. He was Hungarian, descended from an old and aristocratic family. He lived in Budapest until after World War II. At seventeen, he immigrated to America to escape communism and dictatorship.

Deak was a chaired professor, older than I, in excellent physical condition and profoundly intellectual. He jogged most mornings, was a frequent contributor to the *New York Review of Books*, and had published several important histories. One day, a student in the class, a PhD candidate in Polish history and culture, remarked that Poland was the only nation to defeat Russia by conquering Moscow. Deak provided the date of the siege of Moscow and dismissed the contention: "Russia was, at that time, not a unified state but a conglomeration of provincial towns of which Moscow was one." I was sure that if a student had asked a question about Chinese culture in the fifth century B.C., Deak would have known the answer. He seemed to know everything!

I had been a history major at Colgate. After college, I continued to read histories, particularly books on World War I and II. To gain different perspectives on the wars, I read accounts written by English, German, American, and Russian historians and generals. I felt at home in class. I participated in discussion and often stayed after class to talk with the other students and Deak. But, I made no friends. How could I? They were so much younger than I. This lack of collegiality posed an academic problem.

Deak asked that we form teams of two. Each week, one member would debate the pros and the other the cons of a subject related to that day's reading assignment. Students were required to participate in two debates. Through a Columbia Internet site called Course Works, I posted a message to the class seeking a partner. I got no responses. I asked several students both before and after class if they were interested in partnering with me. No takers. I was the odd man out, the only one without a partner.

I described my plight to Deak and asked if I could partner with my doppelganger and take both sides of a proposition. He agreed. I selected the pros and cons of the German military plan for World War I, prepared in 1906 by the Chief of the German General Staff, Field Marshal von Schliefen, and tweaked by his successor, Field Marshal von Molke.

I had fun debating with myself. My doppelganger began the contrary argument by saying, "My learned opponent has missed the point." My personality was split. Each side made fun of the other. Deak liked my presentation, except for the comedy routine and one point. The Austro-Hungarian army contained people of many different nationalities, including a large Slavic force. The enemy forces on the eastern front were Russians and Serbians, who were also Slavs. I commented that the Slavs in the Austro-Hungarian army deserted in mass to their Russian and Serbian brothers and cousins. Deak interrupted and said I was wrong: "A thesis written by a PhD student advised by me exposed that myth." I replied, "My statement is supported by one of the leading military historians, John Keegan." I had Keegan's book with me and read out his pertinent sentences and said, "I stand by my statement."

Deak rose to the challenge. He calmly summarized his student's thesis and added that the Slavs fought valiantly. He knew. His father, who had served as an officer in the Austro-Hungarian army, had told him so. Deak was relying, in part, on an eye-witness report from a highly credible witness. His father was a member of a Hungarian family with a reputation for integrity. He would not deceive his son. Further, Deak is a scholar and a dedicated teacher. He would not have approved of a thesis espousing an erroneous point. I suppose I should have quietly bowed to his authority. The military plan, not the loyalty of the Slavic forces in the Austro-Hungarian army, was central to my debate. But it is hard for me, a confrontational lawyer, to submit meekly. So I continued. I pointed to the vast number of prisoners of Slavic origin taken by the Russians and said, "The statistical evidence is persuasive. The percentage of Slavic prisoners to the whole was disproportionate to the number of Slavs in the army."

Deak had the last word. He graciously acknowledged that my view was the popular one but, in his opinion, wrong. He said the class should make up its own mind and that he would make available a copy of his student's thesis. He looked directly at me. I had raised the point. In retrospect, intellectual curiosity and respect for a distinguished teacher should have led me the very next day to his office for that paper. I regret that I did not do so the next day, or any day thereafter.

Deak said our grade would depend on a paper submitted at the end of the term. While class discussion was not graded, he cautioned, "No one will get an A who does not participate in class." He then set a schedule for the submission of an outline, draft, and final paper. About the outline, he said, "Pretend that you are submitting it to a publisher as the subject of a book. Make it enticing and amusing."

I selected German hyperinflation following World War I as the subject of my paper. My outline's title was, "When a Humble Kohlrabi Cost One Million Marks." I discussed the twin causes of the inflation, the issuance of currency in excess of the gold supply and the military defeat. In an attempt to be humorous, I added, "The Germans reacted to defeat and the destruction of their currency in a bizarre way. They drank excessively, danced and partied all night, and engaged in acts of sexual depravity. This paper should not be read by children under the age of sixteen." I concluded with another wisecrack, "The author will not accept advances in Weimar marks."

Deak's comments were mixed. He liked the content and complimented me on my grasp of the economic conditions. He did not like the humor: "In class, you often make comments to amuse [I think he was referring to my earlier debate with myself], a process you continue in your outline. Be warned. Make sure your paper is serious."

I interpreted Deak's comment to be critical of the light touches in my outline. In an e-mail, I reminded him of his instructions to use humor. Deak may have thought his comment too harsh. At the next session, he brought to class a Weimar Republic one million mark bill and said, "This is for Sidney. Use it to buy a kohlrabi." The class laughed.

Deak relaxed the two-debate requirement by allowing students to distribute a paper to the class in lieu of a second debate. Since I could not find a partner, I decided on a paper.

I selected the topic of whether the Polish population was generally united in opposing the Germans during the Warsaw uprising. I discussed the divisiveness between the home army, supported by the London government, and the Soviet-controlled Polish Communists. The cold war started in Poland, years before World War II ended. I then turned to a third group, the Jews living in the Warsaw ghetto. They too staged an uprising. Neither the home army nor the Communists gave the Jews any support, although all were fighting a common enemy. The Jews fought valiantly, but the German forces were overwhelming. The uprising ended with the fire bombing of the ghetto and the death of most of its inhabitants.

A friend of mine, Yehuda Nir, fought with the Polish underground and agreed to be interviewed. I e-mailed Deak with my proposal: An exercise in oral history. Deak approved.

Nir lived in Poland during World War II. His father was killed by the Germans. He, his mother, and sister escaped the fate of their father, as did other Polish Jews, by concealing their Jewish identity. Yehuda wrote a book about the experience, *Lost Childhood: A Memoir* (Harcourt: New York, 1989). His life in Poland was a nightmare. Nir, a boy of fourteen, joined the Polish underground, passing as a Catholic. In our interview, he described his work for the underground: "I carried weapons and ammunition.... It was very dangerous to walk on the streets because of snipers. I went through cellars and the sewers of Warsaw to deliver ammunition and intelligence reports to those fighting the Germans in the streets of Warsaw. I almost got killed several times."

Among his most vivid memories was the vicious anti-Semitism of the Polish people. Nir described the pleasure the Polish freedom fighters derived from watching the Germans put down the Jewish uprising in the Warsaw Ghetto. "I remember, it was April 1943, the time of the Warsaw Ghetto uprising. I was living with a family in Warsaw. One member of the family was in the underground. His aunt proposed that we watch the Germans burn the Jews in the ghetto and said it was the only amusement the Germans were providing."

Nir was convinced there were no good gentiles. He said, "I remember a remark by a national underground member that the only good thing about the Germans was that they were killing the Jews." He also related that his family, while hiding in Krakow, were recognized by "a former neighbor from Lwow who ... threatened to report [us] unless my mother gave her money. My mother gave the woman money and jewelry. Nevertheless, the woman reported my mother to the police, who came to arrest us shortly thereafter. We had a narrow escape and moved to Warsaw."

Deak regularly reviewed Holocaust books for the *New York Review of Books*. His take on his fellow gentiles, based on the entire record, although highly critical, was far less severe than Nir's. Nir wrote letters criticizing many a Deak review. Unbeknownst to me at the time, Deak disdained both Nir's harsh criticism and his lack of scholarship.

After class, Deak asked me to stay. He believed my presentation lacked objectivity and criticized my scholarship. The following exchange took place.

> Deak: "Do you believe, like your friend Nir, that there were no good gentiles?"

> Me: "The Germans made it a crime punishable by death to assist a Jew. Nir claims that not a single gentile was indicted for crimes against Jews, let alone convicted. He was a victim. I respect his view, but I have visited Y'ad Vashem, the memorial in Israel commemorating gentiles who helped Jews."

> Deak: "You are a lawyer. You should have cross-examined Nir. Would you allow a witness in a trial to get away with misstatements?"

> Me: "Of course not. But this was not a trial. I would not under any circumstances cross-examine Nir. He was a victim of the Holocaust. Further, my paper is an oral history recording his experience and views."

> Deak: "I accept it as an oral history and will reserve judgment on your scholarship until I read your final paper."

I tried my best to make my paper scholarly. I changed the flippant outline title to: "A Study of Hyperinflation in Germany with a Note on Poland." My bibliography referenced the dozen books and articles I had read. The paper ran twenty-three pages and contained sixty-seven footnotes.

A recent book made an outstanding contribution to the history of the inflationary period. The author, Gerald D. Feldman, a history professor at Berkeley, spent twelve years researching and eight years writing it. The book, *Great Disorder: Politics, Economics, and the Society in the German Inflation, 1914–1924*, was over one thousand pages. It covered social, political, and economic issues in such depth that, at times, it left me breathless. At first, I got a copy from the Columbia library, but then bought it. I had to own it.

When I mentioned to a bright young classmate that my paper was on German inflation, he asked if I was aware of Feldman's book. I told him I owned the book and asked how he knew about it. "My father is a history professor at Berkeley and a colleague of Feldman. The book is a source of awe among Feldman's colleagues in the department. They bow to him when they pass him in the hall. My father considers it the best research work of our time," he said.

My son offered advice on structuring my paper He has a PhD in the classics. He advised me to "Discuss the prevailing position, pointing out its strengths. Then find a narrow point of disagreement and hammer it home." I followed his advice.

As is often said, "The German inflation of 1914 to 1923 began in a trot, increased to a canter, and ended in a gallop." I concentrated on the trot. Historians, economists, and bankers were virtually unanimous in blaming the inflation on the means Germany used to finance the war; that is, printing new currency. The additional currency depreciated the value of the mark. By1918, it had lost 50 percent of its buying power. Inflation was ending its trot and beginning its canter. In contrast, England and France imposed new taxes to finance the war. They also borrowed from friendly neutral countries. (Gordon A. Craig, 1978. *Germany 1866–1945*, New York: Oxford University Press, 435.)

The authorities were virtually unanimous on the point: new taxes, not printing more currency, was the proper way to finance the war. I had my point of disagreement. I believed an inflation tax engineered by the Reichsbank, the German approach to financing the war, was sound. It had advantages over conventional forms of taxation. An inflation tax avoids the enactment of unpopular tax laws and eliminates paperwork. And collection is automatic. It applies to all accumulations of wealth and it cannot be evaded. It may not be a fair tax, but that was not the issue. Moreover, the German military plan predicted a war lasting about six weeks. The Reichsbank use of inflation to finance the war was based on the military plan.

In my paper, I discussed the authorities critical of the Reichsbank. I quickly learned the academic protocols about documentation of sources and provided bibliographical data in numerous footnotes and endnotes. All these I have omitted from these memoirs.

Gordon Craig, an Oxford professor and a leading expert on German history, unequivocally declares: "Despite everything anti-republican propagandists were to say later on, the inflation originated neither in the iniquities of the peace treaty nor in the flabbiness of leaders brought to power in November 1918. It was rooted rather in the fiscal policy of the Imperial Government during the war years and, specifically, in its decision to finance the war by loans rather than taxes." Bresciani Turroni, an internationally renowned economist and member of the Reparations

Committee, "blamed the fall of the mark almost exclusively on German financial and monetary policy."

Friedrich Bendixen, a Hamburg bank director and money theoretician, commented in 1915 that the paper emission policies of the Reichsbank were not "worthy of the German name."

Feldman claims that "the inflation itself owed its birth to the war economy and its financing."

I then stated my point of disagreement: "It is the opinion of the author that the hyperinflation was caused by one event and one only: Germany lost the war. If Germany had won the war, the mild wartime inflation would have been corrected. Indeed, even had Germany obtained nothing at all from the Allies and held on to its gains from the Treaties of Brest-Litovsk and Bucharest, the inflation would have been negated by increased production obtained from the annexed territories."

My paper then defended the Reichbank and its officers. It continued:

> Germany's fiscal policies were not determined in a vacuum. The German military plan projected a swift six-week victory in the west, against France, Germany's strongest opponent, and a holding action in the east. After the defeat of France, Germany's entire military effort would be directed against its weaker opponent, Russia. The Russian campaign was also projected to be short; Germany had no intention of advancing into the Russian interior, as its objectives were limited to annexing the Russian kingdom of Poland. Based on the military plan, it made no sense to finance a war of short duration by a complicated, costly-to-administer, and time-consuming system of taxation. The generals anticipated that the war would be over by the time a war emergency tax could be collected.
>
> The war did not, of course, end in a matter of months but extended for more than four years, while inflation spiraled upward. Germany had no choice but to continue to pay all the associated costs. The Reich's principal means of financing the war through short-term loans from the Reichsbank did not change. The mark continued to depreciate and inflation to increase.
>
> Inflation brought about by a depreciation of currency is a form of tax on accumulated wealth. Using 1913 as a base year with the general cost of living pegged at one hundred, the index increased slightly in 1914 to 103 and rose to 313 in 1918. A German who had accumulated liquid capital in 1913 experienced over a five year period a 66.7 percent decline in its purchasing

power. In a real economic sense, inflation assessed the liquid assets of every German at full value and subjected them to an inflation tax at an aggregate five-year rate of 66.7 percent.

An inflation tax has advantages over other forms of taxation. There are no costs of collection, there is no need to conduct an independent assessment of net worth, and there is no means, consistent with one's patriotic duty not to hoard gold or scarce resources, to evade or avoid the tax.

Meeting the demands of an expanding budget by depreciating currency is a practice dating back to ancient Rome. Nero clandestinely reduced the quantity of silver and gold in the denarii by about 10 percent, producing more coins to spend without raising taxes. Subsequent emperors followed Nero's strategy. By the time of Emperor Lucius Septimius Severus, the silver content of the denarius was reduced by 50 percent.

[The officers determining the policy of the Reichsbank] were definitely not Neros. They made every effort to maintain the integrity of the mark. Using the dollar exchange rate as a benchmark, until the war ended they were reasonably successful. The average exchange rate from June–December 1914 was 4.41 marks to the dollar; the average from January–June 1918 was 5.17.

At year end, 1914, the amount of marks in circulation, excluding balances at banks of issue, amounted to 8.7 billion marks; at year end 1917, the money supply had increased to 18.458 billion. Market theorists believe that foreign exchange rates rapidly incorporate all information, public and private, which may affect the currency markets. A Germany victory in the war would favorably impact the value of the mark. The comparatively slight decline in the foreign exchange rate for the mark obviously reflected the emphasis currency traders were placing on the favorable war news rather than on the vast amount of newly issued marks. The traders believed that the mark would return to its 1913 pre-eminent foreign exchange position if Germany won the war. In that event, war booty and reparations would create the surpluses necessary to retire the excess marks issued to finance the war. It appears that traders considered a German victory sufficiently likely to discount the vast increase in the amount of marks in circulation in setting the exchange rate.

> It was not financing the war that destroyed the mark but the defeat.

I submitted my draft. Deak called my draft paper "exceptional." I was proud and happy. I forwarded his comment to our three children. After all, I had read their teachers' comments. Why shouldn't they read mine?

Deak objected, however, to my wholesale endorsement of the Reichsbank. He said, "I am not an expert on taxes or economics, but I think the Reichsbank should have held back some gold as a reserve against defeat." I amended my draft paper, adding: "One could contend that the Reichsbank should have hedged its bets and conserved resources to meet the possibility of defeat. The author believes that there are two complete answers to this contention. First, there was no early indication that Germany would lose the war. In fact, as late as March 23, 1918, the Kaiser declared a school holiday in celebration of the 'victory' in the west. Second, after the war ended, the advocates of a Carthaginian peace prevailed and reparations and other costs were heaped upon Germany without regard to its ability to pay. Regardless of how the war was financed, the German economy could not have survived the peace."

Deak offered a second criticism: "You relied too heavily on one source, the Feldman book." I answered in an addendum, "The author of this paper acknowledges his dependence on Professor Feldman's book. Any study of German inflation that does not rely extensively on Professor Feldman's work is either dishonest, not scholarly, or both."

In retrospect, my statement was both extreme and unnecessary. I should have agreed with Deak and acknowledged that my heavy reliance on one book was unscholarly. But, I was too full of myself then and unable to admit to an error. I even find it difficult now to write that sentence.

Deak had asked me to add a few pages on inflation in a Central European country. I selected Poland. In 1815, Poland was divided among Prussia, Russia, and the Austro-Hungarian Empire. After the war, it reemerged as a nation with a new currency. The cause of its inflation was baffling. My draft had only a heading on Poland's inflation and a note that my final paper would include a section on it. Deak said, "You can forget about Poland. You have done enough work."

German inflation could be traced to the war and defeat; Polish inflation had no apparent cause. I suspected government corruption. The subject was fascinating. In writing on the subject, I committed a blunder. I wrote that Poland emerged as an independent nation in 1918, under the terms of the Treaty of Versailles. In fact, the treaty was signed in 1919. To a scholar like Deak, my mistake was serious.

Deak had commented extensively on my draft. On the final paper, he made only one comment, "You made a historical error. Poland became a state in 1919, not 1918. Your grade on your paper and the term is A-. I am sick. Please do not fight with me."

I did not fight. Instead, I sent him a gift, an out-sized bottle of very expensive Polish vodka. My note said, "I hope there is one thing about Poland we can agree upon: it makes a world-class vodka. Thanks for your patience and wonderful instruction. Get well soon." I should have stopped there but could not resist a wisecrack: "I would have sent a case if you had given me an A!"

I am happy to say both that Deak recovered from his illness and was not offended by my remark.

History, economics, money, and banking were familiar subjects. The course did not provide an answer to a new troubling question: should I remain in graduate school? The second course on Spinoza was more instructive.

I had taken no courses in philosophy in college. For me it was a new subject. I had to tackle successfully a course outside my limited sphere of knowledge. Philosophy represented intellectual growth. It would provide a test as to whether I could grow. If I failed, my time in graduate school would end.

There were many philosophy courses offered. I picked a survey course, Morals and Ethics, in the belief that it would served as an introduction to philosophy. I met with the professor before the class began and told him philosophy was a new subject for me. He said, "Philosophy is different from other subjects. A course on morals and ethics covers the thinking of several different philosophers. Rather than serving as an introductory course, it presumes familiarity with their overall thinking. You will not get much out of the course. I advise you to study individual philosophers and then take a survey course like this one. Spinoza is a good starting point and Allen Gabbey is teaching a course on Spinoza the same day and time as my course. Switch and come back to me when you are ready." I accepted his advice and enrolled in Spinoza.

I could not grasp Spinoza's work. The class discussion provided no help. The major work, *The Ethics*, presented Spinoza's philosophy in a series of definitions, axioms, propositions, and proofs. I spent hours reading Spinoza, but got nothing out of it. Gabbey lectured on the assumption that the students understood the assignments. He was right except for one student, me. The comments of the others served as departure points for class discussion. For weeks, I was unhappy. Then, I applied the advice of a friend: "Every philosopher has one idea that pervades his work. Find the idea; it is the Rosetta Stone."

Common sense told me that Spinoza had begun with a full-blown philosophy which he then stated in the form of syllogisms. Cambridge University publishes collections of essays on leading philosophers. I purchased the book on Spinoza and read until I found his major idea: God is nature, natural law is divine law; divine law is truth; since miracles violate natural law, they cannot occur. I then re-read the chapters in *The Ethics* which I had not understood. Now they began to make sense. There is, of course, a lot more to the thinking of Spinoza than the kernel I plucked. It provided no more than a ray of light into the complicated thoughts of this great thinker.

One day, we discussed the difference between a square circle and a unicorn. The former can not even be imagined. Although a unicorn also does not exist, unlike a square circle, it can be visualized. Gabbey concluded the session by saying, "Philosophy is not simple. You cannot put it into a neat package and tie a bow. Maybe, that is why we study philosophy." He glanced at several of the best students. Then he turned to me and smiled. That smile implied that I knew full well philosophy was difficult.

Gabbey required two papers. I wrote my first on Spinoza's *Tractatus Theologico Politicus*. The thesis of this work is that the Old Testament, a.k.a., the Pentateuch or the Five Books of Moses, was not the word of God transmitted to Moses. God's word is truth, yet the Bible contains many errors, inconsistencies, and outright contradictions. Spinoza pointed them out. He also showed that the Bible was not the work of one person but was written over a long period of time by many hands. Spinoza admired the story but branded it fiction.

Two samples of Spinoza's critique, discussed in my paper, are set forth below. The first invokes the Second Commandment admonition against the worship of graven images. The Torah teaches that God is incorporeal and that the children of Israel must worship him and not graven images. Inconsistent with the true word of God, the Torah makes repeated references to anthropomorphic characteristics of God. He is seen as "seated" as an "old man clothed in white garments," as possessing eyes, a face, and a mouth. If the Torah reflected the word of God then there would be no reference to God having any resemblance to things in heaven or earth or in the water. Otherwise, God would be the very idol that he interdicts man not to worship. Since God is truth and the references to corporeal characteristics of God are false, they cannot have been conveyed by God to Moses.

The second question was whether Moses could be the author of the

Torah since it reports on events after his death. In my paper, I wrote: "The Torah recites, 'So Moses the servant of the Lord died there in the land of Moab over against Beth-peor, and no man knoweth of his sepulchre unto this day. And the children of Israel wept for Moses in the plains of Moab thirty days.' [H]e could not have reported that his place of burial was unknown or the number of days that he would be mourned would be thirty. Spinoza emphasizes the portions of the Torah describing his place of burial and the period of mourning as circumstances indicating that the Torah was not dictated by God to Moses.

I was uncertain as to whether my paper was any good, so I accepted Gabbey's offer to read a draft in advance of submitting the final version. The next week Gabbey said my paper was fine, I submitted it and got A-. He cautioned that my final paper must discuss a topic covered in Spinoza's main work, *The Ethics*.

My final paper discussed the metaphysical question of: Does God exist? It was entitled "Miracles, Wonders and Signs."

Spinoza postulated that there had to be a first cause of everything. Thus, if God were the first cause of the universe, there had to be a first cause of God and a first cause of the first cause *ad infinitum*. To avoid an infinite regression, Spinoza proposed an immanent thing, a thing composed of itself. He called it substance, God, and finally, nature. In my paper, I summed up Spinoza's argument that the Judeo-Christian God does not exist. In fact, God cannot exist, only substance. Spinoza's proofs lead to the conclusion that substance or God is nature, the universe, or extended space. Infinite modes, the effects of the infinite attributes, thought and extension, are the laws of nature and finite modes, the things that exist in nature. Spinoza's God is not a supreme being existing outside the "causal order of nature." Indeed, he is not a being at all, but *Natura naturans,* the very essence of the universe.

Spinoza's pantheistic view of God is a rejection of God as he is understood in the Jewish and Christian religions. The geometric method, modeled on Euclid's elements, employed by Spinoza in *The Ethics* proves the opposite. Spinoza says God does not exist.

In the conclusion to my paper, I related Spinoza's view to a current dispute. I wrote:

Conclusion

The *New York Review of Books* on October 4 and 18, 2001, published two essays by Frederick Crews, entitled "Saving Us from Darwin." The essays incited a dispute about the respective domains of religion, evolutionary biology, and metaphysical naturalism.

In a letter appearing in the *NYRB* on November 29, Alvin Plantinga, a professor of philosophy at Notre Dame, asserted that evolutionary biology does not imply "that there is no God, or that God has not created human beings in his image." Professor Plantinga claimed that only when it is joined with evolutionary biology can such an inference be drawn. He concluded that the same inference could be drawn if metaphysical naturalism were aligned with, say, the *Farmer's Almanac.*

In the same issue, Benjamin Kissin suggested an accommodation between science and religion. Let the religious confine themselves to their belief in God and associated religious practices and leave everything else to science. Professor Kissin, a professor of psychology, pointed out that 40 percent of scientists believe in a personal God.

In his reply, Crews finds Professor Plantinga's belief in miracles, "God's special revelation, in the Scriptures and through his church, of his plan for dealing with our fall into sin," incompatible with evolutionary science. Crews says that while evolutionary biology does not require a rejection of God, it does demote God to a "*deus absconditus,* and even this faint whiff of divinity is more than the theory of natural selection strictly requires."

More than three hundred years after the death of Spinoza, the dispute rages on.

I got a B+ on the paper, but an A- for the term. The A- was a gift. The grade on the final paper was more important than the earlier one. My participation in class was not particularly good. Further, Columbia has a policy against grade inflation. Professors are cautioned to award very few As less they lose their significance. There was, I concluded, no good reason other than charity to increase my grade over the mark received for my final paper. But I certainly earned a B+. Grades are important to me. They are a sign that I learned. And learning is why I am back in school.

Spinoza focused my attention on the existence of God, a subject I had deliberately avoided. If asked, I deflected the question by saying, "I live in the real world. I am concerned with practical, not metaphysical questions. I'll worry about God when I get to the other side." I did, however, observe the rites and rituals of Judaism, and for a number of years was on the board of trustees of my synagogue. Since studying Spinoza, I observed fewer rites and rituals. Now I am absorbed with a metaphysical question: the existence of God.

I discussed my grades with everyone I met, even casual strangers. "I got an A- in Spinoza. I deserved only a B+. But the professor was generous and I had no background in philosophy. So, even a B+ would have been a prize. I had majored in history at college and continued to read histories. I wrote an exceptional paper; at least, that is what the professor said. But, because I made a historical error, he gave me only an A-. But for my careless error, dating the Treaty of Versailles in 1918 instead of 1919, I would have gotten an A. However, a balance was struck. I got more than I deserved in Spinoza and, because of the careless error, less in German history."

In the middle of November, the Telxon case was placed on a fast track. The judge set a date for the conclusion of discovery, a second date for dispositive motions, and a final date for trial. To give you an idea of how fast the track was, the trial would commence in the middle of April. The judge also announced that no request for adjournment would be entertained.

My options were clear. If I continued with the case, I would have to shortchange my school work. We have a home in St. Croix where I was planning to spend the winter. I would also have to give up my winter vacation. I called Symbol's counsel. I told him the fast track was a signal from the judge that our case had merit. I also told him of my classes and my desire to take the winter off. I concluded by saying, "When I accepted the case, you said your outside firm would help. I need help. Would it be all right if I turned over the case to them?" The attorney thanked me for my work and graciously relieved me of any further commitment.

I had worked very hard in both classes and was tired at the end of the term. The engine needed recharging and St. Croix was the right place at the right time. I spent the winter swimming, golfing, reading, practicing chess, and napping in the afternoon. For the first time in decades, there were no law cases to worry about. I was sixty-nine and at peace.

FALL 2002

Philosophers LIVE IN IVORY towers. They ponder esoteric issues, not bread and butter ones. Right? Wrong! Karl Marx was a philosopher. His central philosophical principle argued for state ownership of all resources and the means of production. This economic system is, of course, called Communism. It was adopted by Russia in 1922 and transformed an imperial nation into a socialist state. In 1991, almost seventy years later, the Soviet Union imploded; Russia and capitalism were reincarnated. The rise and fall of the Soviet Union was one of the major events of the twentieth century.

The Economics Department at Columbia offered a course entitled, The Organization, Development, and Collapse of the Soviet Union. I wanted the course, but there was a problem: a prior course in macroeconomics was a prerequisite. One aspect of macroeconomics involves the preparation of a business plan for the future. Such plans are called projections and generally cover a five-year period. The Soviet Union's economy was run strictly on plans; hence, the reason for the prerequisite. Although I had no formal training in economics, I did have empirical knowledge gained through lawsuits involving the bona fides of projections. I enrolled and took a chance. The subject was fact-intensive and the professor, Richard Ericsson, was equal to the challenge. His lectures were perfectly balanced and insightful. I read the assignments and not only followed the lectures but listened so intently that sometimes, in my mind, completed his sentences. Ericsson arrived about fifteen minutes before class began and fielded questions from the early birds. He also permitted interruptions at any time, by any student, for any reason, but we infrequently raised questions during the class period. There was a lot to cover, time was short, and his lectures were clear.

In graduate school, term papers are the standard requirement and basis of evaluation. They replace exams and determine your grade. Ericsson required a final paper but added a take-home final exam consisting of two questions. Our answers would be due within forty-eight hours.

Term papers are not daunting as there are no time limits. I can spend as much time as I want researching and writing. Time is my most plentiful commodity. Furthermore, a term paper bears a resemblance to a legal brief. In an academic paper, I began by stating the problem, the position taken by the leading authorities, and, as I had been advised by our academic son, my point of disagreement. In the middle, I presented the position of the leading authorities and their reasoning. Then, my differing position, the reasons for disagreeing, and any outside support. In the conclusion, I summarized my attack on the majority position and argued that my point was correct. In writing briefs, I used a similar format; stating the issues, distinguishing the contrary decisions and authorities, and arguing the merits of my client's position.

An exam, however, filled me with anxiety. I had not taken one in forty-five years, since the bar exam in 1957. I could not possibly research two, or even one new area, and write two essays, all within forty-eight hours. Early in the term, I conceived a plan that put my fears to rest and allowed me to relax and enjoy the course. The curriculum listed the required weekly reading assignments. These were contained in several texts which I had purchased. In additional there were about fifty articles, designated as suggested reading, available in the reception area of the department's offices. I got the articles copied at Columbia's copy center and took them home. Midway through the term, I read the suggested reading material, but only as it pertained to the conversion to capitalism. I then made an educated guess as to three, not just two, questions that could be the examination questions. Two dealt with the system, how it worked and the reason it failed; the third was the controversial means used to convert Communism to capitalism.

The second step in my plan was to pick a topic for my final paper that would cover the first two likely questions.

Most of the term was spent on Communism and less than 20 percent on the aftermath. To me, the planners, consisting of thousands of trained persons with expertise in many different fields, were at the heart of the system. The many thousands of pages of their written plans accounted for the production of every nail, screw, axle, tire, car, tractor, truck, loaf of bread, and bottle of milk, from its origin to its final use. Nothing was overlooked. A study of the planning process would reveal the workings of the system and its weaknesses. There were excellent articles on the planners and one extraordinary book by a high-ranking planner who defected.

My paper discussed the operation of Communism as the necessary predicate for my main theme: why it failed. I titled the paper, "Who killed the Soviet Union?"

The Sovietologists placed the blame on socialism, contrasting its weakness, an absence of competition, with capitalism. Capitalism, for example, forces obsolete, inefficient, and poorly located factories to close. They are replaced by modern efficient ones, located close to the markets served. In contrast, the Soviet Union ran the economy as a welfare state. No factory was ever closed, no matter how inefficient, costly to operate, or poorly located. The life of the workers revolved around the factories. Their homes, schools, shops, and entertainment were tied to the factory. Closing a plant would have a devastating effect on the workers. They would lose their way of life. Because plants were kept in operation long past their useful lives, inferior goods were produced at excessive costs. And while free enterprise provides incentives for hard work, Communism provided none. Productivity suffered.

I restated the traditional arguments and cited the authorities, including an article by Ericsson, my professor. Then I turned to my dissenting point. Communism failed because, after World War II and for the duration of the cold war, military and defense expenditures consumed about half of the country's resources. Over the same period, defense got about 8 percent of the resources of the United States. The Soviet economic plan mandated that consumer goods be designed for possible conversion to military purposes. Tractors had treads, not wheels, so that they could be recycled as tanks. They were inefficient as tractors. Trucks and planes were outsized, wasteful for ordinary use, but adaptable for military transportation. Too little resources were devoted to goods designed solely for consumer use. Shortages of food, clothing, and housing were endemic.

What good did it do to have rubles if there was nothing to buy? If only the Soviet leaders understood that the western world's foreign policy was containment, not fomenting revolution within the Soviet Union's sphere of influence, the cost of burying us might have been better spent improving the quality of the life enjoyed by Russia's citizens. A misguided foreign policy was, I concluded, an insufficiently recognized cause of the failure of Russian Communism.

As the term approached the finish mark, the students used the period before class to ask questions about the exam. They too were apprehensive. Ericsson is fair. He sensed the overall anxiety, waited until the whole class was present, and then provided useful hints. "The exam will consist of two questions, one on the operation of the Communist state and the other on the transformation of Russia to a market economy. Both questions will be broad, and you will have forty-eight hours to answer. Each question must be answered in no more than two typed, double-spaced pages."

When the Soviet Union collapsed, the government raced to sell state-owned assets. In a process, one of the most corrupt in all history, 60 percent of the wealth of Russia wound up in the hands of eight related cartels. I remarked to a young girl, a foreign student from Russia, that if I were living in Russia, I would favor revolution. She said the present system with all its faults is better than Communism, but added, "My father agrees with you." A lot of knowledgeable people would say she was right, but I agreed with her father.

Among the articles I had earlier copied was one by Ericsson. He criticized the rapid transformation and lack of systematic planning that enabled corrupt forces to seize the wealth of the nation. But then, in class, he seemed to approve of the speed with which the government converted to capitalism. He said it might have been necessary to prevent a relapse. I e-mailed him, and asked, "What's a poor student to believe? What his professor writes or what he says?" He replied, "With all the arguments presented, the student must make up his own mind." I decided on his written word; it accorded with my own belief. There was also another reason. Professors are in some ways like judges. Both are rulers over their respective domains and tend to hold their own published works in high regard. For example, I recalled a particularly brilliant trial judge advising my opponent and me on the legal authority he considered binding. It was, he said, "A decision directly on point by the highest court in the land, or anything in my opinions dealing directly, or indirectly, or even remotely, with the issue." Was he serious or making a joke? We took no chances. Our briefs cited his opinions everywhere we possibly could. Some judges have big egos and so do some professors. It cannot hurt to polish the ego.

The exam questions were handed to students at the moment they turned in their final papers. Then, the forty-eight hours began to run. Mornings are my most productive time. By late afternoon, I grow tired. In order to write my exam during the day, I submitted my paper at 9:00 AM, the earliest possible time.

I smiled as I read the two questions. The first could be read as an invitation to provide the causes of the failure of Communism and the second, with a little spin, called for a discussion of how Russia should have been converted to capitalism. I grabbed a cab (I usually go back and forth by bus) because time was a factor. I spent a day on each question. In answering the first, I blamed Socialism. I said it cannot work and I set forth fifteen reasons. My answer was supported by most of the important authorities, including the professor. One dissenting voice, of course, was the paper I had just handed in! In deciding to ignore my paper in favor of the majority view, I recalled a statement made by a professor in the law school fifty years earlier in a course on contracts. He said, "The best two papers gave opposite answers. What we are concerned about in law school is your analysis, not your answer."

I answered the second question by addressing Russia's most pressing need, a stable currency accepted in the world market. During Communism, the ruble was not accepted as a monetary unit for foreign exchange. In order to pay for imported goods, the Soviet Union obtained credits by exporting goods to nations with sound currency. Russia had vast oil and natural gas reserves. My plan for Russia was this: auction her oil and gas reserves for cash, retaining a production interest or profit participation. Exploration property should be retained. It represents future wealth. Use the proceeds of the auction to make the ruble acceptable in foreign markets. Close obsolete plants and invest heavily in overhauling and modernizing profitable enterprises able to compete in the world market. In my paper, I criticized the mad dash to a market economy as advocated by Professor Jeffrey Sachs, formerly at Harvard and lured to Columbia by the offer of a higher salary and no teaching responsibilities.

I handed in my answers exactly forty-eight hours after I started. I did not have to wait long for the results. On the final exam, Ericsson commented mockingly, "What's a poor professor to believe? What a student writes on his term paper or his answer to the final exam?" He gave me an A for the term!

I enrolled in Columbia to study new subjects. The course on the Soviet Union was fascinating but familiar territory to me. My second course had to be totally divorced from my life. I found the course, Renaissance Literature: Erasmus, More, and their Circle. The professor was Ann Lake Prescott. She is beautiful on the outside and, as the course progressed, revealed even more beauty on the inside. She knew literature: ancient Greek, the Middle Ages, right up to modern times.

The class was a seminar in which students were required to speak. My classmates were mostly PhD candidates. They were well versed in Renaissance literature. They spoke often and well, but not me. I did not say a word. In the beginning Professor Prescott called the roll. She said she would do so until she learned the names of the students. She quickly recognized the ones who spoke and called them by their first name. When she came to my name, she said, "Sidney Silverman?" in such a way as to suggest doubt that such a person existed, let alone was a student in her class. I knew that once I spoke she would know me, but remembered the advice given to a new senator, "Let the others wonder why you did not speak rather than why you did."

Poor me. I knew nothing about Renaissance literature. I was not ready to speak and would have to endure the sound of that perplexed "Sidney Silverman?" until I did. After weeks of intensive study, I got the gist of Erasmus's philosophy. It emerged in two books, *In Praise of Folly* and *The Enchiridion.*

In biting satire, Erasmus exposed corruption in the church, the inanity of pilgrimages, and the worship of ancient relics. He preached the simple life in which salvation is achieved by following the life, spirit, and teachings of Christ.

Erasmus was an Augustinian monk, a patristic Christian, and a humanist. He believed that doing good deeds for one's fellow man was the way to salvation. He attacked the mindless repetition of prayers to the masses in incomprehensible Latin. Instead of pilgrimages to holy sites, Erasmus advocated staying at home and looking after one's family. He dismissed holy relics as frauds. He suggested that if all the wood claimed to have come from Jesus's cross was real, the cross itself would have been big enough to cover the planet.

Erasmus believed that the observance of rites was of little importance, that adherence to them was not the way to salvation. Rather, a good Christian was one who followed the "life and teaching" of Christ. Since Christ lived a simple life and advocated the love of man, his "life and teachings" closely resembled the Ten Commandments. Erasmus made me feel comfortable with a figure that had frightened me, Christ. Although he was a Jew, I believed anti-Semitism started because Jews refused to recognize Christ as the savior. Catholic liturgy and practice were frightening to me. Erasmus took the fear out of Christ.

Now, I was ready to participate in class discussion and in an e-mail to Professor Prescott outlined what I proposed to say. She encouraged me, and at the next session, "Sidney Silverman?" became "Hi, Sidney."

We read St. Thomas More's *Utopia,* and his history of Richard III upon which Shakespeare's play was based.

Utopia consists of two books. In Book One, written after Book Two, the narrator is introduced to Raphael Hythloday, a traveler and philosopher who describes England as two nations, one rich and the other poor. The poor are victimized in many ways but none are worse than those practiced by the criminal justice system. It punishes petty crimes committed, for example, to obtain food to feed one's starving family, and it punishes such crimes severely—by death. Hythloday would condemn society, not the criminal. He says, "For if you suffer your people to be ill-educated, and their manners to be corrupted from their infancy, and then punish them for those crimes to which their first education disposed them, what else is to be concluded from this, but that you first make thieves and then punish them?"

In Book Two, More describes life in the mythical state of Utopia. There the wealth is evenly divided—it is an egalitarian state—and all live virtually identical lives. They work six hours per day, three before lunch and three after. They go to bed at 8:00 PM and sleep eight hours. Meals are taken in a common hall. Everyone eats the same food. They also dress alike, except for distinctions between the sexes and the married and unmarried. The houses and towns are alike: "He that knows one knows them all." Crime is virtually non-existent.

Scholars debate the relationship between the two books, many contending that there is none. I found a connection: an egalitarian society, the supposed cure to poverty and crime, is worse than the disease. Such a society destroys individuality. Its members lose more than they gain.

The students and the professor disagreed with me. She pointed to the area south of Morningside Drive and said, "The people there might prefer Utopia to their present existence and not object to the sameness of life." Others called me a plutocrat and a crass capitalist. They missed the point. My view was More's view. He, too, despised Utopia.

The class loved Prescott. She was exciting, led class discussions with gusto, and her enthusiasm was infectious. It was hard to reconcile her animation with an early statement she made about her health, "I take a lot of pills for a stomach ailment and forgive me if I sometimes fall asleep in class." It never happened. But, one day she did not show up. The first student to speak said, "I get to class very early and she is always here. She must be ill. I'm going to the department office and find out." He returned and said, "She is fine but lost her voice. She is scheduled to read a paper before the St. Thomas More society and wants to stay in bed and rest her voice." We were relieved, but were confronted with a decision. Do we leave or stay? The decision to stay was unanimous. Each session, one student had primary responsibility for leading the class. That week's leader took the professor's chair and conducted the class. The student leader was excellent, but we stayed as a tribute to our professor.

The leading Renaissance figures looked backwards for inspiration to the golden age of Greek civilization. They hoped, by standing on the shoulders of the Greek philosophers, to see farther into the great problems of the day. Our grade depended largely on a term paper. I decided to combine Erasmus's thoughts with that of an ancient philosopher, but knew nothing about Greek thinkers. Fortunately for me, my son, David, holds a PhD in classics. I sent him an urgent e-mail: "I want to write about Erasmus and religion with emphasis upon his book *The Enchiridion*. To whom can I compare him in Ancient Greece." He replied, "There was a Stoic philosopher named Epectitus who wrote a manual on morality, also called *The Enchiridion*. Maybe there is a paper."

The Columbia library had Epectitus's *Enchiridion* and reference material pertaining to Epectitus and the Stoics. I borrowed the books. I was alone in New York with the Stoics. Irene returned on the weekend as we had tickets to an opera. I waited for the appropriate moment to inject Stoic thinking into our conversation and Irene unintentionally obliged. She worried that unusual traffic congestion might make us late for the opera. On an earlier occasion, we had arrived as the doors to our section were closing, but before the curtain was raised. We had to watch the first act on closed circuit TV in a room in the basement with other late comers. I jumped at the opportunity: "We cannot control the congestion and the delays that flow therefrom. Do not be concerned over matters you cannot affect. They will occur regardless of your fears. Instead, direct your energy to bring about desirable results over matters within your control." She asked where I got that from and when I told her from reading Stoic philosophy, she said, "If you make another comment like that, you are divorced! And that is a matter under your control."

Irene did not like that night's opera. Since I selected the operas we went to, she asked why I did not get tickets to her favorites, which she then named. I tried—I really did—not to invoke the Stoics, but they could not be repressed. "Think of life as a banquet. Certain dishes are passed your way. Partake of them, of course, in moderation. Other plates will not come to you. Do not grieve over them, rather enjoy the ones you receive." Irene took one look at the smile on my face and declared, "You're divorced!"

Although I appended a discussion of Epectitus and the Stoics to my paper, the thrust was Erasmus. My theme came from an uncontroversial statement in an unrelated article, stating that people initially formed nations to provide protection from marauding tribes and paid taxes to a central authority in order to secure that benefit. From that statement, I reasoned that people support the church to obtain the benefit of salvation. Erasmus believed that salvation was achieved by good deeds, a simple life, and love for others, not by adherence to religious doctrine. I then developed the thesis that if the mass of people believed as he did, churches, synagogues, and mosques were dead in the water. Why spend time and money praying for salvation when it could not be obtained that way? Erasmus's views were far more destructive of the Catholic Church than Luther's. He deprived the church of the wealth of German princes; Erasmus would deprive the church of the support of the rest of the world.

In a separate section, I discussed basic Stoic philosophy, which advocates strength in turning away from evil, a principle Erasmus adopts in his Enchridion.

I thought my paper was good but had doubts whether Professor Prescott would read it, or any of the other papers. My concern was based on a conversation between the professor and a student. He submitted a draft of his paper to Prescott and when two weeks had passed without comment, he gently asked her whether his paper was acceptable. She replied, "It's fine. I have it somewhere in that pile of papers. I made no written comments on the paper so I guess there is no reason to return it." I'm afraid that I thought she never read the paper.

At the last session, I handed in my paper, along with a self-addressed, stamped envelope. "How considerate Sidney is. He knows the English Department is starved for funds and has stamped his return envelope. I will return your paper. Thank you, Sidney."

I did not expect to see the paper again. I was right. Months passed and no return envelope or grade arrived. Without a grade, I could not get credit for the course. When we returned from St. Croix, I sent an e-mail: "Paper not returned; no grade; no credit." She replied, "You got some form of an A." I told her, "Your e-mail is not sufficient. You have to submit a formal grade." Well, she did. I got an A!

I fired off e-mails to my children: "Last year, two A minuses. This year two As. Next year two A pluses. I stand first in the class. The evidence is conclusive: my genes made you brilliant."

My kids *are* brilliant, but the genetic evidence points to Irene. She graduated magna cum laude from a top women's college, Smith. I was advised not to apply to the top colleges and my record at Colgate was less than distinguished. More important, Irene did not need graduate school; she was well educated and it showed. She is intellectual and knows that I am not. My grades confused her. "I edit your papers. I don't understand them and neither do you. You are not an intellectual. The teachers must feel sorry for you and that is why you get As." Well, I am not nearly as intellectual as Irene, but I have had lots more experience at arguing. "You've never been to graduate school, so I forgive your naive statement. If you had the good fortune to attend a great university like Columbia, you would know grades are based on merit and nothing else. But, I understand your position. For years, I hid my light under a bale of hay. There was no reason for me to show my true worth. Now, there is. I'm brilliant!"

I also bragged to relatives and friends. "You know grades are important. They measure how much you learn. There are old folks who audit classes. They cannot participate in class discussion, do not submit papers, and are not graded. They sit there half asleep, with contented little smiles. When I speak with these old codgers after or before class, it is clear to me that they have learned nothing. Why go through the motions? I suppose it fills otherwise empty hours and provides fodder for cocktail talk. 'Oh, what do you do now that you are retired?' 'I go to college and take courses.' 'How wonderful.' Well, it is not wonderful. Either do it right or not at all. I work hard but the hard work produces benefits. I really learn. How do I know? Try to stump me. Ask me a question about Spinoza, or Germany and East Central Europe, or the Soviet Union or Erasmus, More, or Rabelais. I'm proud of my record of As. Now two were only A minuses in '01 but I improved in '02 to two As. Next year, who knows? Maybe A pluses."

FALL 2003

WE WENT TO ST. Croix at the close of
the fall term and returned to New York in the spring. I was eager to start
classes. I looked over the listings. In philosophy, it seemed like an Immanuel
Kant festival. There were three classes: introductory, intermediate, and an
advanced course called Kant's Moral Philosophy. That course focused
on Kant's *Grounding for the Metaphysics of Morals,* a work claimed to be
one of the most important books in modern moral philosophy. Patricia
Kitcher, the chair of the philosophy department, taught the course.
Although Professor Gabbey, my Spinoza professor, advised I start with the
introductory course concentrating on Kant's *Critique of Practical Reason*, I
enrolled in the advanced course. I only had room for one course on Kant;
I wanted to study his moral philosophy. To prepare for the course, I read a
collection of essays by Kantian scholars on that subject.

For many advanced classes there are prerequisites, courses that must be
completed before taking the higher course. In others, students must obtain
the approval of the professor. The course in moral philosophy required
neither prior courses nor professorial approval. I took that to mean the
class was open to all graduate students. In retrospect, I realize I overlooked
the self-selecting rule by which only qualified students enroll in advanced
classes. The other students followed the rule. My new classmates were PhD
candidates, all of whom had studied Kant. Several of them were writing
their theses on him.

Intrusion into a class where I did not belong should have made me self-effacing and quiet. Instead, I spoke often, sometimes out of turn. I even taunted the professor. By the end of the term, I realized Kant would have condemned my behavior.

The first day, I made my presence known. I raised my hand. The professor smiled and indicated that I could speak. I began, "Good afternoon, Professor Kitcher. [She frowned.] In making moral decisions, Kant admonishes us to ignore the teaching of religious leaders, parents, friends, and teachers…" She cut me off, saying, "Of course," and continued her lecture.

She was not being rude. My comment was sophomoric. I was stating an elementary principle of Kant's moral philosophy: we possess the innate ability to decide between good and evil. We must learn to rely on ourselves and not on others, who may not be present at decision time. The other students knew this. Showing that I did too served only to waste class time.

As the term progressed, I continued my practice of commenting whenever I wanted to, but I eliminated the salutation. I reasoned that I was an active student, not an auditor. Perhaps, I spoke to make it clear I was not one of the old fellows auditing the course.

Professor Kitcher was interested in comments made by the PhD candidates. What they said became springboards for further discussion. On one occasion, a prized student made a comment remarkably like one I had made earlier. Although she told me I was wrong, she applauded his comment.

I had said that two rational, reasonable people could reach different moral judgments, known in Kantian terms as maxims. "No," she said, "Kant believed that the burghers of Konigsberg would make the same decision." Several weeks later, another student raised my point. She responded, "That is an interesting question. If both use pure practical reason, they can reach opposite maxims." I joined in. "When I made a similar remark, you said that all the good burghers could be relied on to reach the same judgment. Remember? I was disturbed by your response and happy to know that you have changed. Would you agree that the recent five-to-four decision of the Supreme Court on affirmative action is an excellent example of rational persons reaching opposite judgments through the exercise of pure practical reason?" The expression on her face was one of scorn, and she said, "No. Affirmative action is an administrative problem, not a moral one." On this one occasion, I believe she was wrong. Affirmative action is a moral question.

One day, to illustrate a point Kitcher drew an analogy to chess. She said, "I know nothing about chess except that the queen is the strongest piece. It is important to move the queen early in the game." I jumped right in, "I am a chess player. Moving the queen early in the game is usually a mistake and may be a blunder. Her royal highness will be chased by other pieces, even a lowly pawn. Moving the queen to safety wastes moves and allows one's opponent to grab the offensive." She turned red but quickly recovered her composure. "Well, as I said, I know nothing about chess." She then continued her lecture without reference to chess. In difficult situations, I often talk to myself: "Listen, Sidney, cut it out. You are in danger of flunking."

I decided to review the readings and my notes of the lectures and keep my mouth shut in class. I read the first assignment and typed my notes of Professor Kitcher's lecture. I understood so much more than I did that first day. I repeated the process for each subsequent class session. When I finished, I understood Kant's moral philosophy. You always know what is right and what is wrong. Disregard decisions on trivial matters; they have no real moral significance. Think about dilemmas where doing the right thing hurts. Why does it hurt? Because it conflicts with your own interest. Now test your decision for arbitrariness: would you like to live in a world where everyone, no exceptions, lived by that rule? If so, when you do the act called for by your decision, you have done your duty.

What if it is in your selfish interest to do a good deed and you perform the act? It is a just act, but it does not "shine like a jewel" because you were influenced by inclination, not solely by duty.

As I worked my way through the lectures and assignments, the idea for my term paper started to unfold. Feelings and emotions have no role in Kant's moral philosophy. We do what's right for one reason only: it is our duty.

The secondary material on Kant is vast. I spent several hours searching the library stacks and hundreds of hours reading the selected books. By the time I was ready to start writing, my typed notes, not including those from the lectures, ran over a hundred pages. Before writing, I placed the books on the floor in alphabetical order by author and kept the notes on my desk. Hours passed. I read and reread my notes, but could not write a word. Then, I talked to myself: "Idiot, how did you write a brief? Well, I knew the case inside out. I drafted a brief without consulting a note or legal source. When I finished the draft, I plugged in references and quotes from the trial record. Do you know Kant's moral philosophy and the role of inclinations? Yes. Then toss the notes on the floor and write." I did. And, a week later the paper was done.

I used analogies to further my analysis. To illustrate the purity of motive, I gave the following two examples: A man, well known to be very rich, is drowning and is rescued by another, motivated by the expectation of a reward. The rich man is saved but the rescuer has not done his duty because he acted, not out of respect for the law, but out of self-interest. In a second example, a rescuer tries but is unsuccessful in saving a drowning man; a riptide carries the victim out to sea. The rescuer acted solely out of duty, i.e., to save the life of another. Even though he was unsuccessful, he did his duty.

I argued that Kant approved of autonomy, a form of self legislation. It allows that two people of good will can reach opposite judgments on a single matter and, although their acts are contrary, both perform their duty. I drew upon our earlier dispute on affirmative action and gave the following example: Two candidates for admission to Columbia University, one white and the other black, know that if affirmative action is applied, the black student, but not the white, will be admitted; and if affirmative action is not applied, the white student, but not the black, will be admitted. Columbia tells the two applicants that they must decide whether the admission process will take race into account. The white student rejects self-interest and decides in favor of affirmative action. He tests his decision; would he like to live in a world that favors a disadvantaged class in order to compensate for past injustices? His answer: yes. The black student also comes out against self-interest. Admission to Columbia should be based solely on merit. He, too, tests his decision; would he like to live in a world where merit ruled? His answer: yes. Both students have acted with good will and Kant would approve of both, even though they reached opposite decisions. (In fact, Kant was a racist and a sexist. He believed that blacks and women were inferior to white males. He also believed that sexual intercourse defiled a woman even if consensual and between husband and wife. He also thought that men who masturbated should be castrated. Kant was a mean, bigoted man. But his moral philosophy was revolutionary and important.)

It is easy to confuse Kant's message by merging the decision to perform an act with the act itself. Schiller did so in verse:

Scruples of Conscience
I like to serve my friends, but unfortunately I do it by
inclination and so often I am bothered by the thought that I am
not virtuous.
Decision
There is no other way but this! You must seek to despise them
and do with repugnance what duty bids you.

I analyzed Schiller's verse in my paper and disparaged it. The decision to act cannot be influenced by inclinations, as they are subject to change. However, when performing the act, love, passion, and friendliness can and should be displayed. Kant disapproves of the performance of a good act with hate, as it undermines good will.

Some Kant scholars have tried to humanize his view that the motive for doing one's duty is "respect for the law," or doing good for its own sake by searching for motives closer to feeling. The leading advocate of this position is Professor Barbara Herman of Harvard. She developed the theory of overdetermination, in which a decision can have a second, joint determining factor, an inclination such as beneficence.

I attacked Herman's thesis. Kant should be strictly construed. There is no room for allegorical or metaphorical interpretation of what he wrote. Kant means what he says and says what he means. If overdetermination were a viable principle, Kant would have said so.

Kitcher encouraged us to submit drafts of our paper for review. I sent mine to her by e-mail. I was both eager and anxious for a response. We were off to London for a week before the end of school, and I wanted to clear my paper before we left. I was uncertain how she would evaluate it. When two weeks passed with no response, I asked whether she received my paper. She replied, "A colleague is sick and I have filled in for him. No time to download files." I asked, "Would you prefer that I give you a hard copy?" "No," she said, "I'll get to it during the week." On the last day of class, she appeared, loaded with draft papers and distributed them. Mine came last. I turned to the last page and read her comment: "You show a thorough understanding of Kant's moral philosophy and some excellent insights. My only criticism: some paragraphs lack connection."

I departed for London in high spirits. Who knows? Maybe another A. On our return, I had a full week to work on the paper. I accepted her few suggestions, made sure every paragraph was connected, and, after reading my notes, added some additional points. I knew that if she liked the draft, she would love the final version. It was clearly an improvement. At first, I wrote a long letter to accompany the final paper, pointing out the changes and additions. Then, I rejected the letter. In the end, I simply submitted the final draft to her box in the philosophy department.

I did not have to wait long for my grade. I got an automatic e-mail from Columbia stating that my grade had been recorded. I opened my account; the grade was a B+.

How did I feel? A grade of B+ in the advanced course for an old guy with no background in Kant was a great achievement. To myself I said, "Sidney, old boy, I am proud of you. Nice work."

I continued to think a lot about Kant. I applied his thinking to the decisions I made in preparing and trying a case. I always knew what was right. I did not need second opinions. When, for example, as required by the rules of litigation, I turned over a document to an adversary that hurt my case, I experienced pain. Later, when I looked my opponent in the eye, I was pleased to have turned over the document. Kant was right. True pleasure is derived from an act done for no other reason than it is one's duty to do so. I also recalled an early experience with Whitney North Seymour, Jr., a prominent New York lawyer from an old and distinguished New York family.

I was a sole practitioner with an office in the Singer building in lower Manhattan. Seymour was a partner in the leading firm of Simpson, Thatcher, and Bartlett. The case was a stockholder's derivative case brought on behalf of Banff Oil and Gas, a Canadian corporation. Seymour was the principal defense lawyer. His clients had already produced several boxes of documents when Seymour appeared unannounced in my office. He said, "I have just returned from Canada where I reviewed all the relevant documents. I found one my client failed to produce." He handed me the document and left. The document was very damaging to the defense. I went on to win the case, a result that could not have been obtained without it.

Some years later, President Nixon appointed Seymour as the United States Attorney for the Southern District. In the Watergate affair, Seymour took courageous action. While an independent counsel was conducting an investigation, Seymour, acting on his own and against the wishes of the administration, obtained an indictment against his immediate boss Attorney General John Mitchell. Seymour was a paradigm of Kantian moral philosophy. I wondered whether he had studied Kant.

Charles Dickens was my choice for a second course, but the approval of the professor, Maura Spiegel, was needed. She said that she would like to take me but the class was full. She suggested that I attend the first class and see if there were any cancellations. At that session, she said we would be expected to read about four hundred pages a week and submit a short paper discussing the reading. The first assignment was *Oliver Twist*. I read the book and submitted the paper. At the second meeting, several students dropped out, and I dropped in.

I loved the course and particularly the requirement of writing a weekly paper. It forced me to concentrate. I thought my papers were good, but there was no feedback. Then, I got an e-mail: "Thank you for your thoughtful comments. I enjoyed them." I forwarded the e-mail to my children. "I may be failing Kant, but I will surely get an A in Dickens. My forte is literature not philosophy."

After finishing a draft of the Kant paper, I began work on Dickens. I consulted secondary sources and decided to write on children. Dickens was the first novelist to make children his central subjects. There is a popular verse about children born on different days in which Thursday's child is "full of woe." Why not write on Dickens's Thursday children?

Professor Spiegel met separately with each student to discuss the subject of the term paper. She was unimpressed with mine: "Your paper lacks a theme. To discuss neglected and abused children is descriptive, but it is not a proper paper. You must interpret and search for meaning, not merely report what Dickens wrote." I told her I was not literary. She agreed, and said, "But, your weekly papers show good analysis and they are honest." She then gave me several suggestions for papers. I rejected her suggestions, and said, "Unfortunately, I am me, not you. I cannot write effectively on your ideas."

My response was a half truth. I could not write on her topics. Also, I had completed a rough draft of my paper at the time of our meeting and was not willing to start all over again. We planned to go to London if I finished my papers. I wanted to go. I revised the draft to include what I thought was a theme. The day before we were to leave for London, I got the draft back. She hated it. I could not begin all over again; radical surgery had to be performed.

I cut out everything about the boys and concentrated on the relationship between abused and neglected daughters and their fathers. The daughters loved, indeed worshiped, their monstrous fathers, and accepted indifference, neglect, and base treatment as the prerogative of the man. Dickens had to exaggerate the evil nature of certain fathers, as they lacked human feelings. The novels were satires attacking the automatic respect for fathers under the Victorian tradition of *pater familias.* It was unjust. A male-dominated society was wrong. The rights of women must be respected, especially by their fathers. Dickens was a feminist!

On the flight to London, I turned the paper around. Now my paper had a theme and a point of view. I was happy until, several days later, I met the curator of the Dickens Museum.

Our daughter had received a fellowship to the London School of Economics and lived in a school-owned apartment on Mecklenburgh Square. The college provided a private residential hotel, located on the same square, called the Goodenough Club, for the parents and guests of the students. We stayed there. A few blocks from the club is Dickens's early home at 58 Doughty Street, now the Dickens Museum. I never noticed the museum before, but on this trip, I made straight away for it.

There, I spied a young man alone in an office off the bookshop. "Are you the curator of the museum?" He frowned and mumbled, "Yes." His body language said, "Please go away now!" I ignored his silent wish and told him that I was familiar with an important Dickens study authored by his predecessor. He barely changed. Then, I discussed my favorite characters and since I had read six books, the references were many. Finally, he spoke, "What is your interest in Dickens?" My golden opportunity appeared. "Look at Dombey. Don't you hate him for the way he mistreated and ignored his wonderful daughter, Florence." His expression did not change. Then, I discussed other rotten father–daughter relationships, and asked, "Dickens hated and wanted the reader to hate a society that allows men to dominate and abuse women. Dickens was an early feminist."

He looked me straight in the eye, and without moving a muscle said, "I never heard that one before." I persisted, "I'm writing a paper on Dickens and his pro-feminist attitude is the dominant theme." He smiled and said, "I guess you can attribute almost anything to Dickens."

Well, that was not exactly confirmation, but it was not an outright rejection. I stayed with the idea and turned in a revised paper.

I did not expect a good grade and was pleasantly surprised when I received a B+. Well, two B+s are not A+s but, as we old Brooklyn Dodgers fans used to say, "Wait till next year."

FALL 2004

I HAD BEEN TAKING TWO courses per semester. In the fall of 2004, I broke with tradition and added a third. After four semesters, I no longer thought about failure. I was in stride, confident, and secure. Taking an extra course also brought me closer to completing the course requirements at the end of the fall semester in 2005. The required thesis would be my project for the fall of 2006. By taking three courses in 2004, I also had an option; I could drop a course I did not like and take three in 2005. Assuming all worked out as planned, I would graduate in May of 2007, at the same time as my fiftieth reunion from law school. A nice double header.

I selected a course in Heidegger, concentrating on his major work, *Being and Time*. The course was taught by Taylor Carman, a young professor on Barnard's staff. The class was held in a large, windowless room in the basement of Barnard's student activity center adjacent to the cafeteria. I had difficulty finding the room and arrived late. The room was filled to capacity. There were no empty seats. I slipped out to the lunchroom, got a chair and quietly slipped back in.

Carman had written a treatise on Heidegger. I had purchased it and tried to read it during the summer. The prose was turgid; I found the book impenetrable. I gave up. In preparation for class, I read several essays in the *Cambridge Companion to Heidegger*.

On opening day, Carman lectured on the reading assignment, the first fifteen pages of *Being and Time*. He then asked for comments or questions.

I let my classmates speak first. When they were done, I raised my hand. "Time is important to Heidegger. It is in the title of his book. Of the three periods, past, present, and future, future is the most important." Carman agreed. Then I asked my question, "Did Heidegger purposely exclude the fourth period, eternity, as a way of excluding God?" I was thinking about God in these days, and groping for a topic for a paper. I thought Heidegger's concept of God was a possible subject. Carman was no help. He said no, offered no reason, and went on.

I understood Carman's rebuke. My comment did not relate to the reading assignment. The other students, on that very first day, raised issues questioning the text. They showed a level of understanding that put the poor professor to the test. Time after time, he deflected a question by saying we will reach your point later on, even though the student had quoted from the assigned text. In all of my classes, there were many brilliant students. In the Heidegger class, maybe because of the size (about forty students) there were over a dozen superstars.

I spoke only once again. I raised a point mentioned by Charles Guignon, the editor of the *Cambridge Companion*, in his essay in that volume. Carman dismissed my comment as wrong and offered no explanation. Later on, he said that Heidegger was not interested in sex. A friend of ours had written a play, derived from a book about the torrid love affair in the 1920s between Heidegger and a brilliant and beautiful young Jewish student, Hannah Arendt. She later emigrated from Germany and taught philosophy at the University of Chicago. I left the class in an angry mood. I was publicly embarrassed. The professor had declared in open class that I was wrong.

I checked the Cambridge book. What I had said in class accurately reflected Guignon's view. He cited several sections of *Being and Time* in support. I read the sections. It seemed clear to me Guignon and I were right. I was redeemed. Now I took pleasure in telling Carman that he, not I, was wrong. I sent him an e-mail. I referred to my comment made in class, his reply that I was wrong, quoted Guignon, and cited the references to Heidegger's work. I then mentioned his remark about sex and said, based on secondary reports, Hannah Arendt would not agree. I decided to end it by reminding him of one of Heidegger's major flaws: he was an outspoken fan of Hitler. I said, "I enjoy the class but will not when we reach Heidegger's Nazi phase."

Carman took a week to reply. He said he disagreed with Guignon, did not want to discuss Arendt, and said that the readings ended in 1927 with the publication of Heidegger's book. As a cautionary note, he said papers on Heidegger will be limited to 1927 and prior times. Heidegger's political period may not be considered. I, of course, had no intention of writing about Heidegger the Nazi. Carman was rude. I could take it. I liked the class, particularly the superstars and Heidegger's philosophy. That's what mattered.

Students were required to submit two papers; one at midterm and the other at the end of the course. Grades would be based on the papers, with the final one counting twice as much as the mid-term.

I learn a lot from researching and writing papers, particularly those in philosophy. I picked a topic involving the essence of the philosopher's thinking, described it, and then concentrated on a narrow issue.

One of Heidegger's major contributions to the field of philosophy was his development of the concept of phenomenology. I thought my midterm paper should discuss phenomenology and, if possible, the role of God in Heidegger's world. The final paper, as Carmen suggested, could be an extension of the earlier one.

Carman proposed possible subjects for the first paper. He said we were not restricted to his list. Since none even remotely dealt with God or religion, I rejected the professor's suggestions and searched the library's catalogue for a reference to Heidegger and God. I found a book published in 1962 containing a Heidegger lecture delivered in 1927. The lecture was titled "Phenomenology and Theology." The book was in the library of the Union Theological Seminary. I had my paper.

In the lecture, Heidegger argues that phenomenology provides a sound basis for the existence of God. I read the lecture. I was unconvinced. Phenomenology is science; it deals with facts, things, substance. A belief in God rests on faith, a concept at loggerheads with science. Heidegger is wrong. Phenomenology and theology are incompatible. I was depressed. Then I had another mood swing: "Heidegger is wrong! That's my paper. Six weeks into the course, I know more about phenomenology than Professor Heidegger!"

It was bedtime. I laughed as I entered our bedroom. "What's so funny?" asked Irene. "I started with one idea, abandoned it when I found out Heidegger was wrong, and then chose another. My paper will uncover a fatal flaw in Heidegger. I'm a better philosopher than the great Heidegger." "No, you're not. Get ready for bed." I think I might have been conceited if I had married someone other than Irene.

The paper took no time to write. I began with an exposition of Heidegger's view that phenomenology was science. Then to my argument that theology was faith, the enemy of science:

Science for Heidegger is divided into two parts, pure ontic

science and fundamental ontology.... Ontic science is the study of matter. Among other findings, science may identify the composition of matter, its properties and the way it interacts, combines and changes. Existence is the *sine qua non* for scientific study. Fundamental ontology provides the facticity of existence. It is the science of science; it deals with our understanding of entities as entities. Because we are able to inquire, i.e., "looking at something, understanding, conceiving it, choosing, access to it," we know the things that exist. Our suppositions become the matter for discrete scientific study.

Heidegger says, "Ontology and phenomenology are not two distinct philosophical disciplines among others. These terms characterize philosophy itself with regard to its object and its way of treating that object." Heidegger not only adopted phenomenology but made it an integral and, indeed, indivisible part of fundamental ontology.

Can theology be part of science? Although Heidegger proclaims that theology is a pure ontic science, like mathematics, chemistry, physics, and other natural sciences, in this paper I will argue that theology is not a science within the Heideggerian framework. Philosophy is reason and theology revelation and blind faith, irreconcilable concepts.

In his lecture, Heidegger recognized that he faced a dilemma: theology cannot be the subject of scientific inquiry as God cannot be placed on an examining table. The philosopher attempted to resolve the dilemma by creating a new definition of theology. It means something other than the study of God: "But God is in no way the object of investigation in theology, as, for example, animals are the theme of zoology. Theology is not speculative knowledge of God."

Theology to be a science has to be based on fact identified by the science of phenomenology. Heidegger claimed to find the missing fact in what he termed "Christianness," the crucifixion of Jesus. That a person called Jesus was crucified is a fact. The redefinition does not, however, advance analysis. It too rests on a belief not subject to scientific enquiry, the belief that the person crucified was the Son of God.

I finished my paper about a week before it was due. Apparently, some students were unable to meet the deadline and appealed for more time. Carman obliged. He announced papers submitted a week late would be considered timely. On the due date, one student arose and handed in his paper. I did not do it to call attention to myself. Rather, I was busy taking three courses and wanted to conclude this project. Okay, maybe there was a mixed motive. I wanted to show that an old man can be swifter than a young one.

Carman returned my paper with a few meaningless comments but no grade. After class, I asked why he did not grade my paper. He said, "I did not know you were taking the course for credit. Give it back and I will return it next week with a grade." The following week, I got my grade, a B. I asked for a meeting. Thanksgiving break was coming up. Carman agreed to meet on the first day after the break.

Irene and I went to Portland, Oregon, to spend the holidays with our two children who live there. I discussed the history of my Heidegger paper with our son David. Before going to Stanford Law School, he had taught at Reed College for five years. He said, "You made a mistake in not writing on a subject suggested by the professor. He is familiar with those subjects and, as you say, it is a large class. Instead, you wrote about an obscure lecture. What did you expect Carman to do? Stop his work, hop over to the seminary's library, read the lecture, and then review your paper? Make sure you write your final paper on a suggested topic. Don't waste his time and yours by meeting with him. Nothing you say will change his mind."

I accepted half of David's advice. I abandoned God as a topic for a final paper and chose truth, one of the topics suggested by Carman. I attended the meeting. To my utter amazement, Carman said my paper was not a philosophy paper. "What? Not a philosophy paper? Heidegger is a philosopher. He gave a lecture to a philosophy class. I show Heidegger is wrong. Why is that not a philosophy paper?" I brought the book containing the lecture and read the crucial portion. Carman asked for the book. His body language said, "You've misread it." In translated texts, important words are stated in parenthesis. Here "*wissenschaft*," the German word translated to science, was included. When he saw that I had not made this mistake, he said, "The translator, not Heidegger, made the mistake. The word *wissenschaft* means intellectual study as well as science. Heidegger meant it in the former sense." I should have stood my ground and said, "The generally accepted meaning of the word is science. I agree with the translator. Further, if Heidegger meant 'intellectual study' there are precise words to convey that meaning." Instead, I retreated: "It's not my fault if the translator made an error." "It is," said Carman. "Can't you read German?" "No," I said. Carman looked bemused. He refused to change my grade. I switched the subject to the final paper. "My son, who has a PhD in classics and taught at Reed College for five years, advises I select a topic suggested by you for my final paper." I did not like Carman; it was also clear he did not like me. He had been rude to me; now it was my turn. "I have decided to accept my son's advice and select a topic suggested by you. It will make your life easier, as the subject will be familiar. I have selected truth, but it seems too broad. Truth runs throughout *Being and Time*." He suggested that I limit my discussion to the material contained in the chapter entitled "Truth."

After the meeting, I checked my barely used German dictionary. *Wissenschaft* means science, but is broad enough to include the humanities. Read in context, Heidegger meant *wissenschaft* to mean science and theology to be part of science. In his lecture, he aligned theology with mathematics, chemistry, physics, and other natural sciences. Too bad that the argument was not in my paper or made to Carman.

Modern philosophy equates truth with correspondence. The assertion corresponds or agrees with the perceived facts. Heidegger rejected the equation. He set forth his reasons in an interpretation of an allegory, the four stages of Plato's famous cave. In my paper, I relied on the allegory to make Heidegger's point that unhiddenness is truth.

In the first stage, prisoners shackled since childhood live in darkness in the cave, unable to turn their heads. Behind them a community engaged in various activities passes by. A fire in the background casts shadows of the humans on the one wall visible to the prisoners. They mistake the shadows for the beings. The meaning of the first stage is that the prisoners, denied light, see illusion, not reality; they see untruth, not truth.

In the second stage, one prisoner is unshackled, forced to face the fire and confront the beings. The sudden exposure to direct light is painful. The flickering light blurs his vision. With difficulty, he sees beings, but believes the shadows more real than the beings he imperfectly sees. The second stage marks a transition from darkness to light. The prisoner sees the beings for the first time, but because they appear less visible than the shadows, he cannot accept their reality. The prisoner, restricted by circumstances, is unable to uncover the truth: "Truth (uncoveredness) is something that must always first be wrested from entities.... The factical uncoveredness of anything is always, as it were, a kind of robbery."

In the third stage, the prisoner is forced to leave the cave, and live in daylight. At first, he looks only at reflections, and then, as his eyes become adjusted to sunlight, he looks directly at the entities surrounding him. He is liberated. In Heidegger's term, "in the world." The released prisoner is now able to recognize that the unhidden are the beings, not the shadows. The metaphorical sunlight enables the released prisoner to discover reality.

Heidegger uses the lesson of the third stage to demolish the correspondence theory of truth—a fine definition! Truth is correspondence with a correspondence, the latter itself corresponds with a correspondence, and so forth. Judgment is based on knowledge which in turn is based on a prior correspondence with something corresponding, which in turn is based on another correspondence with something corresponding. Since the correspondence theory depends on knowledge and knowledge depends on prior correspondence corresponding, the theory leads to a paradox and not to the essence of truth.

In the fourth stage, the prisoner is returned to the cave. He is unable to see in the dark. He tells his fellow prisoners that the shadows are not real. They do not believe him and are convinced he returned to the cave to regain his vision. Heidegger interprets the return to darkness as death. Living life as an illusion is akin to death. Life exists only for those in the world.

My paper reinforced Heidegger's contention. It argued that truth cannot be equated with perceived knowledge, as yesterday's truths become today's untruths. I illustrated the point by recalling man's changing views of the nature of the universe:

> For 1,400 years, the world recognized as true the Ptolemaic theory of a geocentric universe. Nicolas Copernicus (1473–1543), a Polish astronomer, challenged this theory. From his observations, he developed a heliocentric concept: the earth and the planets revolve around the sun. But it was not until the leading scientist of the early seventeenth century, Galileo Galilei (1564–1642), endorsed the Copernican theory that it gained prominence. Over time, the old truth was discarded and a new truth adopted. More than twenty years prior to the publication of *Being and Time*, Albert Einstein disproved the bedrock of Newton's theory. Einstein demonstrated that gravity was not a force and accordingly, space and time and the universe were relative and not absolute. With the discovery of Einstein's new truth—relativity—an old truth faded away: "Likewise what has formerly been uncovered sinks back again, hidden and disguised."

I liked my paper. I even gave thought to expanding it and submitting it to a philosophical journal for publication. My plan was dashed when my paper was returned. Although Carman said it was better than the earlier one, he paradoxically gave it the same grade, B. This time I accepted David's advice and did not ask for a meeting.

Although I got the graduate school equivalent of a failing grade, I did not even consider for a second that I had failed. I liked the course, and enjoyed writing and researching my papers. My papers were on point. More important, I understood Heidegger.

The brain controls every aspect of our life: cognition, speech, motion, hearing, sight, smell, taste. A lesion in the brain, for example, can cause loss of speech even though the vocal cords, larynx, tongue, and other aids to speech are intact. One's legs may be in perfect condition but unusable if the neurons controlling motion have been damaged.

The philosophy and psychiatry departments jointly offered a course called Mind, Brain, and Space, taught by two teachers, one in the philosophy department and the other in psychology. I was sure the course was for me, but after the first few classes, I gave thought to dropping it.

The philosophy professor conducted the opening sessions. His specialty was logic. He discussed whether the hole in the donut was a part of the donut and whether mirrors reverse left and right. My classmates, a mixture of philosophy and psychology majors, were animated. Not me. I found the subject matter trivial.

Students were asked to make fifteen-minute oral presentations backed up by written papers submitted a few days before the presentation. Those speaking on philosophical topics went first. I did not commit to speak and, in fact, was absent on that day. Irene's cousin once removed was getting married. The groom's parents were hosting a dinner in New Jersey. Irene insisted I attend. She said, "What am I going to tell my relatives? Sidney has a class and cannot come?" I wanted to hear what the philosophy students had to say, but I owed a lot to Irene. So, off I went to New Jersey.

The next part of the course was led by the psychology professor.

I understood the readings in the philosophy phase but not the first assignment in psychology. Then I remembered Max Pollack, a world-renowned neuropsychologist who taught at City College. At a party, I spied Pollack sitting alone on a bench. He was in his eighties and in poor health. I sat down and we talked and never stopped until the party was over. On the way home, Irene commented, "You were not very social. In the past, you hardly talked to Max. At parties, you talk to the wheelers and dealers. This time, you avoided them and spent the whole time talking to Max. You have changed." She was right. I replied, "Max is a brilliant man. He taught neuropsychology at CUNY. Since Max was willing to suffer me, I had no need for other company."

I called Pollack and told him I was having trouble with the Mind, Brain, and Space course. I asked if I could meet with him. He said, "I'm housebound and lonely. I don't sleep well at night, so I stay in bed until about noon. Come any time in the afternoon and a day of your choosing." I chose Monday, the day of the class. Pollack lived on West End Avenue, a few blocks from the subway that goes to 116th Street and Broadway, the stop for Columbia. After Pollack, I took the subway to Columbia and class.

The first reading assignment described case studies of patients suffering from spatial neglect, i.e., they were unable to see or sense on one side. An object on the blocked side emitting a noxious odor could neither be seen nor smelled. When the object was moved, the patient could both see and smell it. Pollack glanced at the case study and exclaimed, "I wrote the seminal paper more than thirty years ago. Let me get it." Pollack held forth for an hour. He was so good. Pollack knew more about the studies than what was contained in the readings. At the end of our session, so did I.

I asked Pollack for a topic for an oral presentation. He opened the *New York Times* to the obituary section and said, "Here is an obit on Pierre Salinger. In his final stage of life, he suffered from aphasia. That should be an interesting subject."

That day, I loved the class. I spoke several times, evoking comments such as, "That's right. Nice insight." And another time, "That's a billion dollar question." To which I replied, "By calling it a billion dollar question, you do not mean that you do not know the answer. You mean nobody knows." "Right," said the professor. "We have had hundreds of years of autopsy of the brain and recently, cat scans and MRIs. Still, there is so much about the brain that we do not know."

After class, I asked if I could make my oral presentation on aphasia. He nodded his head approvingly. Gone were all thoughts of dropping the course.

As required, a few days before my oral presentation, I submitted a written outline of my presentation. I showed it to Pollack on the day of my presentation. Pollack liked it.

My turn came last. The professor said, "I am saving the best for last. Sidney submitted an excellent written presentation. I have made copies for the class. Ready, Sidney?"

The other students used their papers as a crutch. I had the advantage of forty years of experience making oral arguments in court. I talked extemporaneously. My talk followed my written presentation much as court arguments followed my briefs. I paused at times and asked for and fielded questions from the students, and one from the professor. When I finished, both professors clapped.

My research on aphasia led to the topic for my final paper, the relationship between the communication center of the brain and handedness. I entitled my paper "On Parle Avec L'Hemisphere Gauche: Broca's Rule." The title was deceptive. As I explained in my paper, Broca's rule was a theory, not a rule

In 1865, Paul Broca announced that the left hemisphere controls speech. Ever since he did this, it has been referred to as Broca's rule. His findings were based on postmortems of aphasics. They revealed a direct relationship between a lesion in the left hemisphere and aphasia. The rule holds, however, only for right-handed persons. A true lefthander's communication center is located in the right hemisphere. A lesion in the left hemisphere of a left-handed person did not affect speech. One in the right did. This discovery was made after Broca's death. In my paper, I traced the origin of this speech center to handedness. I relied on medical studies, academic papers, and statistical analysis. Below is a section of my paper without the many citations:

> Before speech, hand gestures were probably used as a means of communication. Studies show that at least 90 percent of the population is right-handed. Because of cross wiring in the brain, the right hand is controlled by the left hemisphere. Thus this hemisphere may have assumed an early role in communication. When, as an evolutionary process, oral language replaced hand gestures and freed hands to assume other manual tasks, the left hemisphere may have already been developed for communication: "This preexisting specialization would have favored the development of left hemisphere specialization for oral language and, as communications had previously been relying on gestures, the left hemisphere would also have taken in charge hand control." The deaf speak through hand signs. Their language, codified as American Sign Language, is as complex as oral speech. Some words are expressed with signs made only with one hand ("Class 1"); other words with two hands, but with one hand dominant and the other passive ("Class 2"). Still other words require the active use of both hands ("Class 3").

A rule should admit of no exceptions. Because of the variations of left-handed persons ranging from true to favoring the left, and the occasional location of the language center of right-handed persons in the right hemisphere, Broca's rule is not a rule but a theory. I concluded, "Based solely on postmortem analysis of damaged brains, Broca found a relationship between handedness and the language center. Crossed aphasia, crossed non-aphasia, and anomalous aphasia reduced Broca's rule to a theory. Almost 150 years later, with the advent of modern technology, neuroimaging on living subjects confirms Broca's theory that a relationship between the language center and handedness exists."

The brain is the most important human organ. Because it enables us to think, it distinguishes man from all other entities. Now, as I approached seventy-two, I had, for the first time, some comprehension of the many functions performed by the brain and the physical disabilities caused by internal traumas to the brain.

I got an A. I told my children and anyone else who would listen that Columbia does not give a grade higher than A. How did I know? If an A+ were awarded, I would have gotten one in Mind, Brain, and Space.

My third course was William James, Pragmatism, and Religion. It was taught by Wayne Proudfoot, an ordained minister and a chaired professor of religion. At the opening session, he said that in addition to a final paper, each student must lead a class session on that week's assigned reading material and submit, in advance, a written outline. The outline, he cautioned, must do more than restate the assignment; the student should discuss related but different subjects. He asked for volunteers for the next week's assignment. I raised my hand. By discharging my responsibility early, I would be free to concentrate on the readings and pursue my journey: a search for a rational basis for a belief in God. My reading in pragmatism, that most utilitarian of all branches of philosophy, might provide an answer.

James was a neuropsychologist. He had written the standard medical text book on the brain, still regarded as authoritative on many points over a hundred years later. He was not, however, one dimensional. He was also a philosopher and a leading advocate of pragmatism. The course focused on Jamesean philosophy. My assignment covered eight lectures delivered in 1906 at the Lowell Institute. The lectures dealt in part with the battle between monism and pluralism. I used the controversy as a springboard for my presentation and combined it with a religious essay I had written earlier, published by my synagogue and distributed to congregants over the High Holidays. It discussed how Stephen W. Hawking, the celebrated astrophysicist, discerned the hand of God in the creation of the universe and how astronomers, perched in observatories searching the heavens through high-powered telescopes, claimed almost to see God. God was now in the forefront of my thoughts.

My outline began with James's flat-out rejection of the belief that the Judeo-Christian god alone rules and that all other gods are false. This doctrine, he said, would deny the religious beliefs of most of the inhabitants of the world and credit only that of an elite minority. It would also run counter to the dictates of pragmatism. If a belief in a god, any god at all, a graven image, a sun god, or even a multiplicity of gods, grants the believer solace, than his religion works. As a pragmatist, James chose pluralism, a belief in more than one god. I then reworked my synagogue essay on Hawking:

> Stephen W. Hawking is perhaps the world's leading astrophysicist. In his book *The Theory of Everything*, he states that at the moment of the hot big bang, the universe was infinitely hot, as it had zero size. As the universe expanded, the temperature of the radiation was spread over an increasing area and accordingly decreased. One second after the big bang, the temperature was ten thousand million degrees, about a thousand times the temperature at the center of the sun. About one hundred seconds later, the temperature fell to one thousand million degrees, the temperature within the hottest stars. At this temperature, protons and neutrons combined to make helium nuclei and small amounts of lithium and beryllium. Eventually, as the universe continued to expand and the temperature decreased, electrons and nuclei lacked the energy to overcome the electromagnetic attraction between them and combined to form atoms. Hawking's explanation is based upon the Nobel Prize-winning work of Arno Penzias and Robert Wilson, who discovered the microwave background of radiation. Based on their study, Hawking concluded, "We are therefore thoroughly confident that we have the right picture, at least back to about one second after the big bang."
>
> Hawking states that the temperature at the moment of the big bang and the rate of expansion of the universe were perfectly coordinated to a degree that eliminates the possibility of randomness. He explains that if one second after the big bang, the rate of expansion had been larger or the temperature had been smaller by even one part in a hundred thousand million the universe would not have been able to support life as we know it and would have recollapsed before it reached its present size. Hawking concludes that such precise calibration must be attributed to an "act of a God who intended to create beings like us."

I reserved for my final paper an in-depth investigation into pluralism and the afterlife.

For the balance of the term, I read the assignments and listened to my classmates' presentations. Most were brilliant. What a pleasure to listen!

Towards the end of the term, I began work on my final paper. It held more than academic interest; it presented my personal search for God. I entitled the paper, "The Science of Religion: A Jamesean Solution to the Problem of the Supernatural."

In an earlier paper, I rejected Heidegger's attempt to align science and religion. Science is fact; religion is faith. James, unlike Heidegger, found a factual basis for religion and a pragmatic reason for a belief in the supernatural and the afterlife.

James rejects the absolute position of the empiricists, those who deny God because there is insufficient evidence of his existence. James claims that they in fact believe the evidence is "absolutely sufficient, only it makes the other way." He considers them to be as dogmatic as the "infallible popes." James also rejects the views of the rationalists who are certain that God exists. He finds their position doctrinaire and authoritative. The phrase "must be," made in answer to every religious challenge, is a particular source of irritation to him.

James resolves the controversy between the two absolutes with the word "maybe," the possibility that the supernatural exists. To obtain evidence, James collected the religious experiences of others, which he published as *Varieties of Religious Experiences*. James carefully selected his subjects. All were rational, most were highly intelligent, and many were scientists. As a psychologist, James was qualified to evaluate the experiences. Some he discredited by tracing the experience they described to a source other than the supernatural. There were, however, too many that could not be otherwise explained. As James so perfectly explained it, "[A] universal proposition can be made untrue by a particular instance. If you wish to upset the law that all crows are black, you mustn't seek to show that no crows are; it is enough that you prove one single crow to be white." If only one reported case called into being or could be traced to a supernatural act, James had his white crow.

To a pragmatist, a belief is of no importance unless it has consequences. If God's existence makes no difference, then "the philosophical disputes collapse into insignificance." If his existence does make a difference, "on pragmatic principles we can not reject any hypothesis if consequences flow useful to life." James finds that a belief in the supernatural does make a difference in the lives of the believers: "The real significance of a belief in God is that it can produce religious experiences, and, from these experiences, a communion with God that can change the direction of a person's life." To deny God to those who have experienced his presence "is an awful thing for you, if you are one of those whose lives are stayed on such experiences."

James turned to the afterlife. He addressed the question of whether our personalities can live on after our death and the cessation of the brain. James asks a question that could not be answered in his time and cannot be answered today. What empowers the brain to function? James had studied many autopsies of the brain and knew the results of thousands of others. None answered the question. Since James's time, the brain has been the subject of high-tech examinations. These too have yielded no answer. James suggests that perhaps a third force empowers the brain and after death revives our personalities. I was intrigued and decided to pursue the question.

I asked the psychology professor in my Mind, Brain, and Space course, "Does anyone know what enables the billions of cells in the brain to perform its many functions?" He quickly replied, "Don't even try to take me there. I'm not going." There is, I realize, a fear of the unknown.

Consistent with his rejection of monism, James also believed all mankind will live on in the afterworld. He rejected the claim that only followers of one church can achieve salvation: "Let us at any rate not decide adversely on our own claim, whose grounds we feel directly, because we cannot decide favorably on the alien claims, whose grounds we cannot feel at all. That would be letting blindness lay down the law to sight."

Based on Jamesean philosophy I had my answer: every person has his own personal god living within his wider self. His god empowers his brain during life and his spirit in the afterlife.

I found support for my belief in two instances in which my life was spared by what I perceived as intervention by a third force. The first occurred during the recovery period from hip surgery. The second happened while I was on vacation in Italy.

In 1981, I underwent hip replacement surgery. As was usual at that time, I was to spend two weeks in the hospital. Near the end of the stay, I had difficulty breathing and thought I was running a fever. I called the nursing station and asked to have my temperature taken. The nurse said, "Temperatures are taken at five. You will have to wait." I was indignant: "Have you ever heard of a patient asking to have his temperature taken out of turn? Mark it right now on my chart that you rejected my request." I guess it was harder to add an entry than to take my temperature because a few minutes later the nurse found that I was running a fever. The resident doctor on the floor was called. He said, "Too late to take an x-ray. The facilities close in thirty minutes. We'll schedule it for the morning." I was perplexed. X-rays were still available. Why wait? "No, we won't. There is still time. I want an x-ray right now." Off we went. The x-ray showed that I had a life-threatening pulmonary embolism. My surgeon was notified. He ordered that I be confined to bed, placed in an oxygen tent, and given medicine to dissolve the embolism. Had I not received immediate attention, a second and third embolism would likely have been formed and quite possibly lodged in my heart or brain. Death would surely have followed.

I had no prior knowledge of embolisms, not even an inkling of their relationship to surgery. I also had no idea of a connection between my breathing problem and fever. Nor was I conscious that my condition was critical. Why did I demand immediate attention? At the time, I had no answer. Now I do. A third force took control of my brain. It transmitted the messages that saved my life.

In May of 1998, Irene and I planned to attend an international convention in Florence. We also planned to spend five days traveling around Italy before going to Florence. The Italian members were the hosts. I asked a member of the Italian delegation to recommend a place for us to stay pending our arrival in Florence. He recommended Portovenere, a mediaeval town just south of the Cinque Terre. We stayed in a hotel originally built as a nunnery. The hotel fronted on a harbor where fishing boats were moored. The harbor led to Shelley's Bay, where the poet had drowned.

I was then a strong swimmer, swimming daily almost a mile. On our next to last day, I went for a swim in the harbor. I picked a point on the other shore lying due west and swam for some time before checking my direction. When I looked up, I saw that I had been turned and was swimming at a right angle to my course. I tried to change direction but could not. The current was too powerful and was carrying me out to sea. I spotted an enormous rock slightly off course. I stopped fighting until I was close to the rock and then made a strenuous effort to reach it. As I got closer to the rock, I felt the current abating. I touched bottom and stood. The water reached to my chest. I walked to the rock and rested against it. I was dehydrated, hypothermic, and exhausted. I could see the current rushing by on the windward side, but the water looked almost calm on the leeward. I took a few steps to that side and confirmed my impression. My swim shoes made it possible for me to walk on the stones lining the bottom. Alternating walking and swimming in shallow water, I made it back to the harbor. Irene was waiting for me on the shore. "That was some long swim. You have been gone for more than an hour," she said. I replied, "It could have been a lot longer."

The next day, I walked along the shore until I was parallel with the rock. I saw that it was more than a rock emerging from the sea but a barrier or breakwater giving protection from the current, a phenomenon unobserved and unknown to me that day in the water. Why did I head for the rock? Nothing in my experience or consciousness can account for it. The answer: a third force took control and guided me there.

In pragmatism, it is not necessary for a belief to be rooted in inconvertible facts. It is sufficient if the fact is reasonably based. The alternative to a third force is my own comprehension, a function of my brain. But since we do not know what empowers the brain to function, until that mystery is solved, I will adhere to Jamesean philosophy and credit a third force, a god living within me.

Proudfoot asked us to pick up our papers in his office at the beginning of the spring term. I was in St. Croix. When I returned at the end of March, I did not retrieve my paper. The professor must have found holes in my theory. I only got a B+. What really mattered was not my grade or Proudfoot's comments on my paper. I had found my god. My journey was ended.

FALL 2005

SAD IS HOW I felt as I contemplated my final semester. Sad that this happy period of my life was drawing to a close. Learning in a structured environment, presided over by brilliant professors and surrounded by enthusiastic young students was a near perfect world. Soon it would end.

I liked all my studies but was partial to philosophy. For my final two courses, I indulged in my favorite; I took two philosophy courses: Nietzsche and the ancient schools of Greek philosophers, the Skeptics and the Stoics.

The Nietzsche professor, Robert Guay, was a visiting instructor who had not yet found a home. The prior year, he taught at Temple. Married and with two children, he commuted from Philadelphia. His doctorate was in philosophy. He was also a classicist and fluent in German and Italian. He had a fine sense of humor and was an enthusiastic teacher.

The class had more than its quota of brilliant students. Guay let them shine. He also tolerated the less than brilliant. The combination of Nietzsche's iconoclastic philosophy, the level of my fellow students, and the professor's leadership made the class the high-water mark of my graduate school years.

The assigned reading was *Beyond Good and Evil* and *Daybreak*. Guay provided a list of additional works by the philosopher and essays and treatises about him.

I started with certain preconceptions. Hitler admired Nietzsche and declared him to be the National Socialist Party's philosopher. Hitler and his followers exalted the state over the individual, were intensely nationalistic, chauvinistic, and xenophobic. And, of course, the Nazis were anti-Semitic. Ergo, Nietzschean philosophy was hateful. It provided the justification for the Nazi creed.

Nietzsche was a prolific writer. Further, perhaps more books, essays, and treatises have been written about him than about any other philosopher. I read extensively and, this time, not solely for the purpose of writing a paper. Rather, I wanted to make my own decision as to whether Nietzschean philosophy provided the ideological basis for Nazism, From my readings, I found my preconceptions were wrong.

Nietzsche was a stern social critic who lambasted deep-seated views of Christian morality held sacred for almost two thousand years. He condemned with passion prevailing ideologies of his countrymen. He was also a prophet whose dire prophesies for the future of Germany came to pass. During my study, Nietzsche emerged as a thinker who promoted the individual over the state, aesthetics over ascetics, the creative man of culture over all others. His ideal was the individual who overcomes custom and tradition by questioning assumptions concerning truth, logic, beliefs, culture, and values. Such a person, endowed also with artistic talent and exceptional mental ability, he considered the highest form of man: the *Übermensch* (overman), the embodiment of the philosopher of the future. From my readings, I concluded that Nietzsche was not a socialist or a nationalist, and that he opposed racial thinking. In fact, he opposed every principle of the National Socialist Party, the political party claiming him as the sponsor of its ideology. I examined those prevailing doctrines of Nietzsche's time which carried over to and dominated German thinking in Hitler's time. Nietzsche's outspoken rejection of these tenets commended him to my soul. They are restated below.

Chauvinism and the glorification of the military were fundamental to the Nazi party and Germans of the late nineteenth century; Nietzsche opposed both.

In Nietzsche's time, a loose confederation of German-speaking states, led by Prussia, became one nation through three wars. The first began in 1864, and the last, a war with France, ended in 1870. The three wars transformed the confederation into the German Empire, a nation comprised of all German-speaking states, with the exception of Austria.

Prussia's victories demonstrated the superiority of its army and its military plans. The German populace, however, saw in these wars, particularly the victory over France, a lot more than success on the battlefield. They saw nothing less than the triumph of German culture and moral excellence and the precursor of victories to come. The nation's sentiments were expressed by the novelist Gustav Freytag:

> There never was a struggle fought for a greater ideal than this; never perhaps did Nemesis strike down the guilty so violently; never perhaps did any army have such warmth, such inspiration, and such a deep poetic sense of the fact that the dreadful work of the battlefields served a higher ethical purpose; never perhaps did the working of divine providence in the apportionment of rewards and punishment seem in human terms to be so just and logical as on this occasion. Hundreds of thousands perceived this as the poetry of the historical process.

Nietzsche was not part of the chorus. With a prescience that was to mark so much of his thinking, he predicted that defeat could better serve a nation than a misconceived victory. He wrote:

"Of all the evil consequences following in the wake of the recent war against France, the worst is … to the effect that German culture also won a victory … and deserves to be decorated with the laurels appropriate to such extraordinary events and successes. This delusion is highly pernicious [and] capable of converting our victory into a complete defeat: the defeat, even the death, of German culture for the benefit of the German empire."

Keith Ansell-Pearson aptly described Nietzsche's opinion of the newly formed nation: "Nietzsche now saw the German Reich of Bismarck as a state which prided itself on philistinism advancing its power politics through racist, statist, and nationalist policies. He believed that classical liberal values had been corrupted by the nationalist cause and culture had been overtaken by a dangerous philistinism."

The religious fervor arising from the German victory in the war with France carried over to World War I. That unnecessary war sprang from a belief hatched in 1870, and nurtured by feelings of nationalism and chauvinism, that God was on Germany's side. It was her mission to rule the world.

In the aftermath of World War I, Germany was not only defeated, but the German economy was destroyed. The mark became valueless. The country entered into a period of hyperinflation. In World War II, in effect a continuation of World War I, Germany was a battlefield. After the war, the country, bombed and devastated, was partitioned into two satellite states, one controlled by the United States, Great Britain, and France, and the other by the Soviet Union.

The Nazis were virulent anti-Semites; the Germans of Nietzsche's time despised the Jew; Nietzsche was an anti anti-Semite and in the context of his time, in much of his thinking, he was a philo-Semite.

In the wake of unification, extreme nationalistic sentiments swept through the country. It had an adverse effect on non-Aryans, particularly Jews. Although there were only five hundred thousand Jews living in Germany among a population of sixty million, anti-Semitism became a major political movement. The popular sentiment was that Germany had to be free of Jews (*judenfrei*) lest the Jews control the entire nation.

Nietzsche mocked that sentiment. He wrote, "That the Jews, if they wanted it—or if they were forced into it, which seems to be what the anti-Semites want—could even now have preponderance, indeed quite literally mastery over Europe, that is certain; that they are not working or planning for that is equally certain."

The anti-Semites branded the Jew a parasitic plant undermining the health of the newly formed German empire. Nietzsche turned the metaphor against them. The fertility of a society's soil, he declared, can be measured by the number of parasites it can endure. To Nietzsche, a pure race was sterile, while cross fertilization fosters and drives creative evolution.

Nietzsche divided Jews into four groups: the patriarchs of the Bible, the priests of the Second Temple, the Diaspora Jews of the medieval period, and the modern German Jews. He admired the first, third, and fourth groups, but not the priests. He believed they endorsed a moral code that based good and evil on actions the Jewish priests claimed were aligned with God's will. This moral code was adopted by the early Christians and, in Nietzsche's view, corrupted Christianity.

Critical comments on Jewish theology does not make one an anti-Semite. Just before his mental collapse in 1898, Nietzsche wrote "*Wilhelm, Bismarck, und alle Antisemiten abgeschafft*" (William, Bismarck, and All Anti-Semites Go Away). In the historical context of Germany in the late nineteenth century, Nietzsche was an anti anti-Semite.

Not every anti anti-Semite is a philo-Semite. Did Nietzsche approximate one? He wrote: "The Jews, however, are beyond any doubt the strongest, toughest, and purest race now living in Europe; they know how to prevail even under the worst conditions (even better than under favorable conditions), by means of virtues that today one would like to mark as vices."

Nietzsche's flattering comments about Jews and attacks on anti-Semites incited Eugen Dühring, a German philosopher, contemporary of Nietzsche and outspoken anti-Semite, to refer to Nietzsche as "Nietzsche the Jew."

Nietzsche socialized with Jews. His good friend Paul Rése was a

Jew. Nietzsche was a disciple of Richard Wagner, but broke with him over Wagner's strongly held anti-Semitic views. A rift occurred between Nietzsche and his sister when she married and endorsed the views of an outspoken anti-Semite. In the context of his environment, a country that hated Jews, Nietzsche's tolerant attitude made him a likely philo-Semite.

Insistence on conformity and intolerance of dissent; Nietzsche extolled the individual and the right of dissent

Fascism under Hitler required acceptance of Nazi principles and punished dissent with death and imprisonment. Such conformity was also a dominating principle during Nietzsche's time.

Nietzsche was an individualist who railed against thinking restricted by tradition. Morality based on custom was his principal target. Nietzsche called himself an immoralist. He was, but only in the sense that he did not follow traditional morality. His compatriots were taught from childhood to observe the teachings of Christianity. Nietzsche, in contrast, had only disdain for Christian morality. He traced its roots to the Jewish priests of the Second Temple, who decreed that "all offenses against Yahweh were punished and all devotion to him rewarded." Since it was the priests who interpreted the will of God, they became "indispensable everywhere," and reduced "everything that has any value in itself … to absolute worthlessness and even made the reverse of valuable by the parasitism of priests (or, if you choose, by the 'moral order of the world')."

Nietzsche distinguishes between two categories of morality, the narrow and the broad. The former applies to the tradition and customs of nineteenth century European Christian morality; the latter, to the conduct of life. Since men are not alike, but vary enormously, Nietzsche rejected the universal and unconditional application of narrow morality. He, however, did not propose its wholesale rejection. Certain evil acts proscribed by custom should rightfully be avoided and virtuous ones followed. Further, for weak individuals, who do not possess sound independent judgment and require certainty, a strict or narrow form of morality works. Rules make it unnecessary for them to make independent moral and ethical decisions. Nietzsche endorsed a broad or free form of morality because it recognizes that actions are inextricably bound to one's tradition, upbringing, psyche, and physical and mental state. That form of morality directs the individual to make use of his psychological and physiological attributes and thereby live an interesting, active, and worthy life.

A final paper was required. I gave thought to Nietzsche the social critic, and to making full use of my independent study. Guay, however, provided a list of suggested topics. Social critic was not among them. Although the professor said we could choose a different topic, I recalled my experience with Heidegger and Professor Carman and decided upon a Guay-selected topic. In truth, my outside reading equipped me to choose many of the suggested topics. I chose nihilism.

It is an important philosophical subject and I knew very little about it. The Nietzsche term paper provided an opportunity to learn about nihilism and make good use of my outside reading. I entitled my paper "Nietzsche: No Nihilist."

Nihilism, in strict Nietzchean terms, means God is dead. His death results in the destruction of all values. In so defining nihilism, Nietzsche emphasizes the despair and extreme pessimism of this doctrine and calls it a preference for a "certain nothing to a uncertain something, [a decision] to lie down and die, the sign of a despairing, mortally weary soul, however courageous the gesture of such a virtue may look." Nietzsche ascribes to a nihilist not only the "belief that everything deserves to perish but actually putting one's shoulder to the plough: one destroys."

Although there are currents of nihilism coursing through Nietzsche's writing, I concluded that when his work is fairly construed, Nietzsche was much more a humanist, the antithesis of a nihilist, than a nihilist.

Certain Nietzschean concepts are similar to those held by nihilists; the similarities, however, exist only on the surface. Nihilists reject traditional values on the ground that they have no real value. Nietzsche rejected such values because they were imposed by custom, directed to be followed slavishly regardless of whether suitable for the needs of the individual. Unlike the nihilist, Nietzsche believed that some traditional values should be observed. He urged a constant search for new values that would elevate and enhance man.

Nietzsche and the nihilists both mock truth but for different reasons. The nihilist believes truth does not exist, only despair. Nietzsche held that truth exists but recognized the harm caused when long-held beliefs are proved false and adherents refuse to abandon a false doctrine.

Nietzsche was an educator, a seeker of knowledge, and a lover of truth. His goal was to improve life through a philosopher of the future who would "introduce life-promoting ideals, values, and doctrines." When inconsistencies and contradictions in his works are set aside, and the focus is on his main thoughts, Nietzsche emerges more as a humanist than a nihilist. While Nietzsche was a bitter critic of the nationalistic and slave-like morality of Germans, he posited hope for the future in the form of a "Philosopher of the Future."

Nietzsche's new philosopher projected a bright future through the promotion of new values. Nietzsche described the qualities of greatness possessed by the new philosopher: "...the higher man, the higher soul, the higher duty, the higher responsibility, and the abundance of creative power and masterfulness—today the concept of greatness entails being noble." Nietzsche's vision of hope contrasts with the despair of the nihilist and strengthens my argument that he was not a nihilist.

Many Germans of Nietzsche's time saw in Otto von Bismarck, the Iron Chancellor who unified Germany, the embodiment of the New Philosopher. Nietzsche thought not. "He thinks and knows as much of philosophy as a peasant or a fraternity student." The statesman who piles up "another tower of Babel is strong! strong! strong and insane! Not great." Capping my argument with Nietzsche's denunciation of Bismarck as the New Philosopher, I took pleasure in rejecting Heidegger's claim made in 1940, that Hitler was the embodiment of Nietzsche's Philosopher of the Future. I said in my paper that if Nietzsche had been alive to hear the claim, he would have dismissed it with three words: stupid, stupid, stupid.

I got an A- on my paper and the course.

My love of Nietzsche did not end with the course. In St. Croix, I completed my reading of Nietzsche's published works. In addition, through the Internet, I accessed Columbia's library, and downloaded and printed articles on Nietzsche. Miracle of miracles. I was able to work as effectively on that island paradise as if I had remained in New York and traveled each day to the Columbia library. My plan was to complete my research on St. Croix and write my thesis on Nietzsche. Circumstances changed my plan and instead of Nietzsche, I wrote on Bismarck. More on that subject later.

The ancient Greeks were a strong influence on many of the philosophers I had studied and, yet, I was nearing the end of my studies without any course in Greek philosophy. It was time. The gap was filled by the course on the Skeptics and Stoics.

Socrates famously declared, "Of this I am sure, I know nothing." Socrates's declaration influenced me to return to school. If he knew nothing, what did that indicate about the state of my ignorance. In fact, I missed the point. Socrates was a disciple of the Skeptic school. What he meant was that things were so uncertain that even a wise man could know nothing.

The Pyrrhonian school of Skeptics, founded by Pyrrho after the death of Socrates, mocked his statement. Socrates was not a true skeptic, as he knew something; that is, the fact that he knew nothing. A true skeptic would say, "At the present time I know nothing, but I do not exclude the possibility that at some time I might know something."

The Stoics, represented by the sages Chrysippus and Zeno, were frequenters of the Stoa, an open-air marketplace where teachers and students gathered. They held, in contrast to the Skeptics, that "infallible knowledge of the world is possible, and that all normal human beings have a natural faculty to make secure discriminations between discoverable truths and falsehoods." The cognitive impression, the bastion of the Stoics' knowledge, was likened by Zeno to a closed fist, grasped so firmly that it cannot be dislodged even by the most eloquent rhetoric. The Stoics, however, limited knowledge to the sage, and his knowledge in turn was limited to facts that were indisputably true.

The differences between the Skeptics and the Stoics were blurred by movements within the groups. Some Skeptics believed it was possible to know something while adhering to the belief that most things were too uncertain and filled with doubt. Members of the Stoa, like the Skeptics, found doubt clouding virtually all facts. It was sometimes difficult to know whether a given argument was being made by a Stoic or a Skeptic.

The professor, Wolfgang Friedman, a man in his early forties, behaved as though he lived in the time of Ancient Greece. For example, although e-mail and electronic submissions were common tools at Columbia, he announced that he did not read his e-mail, or send e-mail, and would accept only hard copies of papers.

Two papers were required, a short mid-term paper and a much longer final paper. He asked each member of the class to confer with him in person on the topic of the mid-term paper.

When it was my turn, he greeted me with a hostile question: "What are you doing in my class?" This crotchety, young, intellectual snob who pretended the electronic age did not exist was taking me on. I answered his question literally: "I am a student in this great university in which you are an instructor and have elected to take the course." He was visibly angry and replied, "I am a professor, not an instructor. I see you are enrolled. I teach all the courses in Greek philosophy and you have not taken any. What are your qualifications for taking my course?"

There were no requirements for his class. I refused to back down. I said, "I have underestimated both of us. Almost fifty years ago, I received a doctorate in jurisprudence from the law school. After a successful career in the law, I retired and returned to Columbia. I have taken courses in Spinoza, Kant, Heidegger, William James, and this term, Nietzsche. I chose your course because I wanted to add Greek philosophers."

He actually smiled, something he never did in class. "What a great way to study philosophy. Take courses in all the stars. All right. What do you want to write your mid-term paper on?" I replied that phenomenology as developed by Heidegger was analogous to "signs" as reported by Sextus. I thought I would write on the origins of phenomenology by exploring the significance of "signs." He approved and then broke with his no e-mail rule. "A colleague teaching at Yale published a book on signs. I do not remember his name or the title of his book, although I have a copy at home. I will send you an e-mail with the information." I thanked him before replying with a smile, "What's an ancient Greek scholar like you doing using e-mail?" He smiled too and we shook hands pleasantly. That evening I received an e-mail from him with the information.

I was at the stage in my education where new information served as building blocks on an existing foundation. Heidegger's phenomenology, how things make their appearance, was based in part on Sextus's analysis of signs, a fact Heidegger acknowledged. To the ancient Greeks, the thing itself is apprehended by something else. The sight of a lactating woman is indicative that she has recently given birth. Or is it? Suppose the woman is a wet nurse? Hearing a bird's song arising from a thicket is indicative of the presence of a bird. Or is it a flute or a recording imitating a bird's song? Some signs can be misleading; others are infallible. Pores are in the latter category. They are invisible to the naked eye but their presence is made known through perspiration. If an actual sign, the word "exit," and the signified, an open door, are revealed at the same time, then the sign is not indicative. The sign must come before what it signifies; otherwise, the sign lacks significance.

Clear things do not need signs; they are apprehended by themselves. Unclear things are not apprehended at all. But things unclear for the moment or unclear through nature, such as disease, are apprehended through nature. For example, measles makes its appearance by a distinctive rash and high temperature, considered by the Greeks to be signs of the disease. Such indicative signs were the basis of the diagnoses of other diseases. Their treatment rested on recollective signs, i.e., illnesses were cured by certain recollected treatments. The cure made itself known after the treatment was successfully applied.

Friedman made no effort to reschedule three classes he could not attend. I assumed he had good reason. I missed the classes. He was an excellent lecturer. He also failed, in good time, to return mid-term papers. At a meeting to discuss my final paper, he told me my grade on the mid-term was B+. At the meeting, I discussed using the Ten Modes attributed to Aenisedemus and the Five Modes attributed to Agrippa in a debate between the leading Skeptics, Aenisedemus and Agrippa, and the leading Stoics, Chrysippus and Zeno. Their subject: do the gods exist?

Friedman thought the modes were not important and said, "For that reason, I did not cover them in class." I almost replied, "Well, if you had made up the three classes you missed, the class might have had the benefit of hearing your views on the modes. After all, Sextus thought they were important enough to be included in his writing." Instead, I said, "I'm a lawyer. The modes are useful tools for argument. I wish I had known them when I was active." He reluctantly agreed.

In my paper, I assigned the role of the affirmative to the Stoics. It was consistent with their beliefs. In the debate, the Skeptics do not deny the existence of the gods but, consistent with their philosophy, will suspend judgment as they detect ambiguity. To fortify the argument of the Skeptics, I had them rely on the modes. They raise doubts by challenging, for example, the infallibility of human perception by showing contradictions among the senses. A straight oar in water may appear to be bent. A waxed pomegranate may appear to be a real fruit. A painting, from a distance, may look three dimensional. Similarly our senses may lead us to conclude one way whereas an animal may reach a different conclusion. We may think that grass is green; a dog might conclude that grass is a different color. If we prefer our senses to that of a dog, we are making a biased judgment by preferring our sense of color to that of a dog. On this point, the Skeptics argue:

> The sensory perceptions of humans should not be preferred to those of animals. An animal's sense perception can exceed a human's. An animal, by smell, can track down wild beasts it cannot see (Sextus 1 64). Further, he said, when Odysseus returned home after an absence of thirty years, "[A]s Homer witnessed ... Odysseus [was] unknown by all the people in his household and recognized only by Argus. The dog was not deceived by the alteration to the man's body and did not abandon his 'apprehensive appearance' which he appears to have kept better than the humans."

In the debate, I introduced the modern concept of intelligent design. The Stoics argued that "intelligent design" is a sign that the gods exist. Here is the argument and refutation as I imagined it:

> Chrysippus: My friends, I will offer a new argument which I am sure you will accept. You will agree that the world has an exquisite design, some even call it "intelligent." Is that not a sign that a divine hand made the world?

> Aenesidemus: It appears that the world does have an exquisite

design, but for the world to be a signifier of the invisible, namely the gods, more is required. Would you say that the sign you speak of is so clear and unambiguous that all rational persons, not suffering from any mental or physical impediments, would consider the sign to be indicative of the gods? Do you think the ancient Hebrews comprehend that the world is wonderfully designed? Do you think they recognize Zeus or any of our other gods? Do you hold that the Persians, the Indians, the Scythian see the indicative sign as a signifier of the gods?

I liked the position of the Skeptics; they suspended judgment whenever they perceived a doubt. Many people, unfamiliar with the teachings of the Skeptics, use intuition and ambiguous perceptions as a substitute for knowledge. "It will surely rain. My joints tell me so." "That restaurant is good." They say these things when actually the speaker has no experience first or second hand. Such comments are part of everyday speech, harmless and escape notice except from those who have studied Greek philosophy..

I have been married to Irene for many years. I never questioned her assertions unsupported by facts. In fact, I was unaware of her tendency to state as facts what she really did not know. Then, I met the Skeptics. I adopted their approach. Poor Irene. Every time she violated the principles of the Skeptics, I pounced, "How do you know?" When, after expressing a baseless opinion, she asked my view; I replied, "I have no basis upon which to state an opinion."

I became very careful before stating a fact to Irene, a practice I am sure I had not followed with her or anyone else. Sometimes, she tried to test a view I expressed. With a gleam in her eyes, she asked, "How do you know that?" I replied by stating incontrovertible evidence if she challenged a statement of fact, or simply some evidence if I had expressed only an opinion. After satisfying her challenge, I smugly said, "If I say something, you can take it to the bank. Not like some people."

My grade for the class was B+; Irene gave me an F.

Fall 2006

A THESIS WAS THE LAST leg on my journey to a master's degree. I began researching early in 2006 and planned to complete the thesis during the fall semester of 2006.

Before a thesis can be undertaken, Columbia requires a one-thousand word outline, a bibliography, and approval of the project by two professors, one designated as first reader and the other as second. The thesis cannot exceed sixty pages, nor be less than forty. A student planning a thesis for the fall term must obtain the necessary approvals by August 15.

Nietzsche was my first choice. During the winter of 2006, I completed my reading of Nietzsche's translated works and, in addition, read several books and essays on the philosopher and his time.

In the spring, I wrote my proposal: "Nietzsche and German History: Antipodes." During Nietzsche's life, the German people were intensely nationalistic and chauvinistic. These strong patriotic feelings had much to do with the country's view on immigrants and on those who were not pure Aryans. They were outsiders, hated, and considered parasitic plants undermining the health of the budding German empire. Although Jews were an insignificant minority of the non-German population, they were the most despised. My plan was to portray Nietzsche as a social critic and an outspoken opponent of contemporary German ideology. He was at one pole and German history at the other. Hence, the tentative title of my thesis.

I sent the proposal to my young Nietzsche professor. He declined for a very good reason. He had obtained a tenure-track position at SUNY Buffalo and would be there in the fall.

My only contact in the history department was Itzvan Deak. He was, however, retired, an emeritus professor. To obtain a second reader, I sent the proposal to the chair of the history department requesting an adviser. She recommended Volker Berghahn, the Seth Low Professor of History. He agreed to serve as my thesis adviser, but suggested two changes.

He thought a second reader might complicate a project he could handle more efficiently alone. When I told him my school required two readers, he said, "I'll speak to the dean." When I mentioned my thesis involves Nietzsche and German history, he said he was familiar with Nietzsche.

The second dealt with the thesis proposal itself. He said, "A thesis on Nietzsche and German history is too broad. To treat the subject properly would require at least six hundred pages, enough for six PhD theses. Your topic must be narrowed."

In searching for a narrower subject, I found a reference suggesting Nietzsche and Bismarck may have been responsible for the rise of Hitler. I submitted a revised proposal: "Were Nietzsche and Bismarck Responsible for the Great German Catastrophe?" He dismissed the new proposal as being even more expansive. "I rejected your first proposal. Nietzsche and German history were too grand. Now you come back with Nietzsche, Bismarck, and German history. You cannot do justice to the subject. You are promising me pie in the sky. You must narrow the subject."

I got the point: my thesis should examine one aspect either of Nietzsche's thinking or Bismarck's career. I considered two topics: Nietzsche and the Jews or Bismarck's diplomacy in unifying Germany.

Berghahn's field was German history and Bismarck was central to it. It was also plain from my proposals and discussions at our meetings that I wanted Nietzsche. What was more important, making me happy or my adviser? I turned to Max Pollack for advice.

He said, "You are an unusual candidate for an advanced degree. You are fortunate to have a distinguished professor advising you. His interest is history. Please him and choose Bismarck. You can use your research on Nietzsche to write an article. Submit it to a philosophical journal. It will be read by two experts. If it is any good, it will be published. Abandon Nietzsche for now." In making my decision, I also weighed a comment by an eminent Nietzsche scholar. He said Nietzsche's philosophy would have been the same if he had never mentioned the Jews.

I met again with Berghahn. We agreed on Bismarck's diplomatic efforts in unifying Germany. At the meeting, we also talked about my future plans.

I would not be going on for a doctorate degree; I planned to concentrate on chess. My goal was to become a master in chess.

Berghahn was also a chess player. He understood the fascination of the game. We talked about strategy, tactics, opening moves, and responses. Then, he introduced chess as a way to evaluate Bismarck, the diplomat: "Did he play the diplomatic game the way a grand master plays chess?" I liked the analogy and vowed to use it.

I said I would prepare a new proposal. Berghahn said no; "You have written two proposals. That is enough." When I mentioned the requirement of a proposal approved by August 15, Berghahn said, "We don't need another proposal. Start by analyzing Bismarck's diplomacy in each of the wars, the second war with Denmark, the Austro-Prussian War, and the Franco-Prussian War. Do not include military affairs. Concentrate on Bismarck's diplomacy, and nothing else. Once I approve the middle sections, the beginning and end will, I predict, be easy to write. We will meet again when you have finished your draft on the war with Denmark."

The war with Denmark involved the fate of three independent duchies under Danish rule, Schleswig, Holstein, and Laurenburg. The Schleswig–Holstein question, as it became known in history, was so arcane and complex that Lord Palmerston, the great British Prime Minister and Foreign Secretary, quipped that there were only three men who understood it. One was dead, another went insane, and he, Palmerston, the third person, had forgotten all about it.

Palmerston was right; the issues were complicated. He was wrong, however, in not including Bismarck among the few who understood. Not only did Bismarck grasp all aspects of the question, but he made used of his knowledge to benefit his country.

Bismarck saw an opportunity to wrest the duchies from Danish rule. He knew annexing the duchies would involve Prussia in a war with Denmark. Bismarck did not fear a war with Denmark; Prussia would easily prevail. However, a major power, Prussia, attacking a small country, Denmark, would be seen by the other European nations as an intolerable disruption of the balance of power. They would align with Denmark and enter the war on Denmark's side. As Bismarck recounted in his memoirs, he did not want Prussia to bite on "a nut on which she might well have broken her teeth." Bismarck had to find a way to keep the other European countries on the sidelines.

The Prussian minister devised a strategy to neutralize the other powers using three international agreements and two laws passed by Denmark. The international laws were the ancient Treaty of Tribe of 1460, the Treaty of London of May 9, 1852, and two promises made by Denmark to Austria and Prussia in 1854 (the "Promises"). The Danish laws were the March Patent and a Danish constitution enacted in 1863. Bismarck's plan: persuade the European powers that the newly enacted Danish laws violated the treaties and the Promises.

In keeping with Berghahn's suggestion of measuring Bismarck as a diplomat against the standards of a grand master, I compared the five laws to the major pieces in chess (rook, knight, bishop, queen, and king).

In chess, it is important to move the pieces (with the exception of the king) to their most effective square. There they obtain maximum power, lend strength to coordinating pieces, and enable the chess master to dominate the game. The king starts at the center of the board. As early as possible, his majesty is moved to a safe corner. There he resides until the attacking pieces are removed from the board. Then, in the end game, the king emerges as a dominant attacking force.

I examined Bismarck's strategic use of the five laws, his chess pieces. He manipulated them with an adroitness worthy of a grand master. In the draft submitted to Berghahn, I showed how Bismarck used the many confusing and interconnecting elements of the question to achieve a major diplomatic victory. A brief description of the five laws follows:

> The Treaty of Ribe declared Schleswig, Holstein, and Laurenburg, independent states under the Danish king and commanded the king to maintain them "forever undivided." The principal duchies, Schleswig and Holstein—Laurenburg was tiny and its interests aligned with Holstein—were separated geographically by the Eider River and culturally by two different nationalities, Danish and German. Schleswig was mainly Danish. Its citizens wanted to be part of Denmark. Holstein and Laurenburg were German. They desired to be part of Germany. The ancient treaty did not, over time, correspond to the desires of nationalism that made "forever undivided" more fictitious than real.
>
> In 1848, Denmark, recognizing the nationalist sentiment in Schleswig, annexed it. The act, overwhelmingly approved by the citizens of Schleswig, separated that duchy from the other two and violated the "forever undivided" mandate of the Treaty of Ribe. The act gave rise to the first Prussian–Danish War. The Treaty of London ended the war. Under that treaty, the Danish annexation was annulled and the terms of the Treaty of Ribe reinstated. The London treaty declared an independent Denmark essential to the existing balance of power. To ensure her independence, the treaty preserved the duchies as a buffer

zone and made long-range provisions ensuring that the duchies remained subject to the Danish crown.

After the treaty was signed, Prussian troops remained in Holstein. In order to induce Prussia to withdraw her troops, Denmark made the Promises, the most important being to enact a uniform constitution, for Denmark and the duchies. This constitution, however, required the approval of Danish citizens and, separately, a majority of the population residing in each of the duchies. The Danes and the citizens of Schleswig approved the law. The Holsteiners and the citizens of Laurenburg, overwhelmingly German, voted against the constitution. They held a veto power over the Danish legislature. It could not pass a constitution as long as Holstein and Laurenburg had to approve. Denmark was frustrated.

In response to its inability to govern, the Danish legislature enacted the March Patent of 1863, providing for a constitution only for Denmark and Schleswig. Since the law would not affect Holstein and Laurenburg, their approval was deemed unnecessary. The March Patent was followed by a new constitution for Denmark and Schleswig, enacted in November of 1863, to take effect on January 1, 1864.

The March Patent and the new constitution indirectly failed to comply with the command of "forever undivided" contained in the two international treaties. A separate law for Schleswig would arguably divide the inseparable duchies. A separate law would also directly violate the requirement, contained in the Promises, of a uniform law for Denmark and the duchies.

Although Prussia's interests were not directly affected by the new Danish constitution, Bismarck used it both to disguise his plan to seize the duchies and to taint Denmark. He told the European powers that the integrity of an international treaty (the Treaty of London) signed by the brother of King William, the present Prussian king, was at stake. In addition, the Promises made by Denmark to a Prussian king obligated Denmark to pass uniform laws for herself and the duchies. The new constitution violated both the treaty and the Promises. Bismarck then moved his king from the corner of the board to the center. He declared: the honor of a king of Prussia was at stake; Prussia was prepared to go to war to uphold the honor of her royal family. If, however, Denmark annulled its constitution, war would be averted.

At an international conference held in London, the other

nations attempted to persuade Denmark to repeal its constitution. It refused for what it thought was a good reason, falsely planted by Bismarck. He had led them to believe that if Prussia attacked, England would come to Denmark's aid.

The wily Bismarck converted a naive Denmark into an international criminal and painted Prussia, intent on seizing Danish territory, as the high-minded defender of international law.

Denmark bore the brunt of international disfavor; England, France, and Russia remained on the sidelines.

Bismarck then persuaded the one remaining great power, Austria, to join with Prussia in a war against Denmark. The Danes were quickly defeated. Under the peace treaty, Denmark ceded to the victors joint control over Schleswig, Holstein, and Laurenburg.

The duchies were not the only area in which Prussia and Austria shared influence. They dominated the German confederation, a loose group of German speaking states. Bismarck wanted to exclude Austria from both spheres of influence. Then Prussia, as the sole dominant power, could force unification under Prussian hegemony. These events would have to await the second war, the Austro-Prussian War.

I submitted my draft to Berghahn. He said, "Your treatment of the Schleswig–Holstein question is good. Follow that same approach in analyzing Bismarck's diplomacy in the next war, the Austro-Prussian War." I thought of saying, "See here, Berghahn, I make no promises. I cannot follow a cookie-cutter pattern in dealing with the intrigue surrounding the Austro-Prussian War. I will handle it my way, which may be very different from my approach to the Danish War." Instead, I looked straight into the eyes of this very fine scholar who was devoting time to a student who had no further ambition than to play chess. I said, "Of course I will follow the same procedure in discussing the Austro-Prussian War." I then discussed my plan for the second war.

The Austro-Prussian War

In the war with Denmark, Bismarck used deception to obtain his goal. He posed as a defender of international law and hid his intention to grab Danish land. In the Austro-Prussian War, Bismarck used a multi-faceted approach. Although deception was present, it was overshadowed by other tactics: rigorous negotiation, patience, and an exquisite sense of timing.

The Treaty of Vienna (1864) ended the war with Denmark. It placed the duchies under joint control of Austria and Prussia. Shortly after the peace conference, Bismarck began his negotiations with his former ally to obtain the duchies for Prussia. He played upon Austria's fear of losing its empire in Italy.

Lombardy, an Italian state, was formerly owned by Austria. An uprising by the Lombardians wrested the province from Austria. She feared that her remaining territory in Italy, Venetia, might soon be lost by a rising tide of Italian nationalism supported by Louis Napoleon of France. Bismarck offered Prussian assistance in a war to recover Lombardy or to retain Venetia provided Austria renounced her interests in the duchies. In essence, Bismarck asked Austria to give up her present rights for a benefit in the future that might never come to pass. Still smarting from Berghahn's comment that my written proposals promised "pie in the sky," I applied the expression to Bismarck's indefinite, contingent promise to Austria:

> The Treaty of Vienna, signed on August 1, 1864, ended the war with Denmark. That same month, Bismark and his king met with Bernhard Rechberg, the Austrian foreign minister, and his king in the Hapsburg palace of Schönbrunn to divide the spoils. Bismarck's position was clear. He wanted to annex the Duchies in exchange for an implied promise to help Austria reacquire Lombardy and defend Venetia if and when war with Italy occurred. He argued that it was in Austria's interest to favor Prussia and, for herself, settle for pie in the sky.

When Austria declined the offer, Bismarck discussed another approach, trade Austria's interest in the duchies for Prussian land. Austria made several reasonable offers. Bismarck rejected them. He knew King William would never willingly cede an inch of Prussian territory. Why did Bismarck engage in a charade? He was buying time to prepare for a war against Austria. He also needed time to trick Austria into making a blunder. He would then use her blunder as the cause of the war.

When it became clear to Austria a land swap was not a reasonable possibility, Bismarck adopted another stalling tactic. He offered a "fat sum" for the release of Austria's claim.

At first, King Franz Joseph, as a matter of principle, rejected cash as a prize of war. He reasoned great nations do not engage in war for money. The king, however, was persuaded by Austria's desperate financial condition to reject principle and accept money.

Bismarck enlisted the support of his personal banker, Gerson Bleichröder, to determine the extent of Austria's financial woes. Bleichröder reported that the country was on the brink of financial collapse. International money markets were not only skeptical about lending money to Austria but were themselves in a chaotic condition. In my thesis, I quoted the banker's report:

> Austria's financial plight worse even than generally known … new expenses exceeding the already anticipated "gigantic deficit"; efforts at obtaining help from international banking world unsuccessful because financiers had their misgivings about Austrian solidity and about Hungarian loyalty to the Hapsburgs. Potential lenders were themselves caught in the calamity in which the principal money markets of Europe find themselves at the present time, on the one hand because of the flowering of manufacturing for exports and on the other hand because of the reckless speculation in transatlantic funds and raw material.

If Bismarck wanted to avert war, the conditions were ripe for a financial settlement. Austria had a great need for funds and Prussia was a wealthy nation. Bismarck's negotiators mentioned "a large sum" and a "fat sum," but refused to quantify "large" or "fat." Why? Bismarck refused to name an amount. He was not interested in a settlement. He wanted war.

Austria, frustrated by Bismarck's intransigence, proposed action guaranteed to anger Bismarck. Austria asked the Diet of the confederation to decide the fate of the duchies, including whether a German prince should assume the ducal throne. If put to a vote, the Diet would decide in favor of the prince. Prussia would lose the duchies and have achieved no gain for her victory over Denmark.

Austria's proposal had unintentional adverse consequences for that nation. It violated the Treaty of Vienna which placed the duchies under the joint control of Prussia and Austria. Bismarck used Austria's wrongful act to rally the Prussian people for war against Austria. The minister president also used Austria's violation of an international treaty to persuade the other powers that Austria was in the wrong. They remained neutral, considering it a local squabble between two former allies. Once again, the Prussian wizard made another country commit actions that caused a war that *he* wanted.

War broke out in mid-June of 1866 and was over on July 3 when the Prussian army won a decisive victory at Köningratz. Bismarck and Napoleon had entered into an agreement prior to the outbreak of war. Under its terms, France agreed to remain neutral in a war between Prussia and Austria, and Prussia agreed to remain neutral in a war involving Austria's territories in Italy. After Prussia's victory at Köningratz, Napoleon violated his agreement of neutrality. He informed King William and Bismarck that Austria had ceded Venetia to France. Napoleon offered to mediate an end to the war with the implied threat to intervene if Prussia rejected mediation.

In my thesis, I described the rash action proposed by King William and the Prussian military leaders. They wanted to continue the war against Austria and take on France too. Bismarck, however, counseled restraint. He wanted a peace treaty ending the war with Austria and postponing the inevitable war with France. His views prevailed.

As explained in my thesis:

> The king and his military staff rejected mediation. Flush with victory, they advocated war with France rather than peace with Austria. Bismarck, however, favored peace provided it met Prussia's immediate political needs: 'It is a political maxim after a victory not to enquire how much you can squeeze out of your opponent, but only to consider what was politically necessary.' He considered, as politically necessary, a free hand for Prussia with the North German states and mild peace terms so as not to humiliate Austria and compel her to seek revenge. In his memoirs, he wrote: "We had to avoid wounding Austria too severely; we had to avoid leaving behind in her any unnecessary bitterness of feeling or desire for revenge; we ought rather to reserve the possibility of becoming friends again with our adversary of the moment, and in any case to regard the Austrian state as a piece on the European chessboard ... If Austria were severely injured, she would become the ally of France and of every other opponent of ours; she would even sacrifice her anti-Russian interests for the sake of revenge on Prussia."

The Treaty of Prague ended the war. Prussia achieved Bismarck's objectives. Schleswig and Holstein were annexed to Prussia and she obtained control over the German states north of the Main.

Austria was not the only loser. Although not as obvious, France lost as well. Napoleon had gambled on a long war that would weaken both Prussia and Austria. France would then emerge as the only power on the continent and unite the separate states in the form of a United States of Europe under France's control. Instead, the war was short. Prussia emerged as a military and political powerhouse and a direct threat to France.

Separating France and Germany were the three independent south German states, Bavaria, Baden, and Wurtemberg. Bismarck wanted to join them with Prussia and the north German states, but faced serious obstacles both with the states themselves and their neighbor, France. As to the states, religion was one bone of contention. The southern states were Catholic, and Prussia and the northern states were Protestant. A second was the hostility of the states' ruling classes. Unification would reduce the princes to mere dukes and their subjects to Prussian rule. A third was the southern population's dislike and distrust of Prussia. Separatism was a creed among the citizens of the southern states.

France's objections were neither spiritual, personal, nor status related. Her objection was based on her own security. France felt threatened by Germany, the aggressive and powerful nation to the north. Her safety depended on a buffer zone, the very one created by the independent south German states. Unification of those states with Prussia would eliminate the buffer and endanger France. The Treaty of Prague, which ended the Austro-Prussian War, specifically addressed the southern states and forbade Prussia from interfering with their independence.

Bismarck believed war with France was inevitable. He needed time, however, to organize the north German states, gain military and political support of the south German states, and lure France into a declaration of war.

I handed in my draft of Bismarck's diplomacy in the wake of the Austro-Prussian War. Then, we met. Again, Berghahn said, "I have suggested certain changes. Please consider them. In dealing with Bismarck and the Franco-Prussian War, remember to deal only with diplomacy and not military strategy." He mentioned the Ems telegram and said it was important. I wanted to disagree: "The role of the Ems telegram is overrated. Both leaders wanted war. It would have erupted even if the Ems telegram had not been sent." Instead, I smiled and agreed. I then said, "When we started, I had difficulty narrowing my subject because I did not know it well enough. If I were to begin again, I would write about the role of the Cologne Minden Railroad in the Austro-Prussian War. In that way, my proposal would have had meat and not offered pie in the sky." He laughed. We shook hands and he gave my shoulder a friendly tap. I silently forgave him for his earlier "pie in the sky" slap.

The Franco-Prussian War

Napoleon violated his agreement with Bismarck to remain neutral in the Austro-Prussian War. That act made him the Prussian minister's enemy, a fact Napoleon failed to grasp. Napoleon, at first, reposed trust and confidence in Bismarck. He responded with ploys designed to frustrate, torment, and humiliate Napoleon.

In taunting Napoleon, Bismarck identified Napoleon's Achilles heel. He was a pretender to the throne of France. Unlike a legitimate monarch, Napoleon needed sensation after sensation to maintain his royal position. As Bismarck observed, "A king of Prussia can suffer misfortunes and even humiliation, but the old loyalty remains. The adventurer on the throne possesses no such heritage of confidence. He must always produce an effect. His safety depends on his personal prestige, and to enhance it sensations must follow each other in rapid succession."

Shortly after the end of the Austro-Prussian War, Napoleon sought a sensation. He proposed to Bismarck a new European order. France would acquire Belgium, a French-speaking nation, and Luxembourg and Prussia would acquire the south German states. Bismarck feigned acceptance of the plan. Viscount Benedetti, France's ambassador to Berlin at Bismarck's urging, prepared a draft for submission to William. Since the draft was handwritten by Benedetti, its source could not be impeached. The prime minister then turned on his would-be partner and publicly revealed the proposal. Napoleon's audacious plan discredited him in the courts of Great Britain and Russia. In the process, Bismarck gained their respect as a leader who valued peace and the preservation of the balance of power.

The resulting furor caused Napoleon to amend his plan. He abandoned annexation of Belgium and offered to purchase Luxembourg. It was owned by the Netherlands, whose king was in need of funds. Since there were Prussian troops garrisoned in the principality to protect its neutrality, the Dutch king sought Bismarck's advice. He referred the matter to the Prussian general staff. They advised that Luxembourg was an important defensive outpost for Germany and urged war in the event of a sale. Bismarck was not ready for war with France. He referred the issue for mediation by the great powers. They rejected Napoleon's request to purchase Luxembourg. The powers also guaranteed Luxembourg's independence. Since an international guarantee was in place, the Prussian troops in Luxembourg were not needed. They were directed to leave. Once again, Bismarck frustrated and humiliated Napoleon.

Bismarck entered into several agreements with the southern German states which had the effect of drawing them closer to Prussia. The agreements were perhaps technical violations of the Treaty of Prague, but too minor to justify a declaration of war by France. That would await the Spanish question.

A military coup in 1868 ousted Queen Isabella II of Spain. The rebels sought a new ruler. They offered the Spanish throne to several candidates, all of whom refused. They then offered it to a German prince, Leopold, the eldest son of Karl Anthony. Leopold was married to a Portuguese princess and his brother was the king of Romania. Leopold and his father, Karl Anthony, rejected the offer. Spain was a poor country and its throne the most unstable in Europe. Bismarck, however, urged father and son to reconsider. He said that they had a patriotic duty to accept. Leopold reluctantly changed his mind. Bismarck then unofficially publicly hinted that in the event of a war between France and Prussia over the succession of a German prince to the Spanish throne, Spain would enter on the side of Prussia. France took the bait. Placing a German prince on the Spanish throne was a knife in France's back. France was prepared to go to war unless Leopold renounced the Spanish throne. King William preferred peace to war, never favored Leopold's candidacy, and requested that Leopold renounce. He did. France achieved a diplomatic victory.

Napoleon could not let it rest. He wanted war, not peace. He informed William through emissaries sent to Ems, where the King was in residence, that he must apologize to Napoleon for the affront and promise never to permit Leopold to accept the throne. William was incensed and sent Bismarck a telegram from Ems describing the events. Bismarck rewrote the Ems telegram and circulated it to important Prussian embassies with instructions to publicize the telegram. The telegram persuaded other nations that Prussia had gone far enough in appeasing France in causing Leopold to give up the Spanish throne. France's insistence on additional conditions were not only unnecessary but provocative and an affront to King William.

Napoleon, however, saw it in a different light. Bismarck had tormented, needled, and frustrated him. He needed to even the score. France declared war ostensibly because William refused to apologize and agree never to support Leopold's candidacy.

The German forces were victorious at the Battle of Sedan, which for all practical purposes ended the war. In the aftermath, the southern states joined with the union to form one Germany, crowning William as the King. As one historian aptly put it, "Thus by a tragic combination of ill-luck, stupidity, and ignorance, France blundered into war with the greatest military power that Europe had ever seen, in a bad cause, with her army unready and without allies."

Berghahn approved my treatment of Bismarck's diplomacy leading up to the three wars. I then turned to writing the beginning and the end. In the opening pages, I said Bismarck's diplomacy would be measured against the criteria of a chess player. The thesis began:

Many people analogize war to a game of chess, and of course there are similarities.

An expert chess player has a plan before he makes his first move. He will attempt to control the four central squares with pawns and minor pieces, protect his king by castling early, and only when his king is protected will he open lines for his heavy artillery, his rooks and queen. As the game progresses, he will seek positional and material advantages leading to the capture of his opponent's king.

A weak player knows how the pieces move but does not grasp the significance of a plan and has no conception of positional and strategic play. All too often, he will attack with a few pieces, leaving the others inactive on their original squares and his king unprotected and standing in the middle. The threat will be countered and the beginner will be quickly defeated.

Did Otto von Bismarck, minister president of Prussia, play war like a grand master plays chess, or was he the beneficiary of circumstances?

Bismarck led his country to victory in three wars: the war against Denmark, the Austro-Prussian War; and the Franco-Prussian War. The result was that the German-speaking states, with the exception of Austria, were united under Prussian hegemony and history rewarded Bismarck with the title of Reichsgründer, the founder of the empire.

Bismarck often said that, "history could not be made ... certain basic issues had to work themselves out ... and one could not direct the flow of time into a chosen direction." If one were to accept these political maxims, then Bismarck should neither be blamed nor credited for the wars—he merely rode the tide of an unfolding history.

However, in contradistinction to his latter statements about history and circumstances in the years prior to 1864, Bismarck made clear that he would not be a passive minister-president, but would advocate war and war alone as a means to bring about Prussian unification of Germany. In 1859, while Bismarck served as the Prussian ambassador, he met Disraeli and told him of his new appointment as his country's foreign minister. He told

Disraeli, "I shall declare war on Austria, dissolve the German confederation, subjugate the middle and smaller states, and give Germany national unity under the control of Prussia." Disraeli wisely assessed Bismarck as a man the world should take notice of, "he means what he says."

In his first official speech as prime minister of Prussia, Bismarck informed the elected delegates, "The great questions of the day will not be decided by speeches and the resolutions of majorities ... but by iron and blood."

In this paper, I will analyze Bismarck's diplomacy leading up to the three wars, to determine whether he, or circumstances, brought about the unification of Germany and whether the wars were necessary.

After analyzing Bismarck's diplomatic feats, I concluded that Prussia could have achieved virtually the same ends without war. Bismarck may have been a great diplomat but, in my opinion, he was a poor statesman. Through efforts short of war, Holstein could have been obtained from Denmark, and Schleswig divided based on nationality, the southern part to the German confederation and the north to Denmark. War with Austria could similarly have been averted through the payment of money, far less than the cost of the war. Finally, there was no need to provoke a war with Napoleon to unite the southern states. In time, they would have joined the German nations. Forty-seven pages later, I reached my ending:

Bismarck declared his political credo: "The capacity to choose in each fleeting moment of a situation that which is ... most opportune." In the confrontations with Denmark, Austria, and France, circumstances provided a choice and Bismarck chose war.

Could Prussia have obtained the duchies other than through war with Denmark? Baron Blixen Finecke was an influential and well-connected Danish politician and a friend of Bismarck's since their student days at Göttingen. He recognized that Bismarck ... wanted the duchies "to fill out Prussia's thin body." He proposed a pragmatic solution: cede Holstein and Laurenburg to Prussia and Schleswig to Denmark with concessions to Germans living in Schleswig.

Had Bismarck pursued Finecke's proposal, lives would have been saved, not to mention the 22.5 million taler spent on the war.

Bismarck went to war with Austria to gain the duchies for Prussia, dissolve the confederation, and obtain hegemony north of the river Main. Prussia estimated that war with Austria would cost sixty million taler and thousands of lives. Could the money have been better spent to obtain a peaceful solution?

As discussed … the dispute with Austria could have been resolved by paying Austria a "very high" price. Werther, the Prussian ambassador to Vienna, had unofficially suggested forty million florin and received back an unofficial response: sixty million florin might suffice. Since one taler was worth two florins, a peaceful solution was much cheaper than war.

Bismarck was the mastermind behind the sparks that ignited the Franco-Prussian War. He wanted that war. Prussia's gains seemed great at the time but turned out to be more of a detriment than a benefit.

Although union with the south German states was achieved, they abandoned their independence "only after a grueling month of negotiations at Versailles, where they had repeatedly been threatened. Prussia would either take them over, cut them loose economically, or subvert them with jingoistic appeals to the masses."

Prior to unification, the south and the north were joined militarily by an offensive–defensive treaty and economically by the Zollparlament. The political unity achieved at the cost of freedom has been cited by historians as a cause for Germany's "escape into war" in 1914.

Prussia had an alternative to war: patience. Over time the south German states would of their own free will have embraced the benefits of political union.

Bismarck was the archetypal political grand master of war. He planned the conflicts, devised the strategies, and executed the tactics that led to swift and convincing victories. War, however, is a drastic and punitive act. It is not a game of chess. Bismarck had alternatives to war but did not make the right choice at the "opportune moment."

I was both sad and elated to finish my thesis. It marked the end of my academic career. That part was sad. The happy part was that I received a grade of A- on the thesis, and successfully concluded my quest for a master's degree. In the entire three-hundred-year history of the university, at seventy-four years of age, I was the oldest recipient of a master's degree in Modern European Studies.

In an early meeting, Berhahn mentioned that if he approved my thesis, I would graduate and then facetiously added, "You can celebrate with a big party." To me a big party was no jest. After all, how many seventy-four-year-old men receive a master's?

The graduation ceremony and my law school fiftieth reunion, of which I was chair, occurred over the same weekend in May. A party on Sunday of that weekend would celebrate both events.

I am a member of the University Club. Its building on Fifty-fourth Street and Fifth Avenue was designed by the Gilded Age's most famous architects, the firm of McKim, Mead, and White. The building is an example of Italian Renaissance Revival. Banquet rooms rival those in European palaces. When not in use for club dining, they are available for members' private parties. Typical of good clubs, the rates are low and the service, food, and amenities are first class.

Once I decided on a party, the University Club was the obvious choice. I reserved the Dwight Room, located on the ground floor. In times past, women were allowed only on the ground floor and the Dwight Room was where members dined with female guests.

Irene did not want to host a party in our house. With the Dwight Room reserved, she took over the party. With the help of a printer recommended by the University Club, she designed the invitations. On the cover was a caricature of me drawn several years earlier by Al Hirschfeld, shortly before his death at ninety-nine. On the inside cover was a copy of my master's diploma. The invitation was headed: "S.B.S.: J.D., M.A." The text read in part: "Sidney will receive an M.A. from Columbia next month, during the same week as his fiftieth law school reunion. And you are invited to help us celebrate this doubleheader. Anyone bringing a gift will be turned away at the door."

My professors, the deans of my graduate school and law school, and our relatives, friends, and many of my classmates from law school were invited. Sadly, no invitations were sent to my colleagues in graduate school. I could not remember a single name of any of my classmates.

My Wonderful Family

For most of the party, my wife and children stayed at my side. There was a good reason. Two weeks earlier, my left hip, replaced twenty-five years ago, had been replaced again. I was weak, walked with a cane, and needed to sit. They were there to help me. They also radiated love and approval. My thoughts turn to them. What follows is not an account of their lives or even an attempt to develop their character. It is a collection of snapshots; a full reckoning is the subject of my next book.

Irene graduated from Smith magna cum laude. She began reading when she was five. She reads constantly. Her range of knowledge extends from medieval times to the current fine works of fiction. She is an expert on Alexander Pope, having written her senior thesis on him.

Irene is also an elegant writer. At Smith, she was a stringer for the local newspaper. After graduation, she got a job with the *New York Post*. Jimmy Wechsler, a crusading liberal journalist, was the editor. He adopted Irene. Her first job was as an assistant to the editor. When Dorothy Schiff, the publisher, demoted Wechsler to editor of the editorial page, he also lost his assistant. Irene became a reporter. Her first story was on a Long Island group of migrant farm workers who were victims of a fire. Her story made the front page. It was followed by state and federal investigations of the living conditions of migrant farm workers.

Shortly after Irene's story appeared, we attended a private showing of a movie. Many people from the *Post*, including Schiff, were in attendance. Before the movie started, she made her way to our seats and said, "Irene, your first story deserves a Pulitzer. No wonder Jimmy wanted to keep you all to himself."

Irene left the *Post* shortly before the birth of our first child. Her career picked up years later with the *East Hampton Star*. When Emily and David were old enough for day camp, Irene showed her clippings to the editor, Everett Rattray. He snapped her up. She quickly became the star of the *Star*. She only worked, however, in the summer when we were in our home in Amagansett. Years later, the computer changed Irene's life.

In 1987, the *Star* computerized its operations and articles could be sent to Irene via a modem. She mastered the new form of telecommunications, XyWrite and CrossTalk, and during the fall, winter, and spring edited the newspaper from our home in New York. As the *Star* grew, so did Irene's role. She became associate editor, the highest position in that family-owned paper held by a non-family member.

Emily, our first born, was a whiz at math. Every summer, City College ran a program in mathematics at Hampshire College in Amherst, Massachusetts, for fifteen of New York's brightest and best high school seniors. When Emily was a junior, City College modified the program. It selected fourteen seniors and one junior, Emily Silverman. Emily's talent was not limited to mathematics. Her verbal skills were also astonishing. On her aptitude tests for admission to college, her math score was 800 and her verbals 750. The college advisor at her high school told us, "Emily's grades are excellent, her SAT scores sensational, and, to boot, she is gorgeous.

Emily is the complete package. She should pick one college, apply there, and that's all."

Emily toured the colleges. She liked Swarthmore best of all. She applied and was accepted.

In her freshman year, she chose philosophy as her major. I objected: "Emily, philosophers take fifty pages to say what could be said in one. You are a pure scientist. Stick with math and physics." She changed majors from philosophy to sociology. Again I objected: "Why do you want to spend your time reading why people shake hands? You're too good for that." She stayed with sociology and developed an interest in communal living. In her junior year, she asked if she could spend the summer in Israel living on a kibbutz and experience communal life. We agreed. That summer Emily got hooked on Israel. She returned to Swarthmore, graduated, and then departed for Israel. There she met her husband, an Englishman. They compared their libraries before they were married. Half the books he owned, she owned. The other half she wanted to read.

In Israel, Emily worked for groups seeking peace. She lived for months in an Arab village, teaching English in return for lessons in Arabic. She is fluent in both Hebrew and Arabic.

Her formal education continued when she was awarded a fellowship to the London School of Economics. She received a PhD. The college extended Emily's fellowship for two additional years of post-doctoral studies. While she was in London, the Technion in Haifa, Israel, one of the world's preeminent universities, offered Emily a position on its staff. She accepted and returned to Israel. She is a research fellow and an adjunct professor in the Technion's school of architecture and city planning. She also works as a consultant to the city of Tel Aviv.

David attended St. Bernard's School, an independent school for boys four blocks north of our home on Ninety-third Street. At the initial interview, we were introduced to the headmaster, David Westgate, a man of the old school, an Englishman with an Etonian accent. In his office was an outsized globe. He pointed to a country and asked David, "What country am I pointing at?" When David, five years old, replied England, Westgate asked him how he knew. "Easy," said David, "E-N-G-L-A-N-D spells England." Westgate smiled broadly. Apparently, very few entry-level students knew how to read. He said he would show David around and asked his assistant to give Irene and me a tour. Without hesitation, David went with the headmaster. When we saw them again, they were both laughing. David was accepted.

St. Bernard's ends at eighth grade. The boarding school advisor recommended Exeter. "David's excellent grades, top aptitude scores, and level of maturity make him a strong candidate for Exeter. We will recommend him highly." We took David to visit Exeter. He liked the school and Exeter, in turn, liked him. He was accepted.

At Exeter, David took enough courses in Greek and Latin to be one of five to receive a diploma in classics. Upon graduation, he was accepted at Yale.

David continued his studies in classics, graduated summa cum laude and Phi Beta Kappa. He won a fellowship at Berkeley, where he earned a masters and PhD. At Berkeley, he met his wife, a Stanford graduate who majored in comparative literature. She had taken a summer course in classics taught by David.

Teaching jobs in David's field are hard to find. He got a job at Reed College in Portland, Oregon. However, the job was not a tenure-track position. David's contract was renewable each year. Under no circumstances, however, could he stay at Reed for more than five years. He searched for a tenure-track job, attending a job conference in the spring. No success. He stayed at Reed for five years. Then, with a wife and two small children, he started all over again. This time in law school at Stanford.

Upon graduating from law school, David was offered jobs all over the country. He and his wife liked Portland. He accepted a job with the leading firm in Portland. He specialized in intellectual property and, after seven years, left his firm to become general counsel of an exciting high-tech company.

Julia was born fourteen years after Emily. Like Emily, she attended Spence, a private school for girls located on Ninety-first Street, two blocks south of our home. Then in ninth grade, she wanted a co-ed school. Like David, she went to Exeter.

When Julia was still a baby, Irene, on those nights she had to work late, took Julia to the *Star*. The whole office took turns taking care of Julia. It was during those years, Julia claimed, that newsprint entered her body. At ten, she wrote a column for the local book store on children's books. At Exeter, she was a top editor of the paper, the *Exonian*. At Brown, she was on the editorial board of the college newspaper. She took a semester off to work as an intern for the *Pittsburgh Gazette*. Upon graduation, she went to Little Rock, Arkansas, as a reporter for the *Arkansas Democratic Gazette*. There she met her future husband, a wildlife biologist. After two years in Little Rock, Julia and Jeff left for Spokane, Washington, when he was hired by the Fish and Wildlife Department of the State of Washington. She worked for the daily newspaper, the *Spokesman*. Two years later, he returned the favor when Julia was hired by the Associated Press in Portland. He transferred to a State of Washington Fish and Wildlife office just across the Oregon border and a short drive from Portland. They too liked Portland, bought a home, and married. In October of 2008, they became the parents of twins!

Julia's news stories for the Associated Press, bearing her byline, were regularly picked up by papers throughout the country and in England. Irene has a Google alert and reads Julia's stories. Irene marvels at Julia's leads. When Julia was only twenty-seven, Irene said, "Julia is a much better reporter than I ever was or ever could be. She is really something."

Irene's opinion was confirmed by the AP. After Hurricane Katrina, the AP sent five reporters to New Orleans. Julia was not only among the five, but most of the reports were signed by her. At the AP, Julia's beat is education and politics, two hot-button topics in Oregon. On a visit to her office, her boss mumbled to me, "She is so good."

My sister Yvonne was a gifted student. She ranked first in her class at Skidmore. She majored in philosophy. After graduation, she got a master's in English Literature from Columbia. She wrote her thesis on Faulkner. She then got a job with an ad agency. She hated the work. She married Joel Archer, a doctor, and got pregnant right away. She was happy to leave her job. Yvonne is a gifted pianist, loves classical music, and is a voracious reader

Yvonne is not only an intellectual but also an uncannily smart investor.

In 1969, Yvonne said, "You are looking for a bigger apartment and so are we. Brownstones can be bought for less cash down than co-ops. What do you say we buy a brownstone together and split it?" We agreed and Yvonne volunteered to conduct the initial search. About a week later, Yvonne called Irene: "I found a brownstone on Ninety-third Street, right off Fifth Avenue. It has two apartments, a lower duplex and an upper triplex. It is not right for us. One apartment is great and the other is not. Look at it anyway as it will give you an idea of what I am looking for." Irene looked and told Yvonne, "The lower duplex is great. You're right. Neither one of us would want the triplex." "What?" said Yvonne, "The triplex is great. Not the duplex."

Joel and I then looked. The building had no elevator. The triplex required a climb of three flights to reach the living room, dining room, and kitchen. Two bedrooms were on the fourth floor and three more on the fifth. Joel and Yvonne did not object to the climb.

In the duplex, the living room, dining area, kitchen, and bath were on the ground floor. On the first floor was a huge master bedroom and bath, and two other bedrooms sharing a bath. Joel and I liked both apartments. We agreed to buy the very first brownstone we saw and paid the asking price of $225,000.

Why didn't we negotiate? New York real estate was at rock bottom, as the city was in a financial crisis, with bankruptcy a distinct possibility. We were able to assume the mortgage of $150,000, making our total cash payment $75,000, which we split. Co-ops on Fifth Avenue were selling at $100,000 and up, plus the assumption of a mortgage. We got not an apartment but a whole house, with two apartments, for a fraction of what one comparable co-op would have cost. It was a bargain. We grabbed it.

We raised our families in the house and still live there. In the early years, when I came home from work there were either four kids in my living room, or they were upstairs with Aunt and Uncle. When Irene and I went away on a trip, our kids were happy to stay upstairs. We returned the favor when Yvonne and Joel went away. Unless we went out on the same night, we had little need for a babysitter.

My father was born in 1892 in Rosh Pina, a town in Palestine, then a Turkish territory and now the State of Israel. In the late nineteenth century, the Jews in Romania were the victims of a pogrom. Baron Rothschild rescued them, purchased land from Turkey, and moved the beleaguered Jews to Palestine. My grandfather and grandmother met in Rosh Pina, married, and had nine children. My grandmother taught in the town's one-room school house. She learned there was free education in England. The family emigrated from Palestine to England.

As a young man, my father went into business for himself. He became a merchant, importing goods from many different countries. He moved his office to Buenos Aires and then to New York. In addition to English, he was fluent in German, French, Spanish, and Italian. He loved music and the opera. He died in 1947, when I was fourteen. My memories include hearing my father, while listening to the radio program "Information Please," answer questions before the expert panel could.

The Not Well-Educated Person in my Family

My sister acquired our father's genes. I was not a reader, nor was I interested in music. I played games: stickball, stoop ball, handball, and later on baseball, basketball, and football. I even boxed. My father and mother joked, "Sidney will get into college because he plays football." And it almost happened that way.

After my father's death, my mother's sister Anne got a sales job in a haute couture dress shop in a fashionable location on New York's East Side. She moved from Chicago into our home in Brooklyn. My mother, who had worked for my father and was skilled in foreign exchange, got a job as a bookkeeper in an international auction house on Fifty-seventh Street in New York City. They decided to move to Manhattan and share an apartment. My sister was in college, but I was still in high school, James Madison High School, and would need to relocate.

I spoke to the football coach, Al Caruso, and told him that my family was moving to New York. He asked, "Are you a good student?" "Of course," I replied. "I'm an honor student." "I've a good friend I played with on the Giants. His name is Charlie Avedesian. He's the football coach at Horace Mann. I'll call Charlie and let you know."

Caruso did more than he promised. He called Avedesian, saw to it that my high school promptly send my academic records to Horace Mann, arranged for me to be interviewed, and offered advice. "The school is a prep school. Dress preppie, practice good manners, and speak only when spoken to. Make sure your responses are short and precise."

My mother called Yvonne who was in her junior year at Skidmore and asked, "What kind of clothes will Sidney need to look preppie?" Yvonne advised, "A maroon corduroy jacket, gray flannel pants, a button-down blue shirt, a striped tie, and white bucks." On Saturday, my mother took me to Rogers Peet in lower Manhattan for outfitting.

The interviewer was the soccer coach. He liked me. I was a big, strong kid. He asked me questions about football and school work. He said Horace Mann ran a summer school. Since I had entered high school in the spring term, I could graduate in three and a half years if I attended summer school. "We have a dormitory nearby where you can stay. The summer session will give you a taste of our academic program. Also, football practice starts before the fall term begins. You'll be right there." I was accepted, provided I enrolled in the summer session. I did.

In summer school, I learned that I was behind in my high school education. Horace Mann students read Chaucer in their junior year. I had not even heard of him. I was tutored by Mr. Oliver, a faculty member who lived at the dorm. He taught French but tutored me in other subjects. With his help, I made it through summer school.

I played end at Madison. At Horace Mann, there were two gifted players at that position. Barry Gadden, a former star of the soccer team, and Al Gordon, a post graduate student from Indiana. I was switched to center. My football career at Horace Mann almost ended when I suffered a mild brain concussion early in the very first game. I returned for the last game. I was probably good enough to play on Horace Mann's basketball team and was encouraged to try out. I declined. My studies needed me more than the basketball team.

By dint of hard work, I managed to finish in the middle of the class. That was no mean feat, as most of the students were very smart. At James Madison, I had ranked in the top 10 percent.

The college adviser suggested a number of schools likely to accept me. Colgate was among the colleges suggested. My mother checked with Yvonne. She said, "Many Colgate guys come to Skidmore. They seem very nice. My good friend is planning to marry a Colgate alum. I think the school is right for Sidney."

I applied, was interviewed by an alumnus in New York, and was accepted. The first time I saw Colgate was when I arrived there, two weeks before classes began, to try out for the freshman football team. I made second team at center. To indicate how bad I was, the player who made first team our freshman year failed to make the varsity team in his sophomore year, even though the team carried three centers.

I joined a fraternity. I partied a lot. I played intramural football and basketball. I also studied. I majored in history and graduated cum laude. I was not inspired to grow intellectually, but that, I have since concluded, was my fault. Many years later, I spoke with Russell Lloyd, a Colgate classmate. He told the following story: "I graduated last in our class with a D average. I enlisted in the marines, was a career officer retiring with the rank of lieutenant colonel. I then enrolled in a college in Virginia and got a masters and a PhD. I taught at the college. All right, my degrees were in administration and that was the subject I taught. Last in our class and I become a professor! I had it in me. Colgate failed to inspire me."

I think he was too harsh on Colgate. Many students took advantage of Colgate's academic programs. The fault was in Lloyd and to a lesser degree in me. We failed to avail ourselves of what Colgate had to offer.

After Colgate, I went to Columbia Law School. I worked hard, very hard for the first semester. I was on track for Law Review, the highest honor for first-term law students. Second semester, I was overconfident. I thought I was a natural at law and did not have to study. My grades slipped. I missed Law Review. In my second and third year, I dismissed the thought of being naturally gifted and worked hard. I was a Harlan Fiske Stone Scholar, a high academic award. I graduated thirteenth out of a class of three hundred.

PART THREE

CHESS AND CHESS COLLECTING

CHESS ENTERED MY LIFE on a family skiing trip. We were in Vermont. The day was cold and, by the afternoon, the trails were covered with ice. Irene and I skied in the morning but gave up after lunch. Our two children (Julia was born several years later) skied with a class in the afternoon while Irene and I explored the small Vermont ski town. I stopped at a game shop, and purchased a chess set and an instruction book. I thought it would make an interesting diversion for our children for the several hours after skiing and before dinner. When they returned, I showed them my new purchase and the book. Emily, age twelve, was interested; David, three years younger, was not. That afternoon, she and I began our study of chess. Chess became part of our routine. Every afternoon after skiing, we read the chess book and practiced making moves. On the last day of our vacation, we actually played a game. We made careless mistakes, took back moves, but we played.

Emily's interest in chess did not extend past that one game; mine never abated. On our return to New York, I purchased several instructional chess books and subscribed to *Chess Life*, a monthly chess magazine. In my spare time, I read the books and the instructional articles in *Chess Life* and replayed games played by leading chess players as reported in the magazine. It is easy to replay a game.

Chess moves are transcribed in an algebraic format. Each of the sixty-four squares of the board is marked horizontally by letters and vertically by numbers. The first square on white's left side is a1, the last, h1. On black's side, the corresponding squares are a8 and h8. The pieces are referred to by capitalizing their first initial, except for the knight who is referred to as N. Why? His royal highness, the king, preempts K. A move of a piece, such as the white knight from his initial square of g1 to f3, is recorded as Nf3. Other symbols are used, for example, to indicate the capture of a piece, a king in check, and checkmate. Chess players must learn chess notation both to be able to replay the games of others and record their own games.

When I believed I was ready to play, I challenged a friend, William Rand. He is a lawyer who lives a few blocks from my home. We played many games. He was better than I, won most of the games, and gloated over his victories. After one session of five games of which Rand won all, he cocked his head and said, "Sidney, we have to find a game you can win at." I longed for the time when I could say, "Willy, you know how you once wished we could find a game I could win at? Well, your wish has come true. The game is chess."

In the summertime, I played against Ed Butscher, a neighbor in Amagansett. He is Sylvia Plath's official biographer and a poet in his own right. He has also written a biography of Conrad Aiken. Although Butscher is a better natural player than I am, he loses most of the time. The reason: I read chess instruction books; Butscher reads great books. My reading teaches me to set traps for Butscher; his books provide no help for avoiding them.

Bruce Pandolfini's book *Chess Openings, Traps and Zaps*, describes about a hundred traps. They are generally set in the opening, between the fourth and tenth moves. The trap is usually baited with an unprotected pawn, or even two. A pawn is the least valuable chess piece, but many games are won by being a pawn ahead. So the bait is attractive. Sometimes a minor piece, a bishop, knight, or rook is used. A queen, the most powerful piece, may also serve as bait, but only if checkmate will soon follow.

Before our games, I replayed the opening moves in our most recent games. Then, I checked Pandofini's book to find traps based on Butscher's pattern of play. When we played, I waited for a sequence allowing the setting of a trap. Such a sequence usually occurred in the first game. I then baited the trap.

Butscher must have thought I was stupid to leave a pawn unprotected and promptly seized it. I then sprung into action. In short order, Butscher was defeated and worse, demoralized. In the subsequent games, he played so defensively that I had no need for traps in order to win.

Butscher is mild and non-competitive. It is difficult, therefore, to believe that winning or losing a game of chess could affect his disposition. It did. After a loss, he would pound the table and say, "I'm a stupid imbecile. How could I be so dumb?" Years later, I heard from a frequent guest at Butscher's house that after our games he was depressed, and often moaned, "I'm better than Silverman. How can I let him win?"

I tried to set traps against Rand. He avoided them. Perhaps he had read Pandolfini's book. My irregular play in setting the traps exposed me to strong counterplay. Rand took full advantage of my weakened positions. I gave up setting opening traps in games against him.

It is pleasant to play chess against friends. The real challenge comes in competition with others. For that reason, I joined the Manhattan Chess Club. The club was located in an office building adjacent to Carnegie Hall. I was a member for several months before I paid my first visit. One weekday night, we had tickets to a concert at Carnegie Hall. I left work early and went directly to the club. I asked Irene to meet me there. I was dressed in a suit and tie; everyone else in casual clothes. In the main room were about a dozen tables each topped with a chess set and a clock. Bookcases stacked with chess books lined the walls. There were several games going on. Other members were sitting on well-worn chairs and couches reading books. I inspected the shelves, selected a book, and sat down. I did not, however, want to read; I wanted to play. I noticed a young man in jeans and a tee shirt staring into space. I approached him and said, "Would you like to play a game?" "Okay, a five minute blitz," he said. That means that each player has no more than five minutes to make all his moves. One can lose, the usual way by resigning when your position is hopeless or by checkmate. A timed game introduces a third way, running out of time. Time is kept on a special chess clock having two faces and two levers. After making a move, the player hits the lever controlling the clock face closest to him. His clock stops running and his opponent's begins. The process is repeated with each move. I chose white and played an opening I thought I knew well.

The clock played no part in my defeat. With about three minutes remaining, my position was hopeless and his position overwhelming. "That won't happen again. I was nervous playing blitz. Play another. You can be white." It did not matter what color he was. With plenty of time left, I was so outplayed; I did not even have a move. We played a third. It was the same result, except my young opponent did not wait to be asked to play another. Without saying a word, he abruptly rose and walked back to his chair.

I asked the club manager, "Who is that?", pointing to my opponent. "He's Joel Benjamin, a grand master." I recognized the name and asked, "Why is no one playing with him?" He looked at me and laughed, "Who wants to play chess against Benjamin?" I got the point. Only a fool would challenge him to a game. I asked about the others in the room. He said, "They practically live here. All are very good, but none of Benjamin's caliber."

I spent the remaining two hours until Irene arrived, hiding behind a book. I wisely decided that the club was not a place for me to find a game. I continued, however, to look for other players. In a courtroom, I found Robert Boddington.

Boddington worked as an analyst for a group of investment companies. I represented one of the companies in a stockholder litigation. Boddington was involved in the case. When I told him I was a new chess player, we bonded.

Boddington played on his college chess team and was captain of it in his final year. He claimed he spent more time playing chess than on all other collegiate activities combined. Boddington achieved chess fame when a game he played against Edward Lasker, a famous chess player then in his early eighties, was reproduced in the *New York Times* and commented upon extensively by the chess editor. Although Boddington eventually lost, his position was better than Lasker's and only a careless error cost him the game. Boddington replayed the game for me from memory, explaining the reasons behind the moves and his fatal error.

Boddington was a bachelor. He was willing to play chess with me in exchange for a home-cooked meal. He came to my house about once a month. We must have played about fifty games. I never won. Boddington claimed occasionally, "You made me sweat." I did not believe for one moment that my play caused a problem for Boddington. He simply felt sorry for me.

After one of our games, Boddington said, "Why do you own only this awful plastic chess set? There are magnificent antique sets made of wood and ivory that regularly come up for auction in London. In fact, there is an auction there in a month. I'm on the mailing list and have a catalogue. I brought it with me. Would you like to see it?" I was emotionally attached to "this awful plastic set." It was the very one I had purchased that long-ago afternoon in Vermont. Nevertheless, I looked at the catalogue. Once I saw the beautiful sets displayed there, my attachment to my first set was over.

The catalogued sets fell into two categories: ornamental sets for display only, as they were too delicate for play, and playing sets made of ivory or wood. In the ivory playing sets, one side was left natural, the other side stained red. The wooden sets were made from boxwood and ebony. I focused on the playing sets; I did not understand the appeal of ornamental ones.

A trip to London would serve two purposes. I could attend the auction and also see my friend and client Pat Rooney. He had lived and worked in New York, but recently moved to London. I called Rooney and made a date with him coinciding with that of the auction.

My first day in London, I went to the auction house to inspect the sets to be sold the next day. The playing sets were Staunton design, the standard since 1849, the same style as my plastic set. There the similarities ended. The sets bearing the highest appraised value were made by Jaques & Son in the nineteenth century. The pieces were large, heavily weighted, and beautifully carved. The knights, as is standard in Staunton design, were made in the image of a horse's head. These knights, unlike any I had seen before, had teeth and muscles. When I held a piece in my hand, I derived a sensuous feeling.

I was successful at the auction. I got every set I wanted. My prize purchase was a large ivory Jaques set made in 1869. It came with a mahogany box, lined in velvet with individual pockets for each piece. I also purchased a Jaques wooden set, several chess boards, and an in Status Quo traveling set. The pieces in the traveling set were ivory pegs that fitted into holes in a board. The set was perfect for playing or practicing on a train or plane. The last two items in the auction were identical copies of a book entitled *Chess Men of the World*. The auctioneer asked for an opening bid of twenty pounds. I raised my paddle. Another raised the bid to twenty-five. I waited. There were no other bidders. The book was sold for twenty-five pounds. The same book was the final item. Again, the auctioneer asked for an opening bid of twenty pounds. I responded. As I anticipated, there were no other bidders.

After the auction, I paid for my items and arranged to have them shipped to New York. All of them that is, except for the book on chess men. That book I planned to read on the return trip to learn about decorative sets. As I was leaving, I was invited to a wine and cheese party at a nearby gallery. The party was hosted by a group called Chess Collectors International. At the party, I met Victor Keats, the author of *Chess Men of the World*. Keats, an Englishman, was not happy about my purchase of his book. He said, "Within two minutes, the price of my book declined by 25 percent." Keats asked if I planned to return in the fall for a chess auction at Christies. When I said I might, he invited me to dinner at his house on the night before the auction, handed me his card, and asked that I let him know if I would be able to accept his invitation.

I also met a German named Thomas Thomsen. He was and still is the president of Chess Collectors. Thomsen said that the group sponsored conventions every other year. Since Europeans outnumbered the American contingent by two to one, there were two meetings in Europe to every one in the United States. The purpose of the group was to study the history of chess and chess men. At the conventions, chess sets are auctioned and members give talks on chess-related subjects. "Our next meeting is in St. Petersburg. We plan a private showing of Russian chess sets at the Hermitage. Lothar Schmidt, a German grand master, and Yuri Averbach, a Russian grand master, will co-host the conference." He invited me to join. I agreed.

I was a happy man. In the course of one day, I had purchased beautiful chess sets and boards, was invited to the home of the author of a book on chess sets, and was asked by its president to join an international group of chess collectors. That night at dinner I told Rooney about my triumph. "Listen, Sidney," he said. "You're a mark. They have you tabbed as a rich American. The Englishman and the German want to sell you sets. Be careful." Rooney's observation seemed right. I was on my guard.

I returned to London in the fall and had dinner at Keats's home. Also invited was Yuri Averbach and Ernst Böhlen, a Swiss national residing in

Berne. Keats lived in Hampstead Heath in a large home alongside the park. He claimed he could walk directly to Buckingham Palace without crossing a street. In the parking area outside his house were two vintage Rolls Royces. Keats showed us his chess collection. The most impressive was a John Company set made in India in the eighteenth century. The white pieces represented the East India Company. The king's face resembled the then president of the company. The black forces were Indian and their king, the Maharajah. The bishops rode in chariots driven by a pair of horses. I asked Keats if he wanted to sell the set. He said, "I have no interest in selling. I also have no interest in buying. My collection is complete."

I got to know Thomsen fairly well. He was a guest at my house in New York. In turn, Irene and I spent a delightful weekend with him at his home in Frankfort. Thomsen never tried to sell me anything. I think now that he and Keats had no motive other than to welcome a new member. Chess collectors are a small and friendly group.

At the end of the evening, I offered to take Averbach home. It was a delightful finale to a wonderful evening. On the ride back, I discussed with this great Russian grand master a chess problem I encounter in games with Rand. Early in the game, he pins my knight with his bishop. The pin prevents the piece from moving. A piece that cannot move is useless on defense and becomes a target of attack. Averbach discussed several ways to answer the pin and equalize. He said, "It is not a refutation, but will give you compensation for your pinned knight." I no longer feared the pin, but I had an additional concern. Since Averbach's solutions were straightforward, why didn't I figure them out for myself?

The third guest at Keats's dinner, Böhlen, was to become a close friend. He was a frequent visitor to New York and spent the winter in Florida. He loved to play chess. He was a stronger player than I and almost always won. He downplayed his victories by telling me, "Several years ago I hired a chess teacher and trained with him for a tournament played in Switzerland. I didn't do well in the tournament but my game greatly improved." I filed that comment away. I thought, "Damn, I'd like to do that too, some day."

Böhlen and I played chess in New York, in Florida, and at my home in St. Croix, but our most memorable games were played at his home in Berne. Böhlen was a big drinker. I also liked to drink. In Switzerland, we combined chess and wine. During the course of one afternoon, we drank three bottles of wine and played many games of chess. I am, by nature, aggressive, always looking to attack. Böhlen plays a more balanced game. When the wine took effect, we were both wild and careless. It was enjoyable, but it was not chess.

A "simul" chess game is another diversion from pure chess. One player will simultaneously play games against many other players. He is the leader. He stands and walks from board to board after making a move. The other players are seated. They make their moves only when the leader is in front of their board. The leader then responds and moves on to the next board. During the course of the game, players resign by turning down their king. Occasionally, the leader will resign.

I played my first simul game against Gary Kasparov, who reigned for many years as the world champion. He was in New York preparing for a match against Anatoly Karpov, a former world champion Kasparov had deposed. His publicist, John Scanlon, had a home in Sag Harbor in the town of East Hampton. He invited celebrities living in and around East Hampton to a cocktail party at his house to meet Kasparov. Irene's newspaper received a press pass. The editor knew that I played chess and gave the pass to her.

After she told me about the event, I called Boddington. "Irene got a press pass to a public relations party for Kasparov. The invitation says he will take on all guests in a simul game. What opening should I play?" Boddington replied that the leader in a simul game has the opening move and added, "You can ask to play white. It is irregular but Kasparov won't care. Try the Torre Attack. Rumors have it that Kasparov does not like to defend against that opening. Record the game on an official score sheet. Study hard." Then laughing loudly he added, "Sidney, don't expect to win."

The party was on Saturday. Irene told me about it on Monday. I had five days to prepare. That day at 5:00 PM, I told my secretary to hold my calls. I closed my office door and pasted a please do not disturb sign on the door. I studied the Torre Attack for two hours and again on the bus home. After dinner, I continued to study. I repeated the regimen on Tuesday, Wednesday, and Thursday. On Friday, I took a late afternoon train to Amagansett. I saw a lot of people I knew on the train. I talked to no one. I just studied.

As soon as we arrived at Scanlon's party, I was offered a drink. Remembering the games with Böhlen in Berne, I asked for club soda. There were lots of "beautiful people" at the party, congregated around the guest of honor. When it was my turn, I greeted Kasparov with a broad smile and made an outrageous remark. He's so good and I'm so bad. Why not attempt to equalize our ranks by taunting him? I said, "You're a fairly good chess player because you devoted your life to the study of chess. The only thing you know is chess." Kasparov answered, "You are wrong. I graduated from college with a gold medal." I then said, "Bobby Fischer was a much better player than you." Although Kasparov generally refuses to discuss Fischer, he replied, "We have learned a lot since Fischer's time. If he hasn't kept up with advances, Fischer would not rank within the top twenty today. He was, however, farther ahead of his time in his day than I am today." There were others waiting, so I ended by saying that I looked forward to the simul game and asked if I could play white. He nodded his approval.

When the time came for the game, there were only nine willing to play. I recognized only one player, George Plimpton. I asked him if he was as good in chess as in his many other activities. He replied, "All I know about chess is how the pieces move." Before the games began, Kasparov said that we could choose our color. I took white. When Kasparov approached my board, I moved my queen's pawn two squares, beginning the Torre Attack. Kasparov moved his queen's pawn two squares, the usual reply. He returned to my board four times before commenting, "You have a score sheet but are not recording the moves." "You are no champion," I said. "I have prerecorded your moves." I then showed him the sheet, but only through move five. I had, in fact, recorded his moves through nine. It was not difficult to do. The moves were from the opening book. That is, they were those which over time have been adjudged the best for each side. If Kasparov had deviated from the book, I would have changed the score sheet.

Kasparov is known for his stare. It often intimidates his opponents. He glared at me for a full minute before moving on to the next board. I laughed and thought to myself, "Remember what Boddington said, 'Don't even think you will win.'" Well, maybe Kasparov will get overconfident. Kasparov may well have gotten overconfident but it made no difference. By move fifteen, I was mashed potatoes. Several moves later, I resigned. I took solace in the fact that I outlasted the eight other players, but then they had not studied for five days.

Irene took a picture of Kasparov and me. I had it framed. It occupied a prominent place on my desk. When clients and opposing attorneys came to my office, I pointed to the photograph and said, "The other guy is Gary Kasparov. We played chess together." I got more than my money's worth from that game.

My next simul games were at Chess Collectors conventions held in St. Petersburg, Vienna, and Philadelphia. Averbach was the leader in St. Petersburg. After the match, we had dinner together. I showed him my score sheet. He brushed it aside, saying, "I remember your game. You are a weak player. You defended a pawn I attacked with your queen. A queen is a bad defender as it can be chased. When that happened, the pawn fell and your game collapsed." I asked about the other players in the simul. He commented from memory about every one of the fifteen games played that evening.

At the Vienna conference, Lothar Schmidt was the leader of the simul game. He is a grand master from Germany. He was the referee in the world championship match between Spassky and Fischer. The match was known almost as much for the petty disputes between the players as for their excellent chess play. They could not even agree on the height of the table, the chairs, or the lighting. In fact, the only agreement Fischer and Spassky reached was the selection of Schmidt as the referee. It was easy to see why. The man is the epitome of fairness and equity.

The simul match was set for 5:00 PM. There were no convention activities scheduled for that afternoon. Irene and I were spending our time walking around the old city, shopping for gifts for our children and sweaters for ourselves. Around 3:00 PM, Irene noticed that I was distracted. "You are not paying attention to the beautiful shops, the splendid old buildings, and the interesting-looking people. What are you thinking about?" There was no sense dissembling. I confessed, "For some time, I have been replaying my moves if Lothar opens with the king's pawn. In that event, I will play the Sicilian defense. But what do I do if he opens with the queen's pawn? I know two good replies, but cannot decide between them. I'm nervous. I need to consult my chess books." Irene was incredulous. "Here we are in the magnificent city of Vienna. It is a beautiful afternoon and, what are you thinking about, the stupid chess game. Let's be frank. Regardless of whether Lothar opens the king's pawn, the queen's pawn, or the horse's behind pawn, you will go down to ignominious defeat. All right, go back to the room and study. I'll see you after the game."

Schmidt opened with his king's pawn. As planned, I responded by moving my c pawn, that is, my pawn on the third row from my right, thus initiating the Sicilian defense. A few moves later, I unintentionally deviated from the book by failing to take his d pawn. I could not believe I had made that mistake and so early in the game. I waited for punishment, but it never came. Thereafter, aware that I had erred, I played cautiously.

I was one of a few boards left. The others had resigned. The defeated players congregated behind the active boards and kibitzed. Since there were only a few left, it seemed that Lothar was back at my board a few seconds after he left. I was playing blitz against a grand master! Of course, I lost.

After the game, I commented to Schmidt, "You were lucky your knight was on the right square and that I could not dislodge him. Otherwise, I had a plan to checkmate you." He replied, "My pieces are always on the right squares." To a chess player, Schmidt was not bragging, but making a sound statement. As a game progresses, there are good and bad squares for pieces. An excellent player always has his pieces on the good squares. A weak player like me does not recognize the good squares until it is too late.

Every night the members ate dinner together. That evening, Schmidt came to our table and said to Irene, "Sidney played tough today." I smiled and, after he left, thanked her for releasing me early from our afternoon walk. In fact, the extra study time, as Irene had prophesied, had made no difference. I should have stayed with her.

When I returned to New York, I replayed my game against Schmidt for Boddington. When I came to my early mistake, I asked why I had not been punished. Boddington said, "It was not a mistake. You played a closed Sicilian. It is a book move and a good choice against a grand master."

Boddington played my position through to my defeat. Even with the luxury of time, he could not prevail. "Although material was even [we had each captured similar pieces], Schmidt's position was superior. There was no way for you to win."

My final simul game was played at the convention in Philadelphia. In that game, Averbach and Schmidt played as a team, taking turns making moves. Alternating moves is tougher on the leader, as he not only has to formulate a plan, but must communicate his plan to the other leader without talking.

I remembered my concern in Vienna over how to meet the queen's pawn opening. I was prepared in Philadelphia. I read about an opening move by black that can be used against all white's openings. The system is called the modern defense. The book advised, "Learn the modern. No longer do you have to worry about white's opening. Your moves are the same regardless of white's choice and your move, not white's, determines the opening phase." I studied the modern and used it in every game when I was black. I also played many games against the computer using the modern. I thought I knew every variation until I encountered the team of Averbach and Schmidt.

Early in the opening, Averbach moved a pawn to c4. It was an unusual move. It had not been used in any of the prior games. Although my book discussed the move, I had forgotten the suggested response. I had plenty of time to think but made the wrong move. I was the earliest board to resign.

The convention was a success for all except for me. I was depressed by my poor play. I was happy when the convention ended.

Although I continued to study and play games, there were long periods when I did neither. I blamed my failure to improve on one of two factors. Either I lacked talent or the long pauses between playing and studying chess, caused by my focus on work, were holding me back. Even when I played or studied my mind wandered to my law cases. The time was not ripe for chess.

By the end of 2005, I had concluded all my courses for a master's. I had only to write a thesis to graduate. I estimated that writing a thesis was the equivalent of one course. Since I had taken at least two courses each semester, I decided to make chess my second course.

Throughout the spring, summer, and fall, I divided my time between work on my thesis and chess. Then, when my thesis was finished, I concentrated solely on chess.

I read chess books for hours. In fact, over a six-month period, except for the *New York Times*, I only read chess books. I also purchased Fritz, a powerful computer chess program. Unlike human beings, Fritz was willing to play whenever I turned him on. At full strength, he is a monster capable of competing against the very best. He can, however, be downsized by removing most of his brains. When we started, I chose a level called friendly mode. Fritz started at 225, spotting a high handicap. Even in that brain-deprived state, Fritz won. After months of constant study and play, I improved and began beating Fritz. With each defeat, Fritz increased his strength. After playing with Fritz for a year, his handicap dropped to fifty-seven.

In my studies of chess, I had a secret weapon named Lev Alburt. He is an International grand master from Odessa, the Ukraine. In the 1980s, he defected from the Soviet Union and immigrated to the United States. Here, he was three times United States chess champion. Alburt is the author of many chess books, writes a monthly column for *Chess Life*, and is renowned as a chess teacher. Among his many books were two recent ones, *Chess Openings for White Explained* and *Chess Openings for Black Explained*. Alburt agreed to tutor me.

We began our lessons working on opening moves. They can extend for as few as five moves and as many as twenty. It was not, as I had previously thought, enough to learn one or two openings. To advance in chess, one must learn them all. Chess games may start out with one opening, but through different moves transpose into another. Failure to know the right moves and reasons behind them, when playing a variation, can be as devastating as a blunder in an ordinary opening.

I purchased Alburt's books. They cover all the openings, variations, and transpositions. The reasons behind each move are explained. Diagrams are frequently provided so that the reader does not need a chess board to follow the text. My close study of the books strengthened my game. Previously, I had trouble surviving the opening against Fritz. Now I was able to play on an equal level and even, on occasion, gain an advantage as the game headed into the middle game.

Alburt also wrote several books on strategy and tactics. They are important elements of the game. Strategy involves the formulation of a plan, the object of which may be to gain a material advantage by capturing a piece or pieces, or obtain a positional advantage that will ultimately lead to victory. A strategy must be flexible and subject to change depending on the changing positions on the board.

A plan is essential in chess. One who plays without a plan is known derisively as a patzer. It has been widely observed that a bad plan is better than no plan at all.

Tactics are the moves aimed at effecting the plan. When they work, they seem as graceful as a Grand Pas, as lyrical as a Mozart composition. I call them brilliancies. They are what makes chess a unique game and explains the reason it has endured for one thousand years.

A brilliancy usually begins with a sacrifice, known colloquially as a sac. In a sac, one's opponent is allowed to capture a piece only to find that after the capture, he has lost a more valuable piece. Thus, the sac is made to achieve a greater goal than what is immediately lost. Bobby Fischer once discussed a strategy where he sac, sac, sac, and then checkmated his opponent.

The tactical moves bear descriptive names that usually convey violence and invoke the image of war. Yet, chess is a quiet game in which concentration is extreme to the point where the surroundings are ignored. Once, Rand and I, returning from a trip, were playing chess while waiting for our luggage. When we finally looked up, our fellow passengers had left and only our bags were going round and round.

Tactics are different from ordinary moves. They are thrilling to execute. They are the highlights of the games of the great players. They appear, however, with less frequency than in games between average players. Grand masters know some three hundred different positions that give rise to sharp tactical play. When they find themselves vulnerable, they take defensive measures to protect against the attack. Not so the average player. When I lose a game through a brilliantly employed tactic, I praise my opponent. And when I win that way, I invariably receive a compliment. To win a game through tactics is satisfying. A game won by the carelessness or indifferent play of one's opponent is just another game.

The final stage is the end game. In an end game, most of the pieces are off the board and the king, passive during the opening and middle game, becomes a strong attacking force. The rules of chess allow for promotion. This occurs when a pawn reaches the eighth rank, six ranks advanced from its starting position. The pawn, the lowliest piece, can then be exchanged for a queen, the mightiest, or indeed for any other piece. It is rare but not unknown for a player to exchange his pawn for a piece other than the queen. Only a pawn can be promoted.

To prevail in an end game one must learn a difficult and spatially challenging system. Sometimes I get it, but most times I do not. Knowing my weakness in the end game, I try hard to avoid it by striving in the middle game to obtain a material advantage greater than a pawn or two. A good chess player will generally prevail in the end game if he is up by a pawn.

I was eager to test my progress in a face to face game. Fritz is a good opponent but he allows you to take back moves. When you do, he determines who won up to the point of the take back. The games continue, but do not count against Fritz's handicap. In playing humans, take backs are forbidden. Although my studies were far from over, I was eager for a test.

Irene planned to leave our home in St. Croix one January to spend a long weekend visiting a friend in Miami. Rand was a frequent visitor to St. Croix. I invited him for the days Irene would be gone. On previous visits, Rand and I played golf and chess. He generally won in both games. I did not expect to outplay him in golf, but hoped to win in chess.

The night of his arrival we played five games. I won three. I gained confidence from the first day's contest and went on to win most of the chess games while he was visiting me. Rand continued his domination over me in golf. Most days we played twenty-seven holes of golf and at least ten games of chess. We played chess at the golf course in between rounds, chess at home, and chess at the restaurants when we dined out.

Success against one's friends and Fritz count for nothing in the chess world. The only thing that matters is one's ranking. A ranking can be obtained only by entering tournaments and winning. My goal was to obtain the rank held by Boddington, that of 1800, entitling one to be called an expert. There are many higher rankings such as master, international master, and finally, Alburt's rank, international grand master, a rank eclipsed only by world champion. Before entering a tournament, I needed Alburt's advice about where and when I should enter, and whether I was ready.

We have a summer home in Amagansett, in the heart of the Hamptons. Alburt had commented that his wife liked Montauk, a nearby town. He said that they stay at a hotel in Montauk during the week and extend their vacation by spending a weekend in the home of a student. I wanted to invite Alburt, was certain he would accept, but needed an extra inducement to overcome Irene's aversion to entertaining two strangers.

I got past the stranger element when Alburt and his wife attended my graduation party. Irene liked them, though not enough to give up a weekend to play hostess. I needed something else. In came a most delightful package.

Our daughter Emily and her son Noam live in Israel. She suggested that Noam's father bring Noam to Amagansett; she would come four weeks later, spend a week with us, and then take Noam home. He is a handsome, charming young man. That summer he was nine and half years old. He is also an avid chess player. He had spent a week in a chess camp. He would benefit from Alburt's instruction. Noam's visit was enough to persuade Irene. I invited Alburt and his wife to spend a weekend before their vacation in Montauk and during the time when Noam would be with us.

We spent that entire weekend playing chess and solving chess puzzles created by Alburt. One highlight was a game Alburt played against Noam and me. Alburt played the black pieces, a slight disadvantage, and removed a rook, a great one. My strategy was to exchange pieces at every opportunity. After an even exchange, Alburt's starting handicap, down a rook, would be decisive as Noam and I would be up a rook, the only remaining strong piece. A rook with the help of the king can checkmate the opposing king.

Alburt employed an unusual opening, one with which I was unfamiliar. I stuck to fundamentals and survived the opening even though I fell for a trap that cost me a pawn. I then put my plan in operation and traded pieces and pawns. Through a series of moves, I could see a forced exchange of queens. Getting Alburt's queen off the board was crucial to my strategy. But it was Alburt's move.

He failed to protect a pawn, and I saw an opportunity to grab it and make up for my one opening mistake. Before I made my move, I consulted with Noam. That turned out to be my best move of the game. "Grandpa, if you take that pawn, Lev will fork your king and rook and when you move your king as you must, he will grab your rook and material will be even. Do you want to play an end game against him?" I listened to Noam, ignored the pawn trap, stuck to my plan, and exchanged queens. A few moves later, Alburt resigned. Noam and I, but especially Noam, had won, albeit with a big head start.

Noam and I played lots of games against Fritz. As we had against Alburt, Noam and I were a team and, of the two, I came away with the impression that Noam was the more valuable member. He saw the correct moves before I did and was better at anticipating Fritz's moves and plans. Noam declined to play a game against me and I knew why.

On one of Noam's prior visits, we had played and he was soundly beaten. He refused a rematch and, on subsequent visits, refused to play. Perhaps, he did not want to humiliate his grandfather. It is also likely he was disheartened by the initial loss. Noam, like his grandfather, likes to win.

At the time of Noam's defeat, he knew how the pieces moved, but not much more. Since then, Noam has been tutored by the coach of his class team and on his team plays number two board. Although he may not have believed it, he, at a mere nine and a half years of age, could beat me.

Chess Life publishes a listing of national chess tournaments. One was just right. It was scheduled for mid-September at the Marshall Chess Club in Greenwich Village. Eligible players were those whose ratings were less than 1,600, or unrated ones, of which I was one. The format required each player to play four games of fifty minutes each. It was scheduled for a Saturday in late September. Participants had to bring a chess set, board, and clock. Unless otherwise terminated by checkmate or resignation, a player, even if ahead, loses if he runs out of time. The fifty-minute rule brings sudden death.

My first opponent was a man about my age with a 1,500 rating. I played the opening well enough and as we entered the middle game; I captured a pawn with my bishop, allowing him to capture my bishop with a pawn. Chess pieces are assigned a numerical value. A bishop is worth three points; a pawn is worth only one. If he recaptured my bishop with a pawn, I planned to recapture his pawn with my knight. I would be down one point but my knight then threatened his queen. He would be forced to waste a move to save his queen. Two pawns plus an attack on his queen appeared to be a good sacrifice. I could not, however, analyze beyond two moves. A good player would have looked at least four moves ahead.

My opponent decided, however, not to capture my bishop, leaving me a pawn up. I could have continued play by taking another pawn with my bishop and thereby force the recapture of my bishop, but instead I moved it to safety and settled for a pawn up. As we entered the end game, I had less than two minutes remaining on my clock. My opponent had five. He offered a draw which means that the game ends in a tie. Knowing how weak I am in an end game, I accepted, even though I was ahead in material by one pawn.

My second, third, and fourth games were against children ranging in age from eleven to thirteen. I lost the second through bad play and was outplayed in the fourth. The third was my best game of all. My pieces were just where I needed them. With twenty minutes left on my clock, my opponent, hopelessly down in material, resigned.

For the game I won, I received one point; for the draw, I received half a point; for a total of one and a half points out of a possible four. Not good, but good enough for a temporary rating granted by the United States Chess Federation of 1270. Many tournaments exclude unrated players; none exclude rated ones. I was now eligible to enter chess tournaments anywhere in the world.

The next day, I reviewed my games with Alburt. He liked the way I attempted to sac my bishop for a pawn, but showed me how; if I had completed the sacrifice by taking another pawn with my bishop, forcing him to retake my bishop, my position would have been stronger. He knew my opponent. He said Cohen [my opponent] had once been an 1800. He was pleased that I had played to a draw. He was not so pleased about the two losses.

Alburt showed me how both games could have been won. The grand master was right of course, but if I possessed his playing skills, I'd have a ranking of 2500. He was not impressed by my win, dismissing it by saying, "Your opponent was a weak player."

I called Noam to tell him the news. I said the format was new and I was nervous. Words of wisdom flowed from his lips, "Grandpa, next time relax your mind and think, 'If I make that move what will he do.'"

The Marshall Club closed the main playing area for refurbishing. The club scheduled no more tournaments until the area was reopened several months later. When tournaments next resumed, I would be in St. Croix. There were tournaments scheduled in Brooklyn, Queens, and New Jersey, but I decided against a trip when I learned that I could join an online chess club, play competitive games, and enter the online club's tournaments to increase my rating. Why travel when I could play against a human opponent simply by turning on my computer and putting in the appropriate commands?

I joined the Internet Chess Club, the largest online chess club. I entered my rating and requested a game. All I could get were opponents who wanted to play blitz. Alburt wanted me to play ninety-minute games and thought the fifty-minute games at the Marshall were too brief. He preached taking my time. "Blitz," he cautioned, "is not a game for you."

I could not find an opponent online willing to play a long game. Perhaps I did not enter the right commands. I played five blitz games and lost all of them. My confidence level started to decline. It continued to decline when I split games against a friend, Dick Eisner. Before my intensive study, Eisner and I were about even. The evidence was clear: I was not improving enough to justify the effort. Maybe I should give up my dream of becoming a competitive chess player. I would make my decision when I returned to New York in April.

When we returned, I made the decision not to pursue chess. I did not possess the qualities necessary to become a good player, that is, the ability to decipher my opponents' plans, the patience to slowly build an attack, and the spatial vision to see many possible moves. Studying was not enough. One must have an innate feel for the game. I did not have the natural talent to succeed. Once I made my decision, I also lost interest in my chess collection.

The leading collectors did not play chess. The world's best chess players are not collectors. I cannot explain why my decision to forego chess competition turned me away from my collection, but it did.

After fifteen years of collecting, I owned about seventy sets. Among my prized possessions were John Company sets like the one I offered to buy from Keats. They are ornamental sets, not playing ones. Complete John Company sets rarely come on the market. Even sets missing some pieces are infrequently offered. To me a partial set was as beautiful as a full one. What difference does it make that the set has fourteen pawns instead of sixteen? Or that it has three rooks instead of four? I have two complete and three incomplete sets, perhaps the largest collection of such sets in the world.

I recently sold fifty sets at an auction in London. I retained my very best sets, but I am thinking now of selling them. All that is except for my two Jaques sets acquired at my first auction. I will give them to Noam.

Part Four

Health and Care

MY WEAK HEART

A FRIEND ONCE QUIPPED, "MONEY
isn't everything, health is 10 percent." I laughed. I thought about the
remark on two later occasions, *only then*, I did not laugh.

The first was when this friend was on his deathbed. Tubes were
inserted everywhere. He could barely speak. I said good-bye. He nodded.
The second occasion was in early April 2006, when I was diagnosed with
severe congestive heart failure.

Towards the end of our stay in St. Croix, I noticed that my left foot
was swollen without any obvious cause. I had a dry cough that persisted
despite repeated doses of cough medicine. I also had shortness of breath.
I entered these symptoms into a computer healthcare site and out came
heart failure. I refused to believe it. That very day, I played eighteen holes
of golf, swam a half mile, lifted weights, and went out for dinner. Yes, I
moved slowly and was tired, but that, I figured, was due to my age, seventy-
three. Surely my condition was not serious, certainly not heart failure. The
next day I went to see a well-recommended doctor on the island.

His nurse looked at my swollen foot and said, "No doubt about it. You
have gout." After a blood test, the doctor confirmed his nurse's diagnosis,
prescribed pills, and advised that I avoid seafood. I checked the Internet
sites on gout. I lacked some of the crucial indicators of that disease. While
one is advised not to eat for four or five hours before the blood test for
gout, I ate just before the test. I was eating a banana in the doctor's waiting
room. Instead of taking the medicine he prescribed, I sent a detailed e-mail

to my doctor, Robert Meyer, the director of internal medicine at New York Hospital. My yearly checkup was scheduled about a week later, on the day after I returned from St. Croix.

At the examination, Meyer attached a device to my finger. We walked along a corridor. The test confirmed I had shortness of breath. I then took a battery of tests on my lungs and heart. When the results were in, Meyer said, "You have a severe case of congestive heart failure. I am referring you to a cardiologist, Joe Hayes." Hayes prescribed medicine and arranged for another test, an angiogram. It is designed to detect coronary artery disease, that is, blocked arteries, the usual cause of heart failure. The blockage can be cleared during the test itself by the insertion of stents or angioplasty, a balloon-tipped catheter. If the blockage is severe, bypass surgery is required.

At the conclusion of the test, the doctor running the test said, "Sorry, Mr. Silverman, I cannot help you." He delivered the same message to Irene and Hayes. Both appeared in the recovery room. Hayes wrote down four phone numbers: his office, his home, his country home, and his cell. "If anything happens, don't call 911, call me." When I asked the reason, he replied, "When they see your ejection fraction, they will not know what to do. Come to my office on Friday." That was the first time I had heard of ejection fraction.

The ejection fraction measures the oxygen-enriched blood contained in the heart and pumped by the left ventricular muscle to arteries throughout the body. The muscle cannot, even in the healthiest of hearts, pump all the blood contained in the chamber. The ejection fraction is the percent pumped. Lance Amstrong's is about 70 percent, at the very top of the range. Normal is any fraction above fifty-five. Mine was twenty-five.

That night, at home in New York, Irene and I both thought I would soon die.

At his office on Friday, Hayes prescribed medicine. He told me my arteries were clear and that is why the doctor said he could not help me. "Well, if my arteries are clear that is good, right?" Hayes hesitated before replying, "If a blocked artery were the cause of your heart failure, it could be cleared and the heart restored to normal. In your case, the cause is idiopathic, that is, unknown. Sometimes the condition responds to medicine. I have a patient whose ejection fraction was also twenty-five. He raised it to forty-five and recently competed in a marathon. He is, however, only forty-five. I am about to retire. I will refer you to Dr. Maryjane Farr. She is the head of the heart failure department at New York Hospital. Can you see her this coming Tuesday at 2:00 PM? And good luck to you." I thanked him and left.

Farr encouraged me to believe that I would live. She doubled the dose of Correg, one medicine prescribed by Hayes. She said she would soon double it again, "Statistical studies show higher doses produce improved results." She added two additional medicines and advised a low sodium diet, plenty of exercise, and no more than a glass of wine per week. "And consider that glass of wine a treat. If you follow my instructions, I will restore your heart to normal function. You are our most active heart failure patient."

I was an avid vodka drinker. I kept a bottle in the freezer. Every night, before dinner, I filled a six-ounce martini glass full of vodka. Sometimes, I freshened my drink with a few additional ounces. It was not unusual for me to have a glass of wine or two with dinner. I did not drink after dinner. Only on rare occasions did I drink before the cocktail hour. I did not believe I drank to excess, but a Web site on the subject said I did. I quit drinking. I did not even indulge in the weekly glass of wine.

I adhered to a low-sodium diet, took my medicine, and increased my exercise regimen. At the next check-up, about a month later, a significant measure of my condition, called BNP, improved dramatically. It measures the degree of congestion caused by the excretion of brain- nutrient protein. At the earlier test, my condition was severe; now it was mild. The most important test, an echocardiogram, was scheduled for late July. It measures, among other things, the ejection fraction.

I learned two friends were also heart failure patients, both like me with clear arteries. Joe Siegel was one. He is built like a fireplug and appears to be very strong. He is a member of my Amagansett golf club and is an excellent golfer. I always ride in a cart with my clubs strapped on the back. Not Siegel. He walks the course carrying his clubs. Even on hot days. I asked Siegel about his ejection fraction. He said, "I'm at forty." I said, "You barely have heart failure. No wonder you can walk the course. How long have you been diagnosed with heart failure?" Siegel, who was then sixty-two, said he has had the condition for five years. Siegel had no disability and seemed comfortable when engaging in strenuous activity. Maybe, I thought, the name of the disease is worse than the ailment.

The second friend was Stanley Diamond. His heart condition was complicated by other illnesses. Diamond did not exercise, was overweight, drank daily but in moderation, and except for not applying salt directly to his food, did not observe a low-sodium diet. When we first discussed heart failure, he said his ejection fraction was about twenty-five. He is three years older than I and has had heart failure for twelve years. I was hard on Diamond, "You must exercise every day. Walk thirty minutes, three times per day, before breakfast, lunch, and dinner. And stop drinking. Autopsies of Bowery bums show enlarged hearts, a heart failure marker, even in young alcoholics."

Diamond did not change. It is hard for old men to change their lifestyle. Diamond recently died of heart failure.

By the time of my next echocardiogram, I had lost fifteen pounds. I take a diarrhetic daily to purge excess fluid. The discharge of fluid caused most of the weight loss. The result was stunning. My ejection fraction was forty, the same as Siegel's. At a rate of thirty or lower, one is susceptible to fibrillations, a condition causing cardiac arrest. At forty, I was safe.

Three months later, my ejection fraction was forty-four. Farr said, "Congratulations. You will not die of heart failure." I attributed the improvement to medicine and abstaining from alcohol. My improved ejection fraction, however, did not last long.

In May of 2007, my artificial left hip was replaced. The operation was successful but debilitating. For six weeks, I could not exercise. For at least two months, I felt weak. When I next took an echocardiogram, my ejection fraction was back at twenty-five. A month later it was thirty-five. Six months later, it was back to twenty-five. I reasoned alcohol was a contributory cause of that low fraction, but not *the* cause. When I stopped drinking, my condition improved, but then the real cause took control. I also had another condition that might have been a contributory cause, a left bundle branch block.

In 1994, I learned I had a bundle branch block. The two bundle branches, left and right, are the electric system starting the pumping action of the heart. They should start at the same time. The block in the left branch caused it to start slightly later than the right. My internist told me I was fine but that the condition should be checked. Tests showed that my heart was functioning well. I ceased to be concerned until Farr focused on it.

She said, "The left bundle branch is winning the battle. I suggest we take it out of play by inserting a bi-ventricular pacing device. It replaces both bundle branches. By causing the pumping action to begin simultaneously, your heart will be re-synchronized. Your ejection fraction should improve. In addition, the device contains a defibrillator. If you get fibrillations, the device will shock your heart and eliminate their life-threatening effects."

In May 2008, the device was implanted. The recuperation period took about two months. According to a Cleveland Clinic Web site, the ejection fraction improves in 70 percent of the patients whose hearts have been re-synchronized.

My ejection fraction improved only slightly at the next test in September. The dramatic improvement, however, occurred a year after surgery. My ejection fraction measured fifty-two a rate normal for a man my age. How did I feel? No different from when it was twenty-five.

Before I was diagnosed with a fatal disease, I never thought of death. We all know some day we will die. It is a thought I suppressed. Since learning I had a fatal disease, I think often about my own mortality. I am not, however, depressed.

The Bible says that the measure of life is seventy years and with added strength, eighty. At seventy-six, I am closer to the end of the range than the beginning. To me, however, it is not the number of years but the extent of one's happiness. On that score, I am 120 and still counting.

MY THREE HIPS

BUT FOR MEDICAL ADVANCES made over the last fifty years, I would have long ago been confined to a wheelchair. My problem began when I was twenty. I was in an automobile accident and dislocated my hip. The hip consists of a ball and socket. A dislocation occurs when an impact causes the ball to break free from the socket. In the process, the socket is chipped. Through surgery, the ball can be returned to the socket, but the damaged socket cannot be fixed. Over time, the impaired socket degenerates and the ball is dislodged. In my case, it took twenty-five years. In the interim, I skied, played tennis, walked for miles, and jogged. Then, I began to limp. I stopped skiing and jogging. I walked only when I could not ride. I continued to play tennis, but quit that too when opponents apologized for hitting shots that made me run. I searched for a mode of exercise that I could do. I found swimming. It is aerobic, puts no stress on joints, and provides a workout.

At forty-seven, I could no longer walk without a cane. My doctor discussed hip replacement surgery. He told me it was advisable only when the pain interfered with my life. I had trouble walking, but was not in pain. The operation, however, was in my future. Rather than see an orthopedist, I made an appointment with a surgeon, Chitranjan S. Ranawat.

I selected Ranawat based on solid information. At a dinner party, the woman sitting next to me said her son was the chief resident at the Hospital for Special Surgery. Special Surgery is the best orthopedic hospital in New York. The residents work with the surgeons. They know who is good. I said, "Would you please ask your son the following question: if your father needed a hip replacement, whom would you recommend?" Several days later, she called, "He says Chit Ranawat."

I made an appointment with Ranawat. Both of my hips were x-rayed. The surgeon showed me the x-ray of my left hip. It was outside the socket. He asked whether I was in pain and when I told him I was not, he advised that I wait as long as possible for an operation. "You are relatively young. The replacement should last between five and fifteen years. A replacement for a replaced hip is a difficult and painful operation. Put the operation off as long as possible." The surgeon also observed that I favored the right hip and that the extra stress made it a candidate for eventual replacement.

I used the cane for several years, walking with great effort but without pain. I was, however, eager to walk unaided, embarrassed by sympathy from friends and strangers, and concerned that I was damaging my right hip. In November of 1982, two years after my first visit, I called Ranawat and asked for the next appointment. A patient had cancelled. He had an immediate opening. I grabbed it.

The operation was successful and, in the beginning, so was my recovery. The usual hospital stay then was two weeks, but I was scheduled to go home in ten days. "You see," I told visitors, "I am in great shape because I swim. My muscles are flexible and respond well to physical therapy." Ah hubris! Sure enough disaster struck. On the eighth day, I felt terrible. My head hurt. I had trouble breathing. I had a fever.

My temperature was 101. My lungs were x-rayed and scanned. They showed I had thrown an embolism which had lodged in my lungs. I was given oxygen to help me breathe and Coumidin to dissolve the embolism. I stayed in the hospital for an additional two weeks.

At first, I walked with Canadian crutches, then a cane, and finally, unaided. Before the operation, I walked so slowly that I was able to count the squares on the sidewalk. When I fully recovered, I walked briskly. I no longer noticed the squares. However, I walked only when necessary. Ranawat had advised, "Think of your replacement hip as money in the bank: the more you use it, the less you will have."

After recovering from the operation, I stopped favoring my right side, but years of uneven pressure had taken their toll. Twelve years after replacing my left hip, I was back in the hospital for my right. The surgeon was not Ranawat. He had left Special Surgery to become the head of orthopedic surgery at Lenox Hill Hospital. I had to choose between the hospital and the surgeon.

I chose the hospital. Special Surgery handles only damaged joints. Its procedure is military in its precision. In addition, during my illness following the first operation, the chief of internal medicine took care of me. I liked him and switched internists. He recommended I stay at Special Surgery and suggested two surgeons. I chose Dr. Sculco.

Sculco said the hip operation had been vastly improved by the introduction of computers. He also said, "Do not worry about your left hip. Advances have been made and a replacement of a replacement is a walk in the park."

The second operation was also successful and, in addition, I had no aftereffects. In five days, I was released and within three weeks, instructed to walk a mile a day. My first long walk in years was from Dr. Sculco's office at Seventy-first Street and the East River to my office at Fifty-ninth Street and Lexington.

My left artificial hip remained in place for about twenty-five years. Over the winter of 2007, it loosened. I was in St. Croix. I had continued to swim and play golf, but only nine holes. By the end of our stay, I was back on a cane. I needed a third hip operation, the second on my left hip.

In searching the Web, I learned that a second operation was called a revision. It is more difficult to perform than a replacement. The recovery period is longer, the result less efficient. Why? A ball, smaller than the replaced ball, is inserted. It is prone to dislocate.

On our return to New York, I called Dr. Bryan Nestor at Special Surgery. He had operated on Irene, when she, racing to answer the telephone, fell and broke her knee. Sculco, then chief at the hospital, was booked solid. He recommended Nestor.

Poor Irene. She could not lower her affected leg. That is, until she saw Nestor. He put his hand on her thigh and said, "Relax the muscle." She did and down came her leg. Although he had a busy schedule, he operated on Irene the very next day. The operation was successful. Within six weeks, Irene was her old self. I thanked Nestor. I told him about my Ranawat and Sculco hips and said, "I'd like to come to you, when the time comes, for a replacement of my Ranawat left hip."

Prior to seeing Nestor, my left hip was x-rayed. He showed me the x-ray. "The old ball is in perfect position and just where Ranawat put it twenty-five years ago. The glue is gone. What I will do is use the old ball and secure it in place." The operation took place in May. When I next saw Nestor, he showed me the x-ray of my revised hip. I noticed what looked like sticks attached to the joint and asked about them. "They are pins," he said. "Your hip will not dislocate."

It took several months before I could return to normal activities. Even then, I lacked flexibility. Full recovery took about a year. I can walk, ride my bike, swim, and play golf. I cannot run, but my mobility is good enough.

My Impaired Vision

I LIKE GAMES. AFTER MY first hip surgery, I took up golf. It is a game designed for cripples. You hit the ball, hop in a cart, ride to the ball, and begin the process all over again. Many years into the game, I developed a problem. I had difficulty seeing my shots. I relied on members of my foursome to find my ball. Several complained, "Why can't you see your ball? The rest of us see our balls." I took a lesson from the pro at the club, primarily to address that problem.

I asked him, "Why can't I see my ball? Is it something to do with my swing or the position of my head? " He answered, "Nothing to do with your swing or your head. Ask your ophthalmologist." I made an immediate appointment with David Abramson. He said, "You have a small cataract in the middle of each eye. That is why you cannot follow your ball in flight. Let's get rid of them." He recommended a doctor who specializes in cataract surgery and off I went.

The specialist examined me and said, "I wonder how Abramson missed this." He called in his staff. "Look," he said "This fellow has a rare disease, Fuchs' dystrophy." He discussed the disease: "It causes the cells, on the endothelial layer, the innermost layer of the cornea, to disintegrate. Their job is to pump water to the stoma and when the cells are impaired, the corneas get too much water and thicken. The corneas admit light and thick corneas admit less light than is required for good vision. The disease is progressive, but slow. It always affects both eyes. The prognosis is blindness. The only treatment is a corneal transplant." He then said cataract surgery should be deferred. "Since corneal transplants are needed, it makes no sense to remove the cataracts from corneas that are going to be replaced." I asked, "How long have I had this disease?" He replied, "At least fifteen years."

He also said that his partner specialized in corneal transplants and asked whether I wanted to make an appointment. I was in a state of shock and said, "Not right now. I have to think about this." I also asked him to send a report to my ophthalmologist.

I called Abramson several times. He was both too busy to take my calls or to return them. I refused, at first, to state any reason for calling. Finally, I decided to play it his way. I told his secretary, "*New York Magazine* designated Abramson as one of five leading ophthalmologists in New York. I know because his walls are plastered with reprints. I want to know how a 'great ophthalmologist' failed, for more than fifteen years, to diagnose an illness leading inevitably to blindness. Tell the great doctor it is in his interest to call me."

You bet he called and right away. He denied that I had Fuchs' dystrophy, mispronouncing it by calling it "Fox." He denied ducking my calls, and said, "I was waiting for the report from the cataract specialist before calling back. I still do not have the report but when I get it, I will send a copy to you."

The plot thickened when I got the cataract doctor's report. It made no mention of Fuchs' dystrophy and falsely said he advised cataract surgery. The doctors were engaged in a cover-up. What to do about it? Sue? The misdiagnoses caused no injury and probably even did not delay corrective surgery. No damage; no foul.

A Web page on Fuchs' dystrophy had a link to the Lions Club of Ohio. Its site described research in progress at Ohio State University in Columbus on a topographical device designed to insure that the replacement cornea was properly positioned. If it is off, even by a nano-fraction, astigmatism results. I contacted the woman heading the project, told her of my problem and my desire to help myself by helping her work, in the only way I knew how, by making a contribution. On the Web site, she said funds were necessary to continue her work. She arranged an appointment with the chief surgeon. She met me at the airport and took me to her lab. She showed me her machine. Then, she introduced me to the surgeon.

I received a thorough examination. One machine simulated a tunnel and then flashed a bright light. In both cases, I saw nothing. The surgeon confirmed that I had Fuchs' dystrophy and said the vision in my left eye was so impaired that I would be denied a driving license in Ohio. In that state, I was legally blind.

I asked when I should get an operation. He said, "Today is Monday. How about tomorrow? Your left eye is virtually useless and I cannot say how long your right eye, which is pretty bad, will hold up." He recommended surgeons in New York saying it made no sense for him to operate, as I would have to return repeatedly for aftercare treatment.

After meeting several surgeons, I chose Dr. Sandra Belmont. She said that some surgeons attached the cornea by making a loop requiring only a few stitches. Her training was unique. She attached the cornea by twenty hair-thin stitches. "It is painstaking work but that is the only way I will do it. I use my own machine to guide me in positioning the cornea." She gave me copies of research papers she had written. I read the papers. They were impressive. But, that was not, to me, an important criterion. I have a theory about surgeons. They are carpenters who cut and sew the human body. Dr. Belmont struck me as a good carpenter and sewer, and that was why I selected her.

New York State operates a cornea donation program. The New York Eye Bank, a not-for-profit organization, distributes corneas free of charge. Unlike organs, corneas are not in short supply. Within a few weeks, I got a cornea from a thirty-five-year-old woman who had died in an automobile accident. The Eye Bank keeps confidential the identity of the donor and the recipient, but transmits an anonymous thank-you note from the recipient to the donor's family. I wrote, from the bottom of my heart, what is probably the corniest and tritest phrase, "Your departed family member is alive in my left eye."

After Dr. Belmont received and approved of the cornea, the operation was promptly scheduled. She referred to it as a triple. The cataract and my old cornea were removed and the donated tissue stitched in place. Four hours later, I was discharged from the hospital. As part of the aftercare and to protect my eye, a metal patch was placed over it. At regular intervals, I applied a steroid, to prevent rejection, and medication to protect against infection.

The next day, I returned to Dr. Belmont. My left eye was tested. I saw the big E, the first letter on the chart. My vision was twenty–two hundred, meaning that I saw at twenty feet what the normal person sees at two hundred. The doctor was pleased. The following week, I was tested again and could not see the big E. It was not until a month later that I was able to see what I had seen on the day following the operation.

A blank lens replaced my prescription lens, so that my left eye went uncorrected until six months after the operation, when it stabilized. The correction gave me twenty–twenty vision, but the correction was severe: I was badly astigmatic. It was difficult to adjust to severe astigmatism. I felt unbalanced with and without my glasses. Dr. Belmont pointed out that before the operation, my left eye could not be corrected any better than twenty–sixty, so the operation was a success. But, we were disappointed by the severity of the astigmatism. She said if the astigmatism did not clear up, I should consider laser surgery. Not yet, I thought.

Ten months later, half of the stitches from the initial surgery were removed. The anticipated change in the degree of astigmatism did not occur. Five months later, the remaining stitches were removed and a patch placed overnight on the eye.

The next morning, I showered and shaved. After shaving, I applied Nivea, a conditioning cream. I looked at the jar in disbelief. For the first time in memory, I was able to read the word "Nivea" without my glasses. I covered my right eye; "Nivea" appeared bright and clear. Then, I covered my left eye and tried, unsuccessfully, to read the word. I placed the jar about twenty feet away and clearly saw "Nivea." The astigmatism in my left eye had disappeared with the last of the stitches. With a correction, my vision was twenty–twenty.

My right cornea has also been replaced. The operation was also successful, but the result not quite as good as my left eye. When corrected, my vision in my right eye is twenty–thirty. My overall vision is twenty–twenty-five, a fine result for anyone, and extraordinary for one who was going blind. The heart, both hips, and eyes were improved though the marvels of today's medicine and surgery. Now I say, "Money isn't everything; health is 50 percent and good healthcare is the other 50 percent."

CONCLUSION

I was born on December 30, 1932, during the depths of the Great Depression. Seventy six years later, the economy again crashed.

Is this the Great Depression II? I don't know. What I do know is that I lived during a mostly favorable period in a wonderful country. It has been a good life..

Our wedding photo. To my left is my mother. Irene's parents are on her right. Her two grandmothers are at either end. May 28, 1961

Gary Kasparov and me. May 1990

Our three children taken at David's wedding. June 1994

Irene and me. circa 2000.